1979

The Right to Participate:

Inmate Involvement in Prison Administration

by
J. E. BAKER

The Scarecrow Press, Inc.
Metuchen, N.J.   1974

Library of Congress Cataloging in Publication Data

Baker, J   E   1917–
    The right to participate.

    Includes bibliographies.
        1. Corrections—United States—History.
    2.   Correctional institutions—United States—History.
    I.   Title.
    HV9304.B34   365'.973   74–7071
    ISBN 0–8108–0727–0

to my wife

MARY ELIZABETH

with love and devotion

FOREWORD

A remarkable feature of much prison management in the United States is the extent to which staff at a single prison regard their experience as unique. This condition has prevailed especially in the many state penal systems which never recruit senior staff from prisons of other states or from the federal system. As a consequence of their isolation, leaders of such prisons assume that conclusions which their experience justifies are unchallengable. Yet, a completely different experience frequently may be found elsewhere, often just across a nearby state border or even in a federal prison within their own state.

J. E. Baker's study of inmate participation in American prison management both confirms the existence of such isolation, and provides an aid in reducing it. He takes us on a tremendous tour through American penal history and penal geography, revealing dramatic diversity in staff knowledge and attitude on participation of prisoners in decisions on even the smallest aspects of their daily life.

Where there is a diversity in fundamental practices, a systematic survey and testing of all feasible alternatives is essential if we are to achieve optimum procedures. Baker's tour is one which all prison officials should take, first via this book and then, with necessarily smaller range, in real life, if they are to be familiar with all relevant experience on inmate participation in prison operations.

Daniel Glaser
Professor of Sociology
University of Southern
California
Los Angeles

TABLE OF CONTENTS

Part II. THE STATES

Part III.   THE FEDERAL PRISON SYSTEM

Part IV.   OTHER JURISDICTIONS

Civil

Federal

Part V.   THE EVOLVING PERSPECTIVE

By 1870, with the holocaust of the Civil War only a scant
half-decade in memory, the present continental limits of
the United States had been attained, and the attention of the
nation was focused on the development of its tremendous
natural resources.   The demands of great national activities,
while creating an unprecedented material wealth, left little
time for consideration of those who for various reasons had
offended the social order.   In the backwash of that society
languished more than thirty thousand human beings in a half-
hundred prisons.   Created as a substitute for brutal punishments, the prison had itself become in many respects a
grim castle set apart from the populace in which the most
unspeakable of indignities were practiced in the name of
reformation and the public safety.   The inhabitants of these
monolithic monuments of inhumanity were deemed to have
suffered a civil death, in which state, although they yet
breathed as human beings, they had no rights other than
what the law in its humanity saw fit to allow.   And the humanity of the law as it pertained to the rights of the individual was at best embryonic.

Social conscience, fortunately, is forever extant, although it
has appeared at times to be comatose.   Throughout the history of the nation, in fact, prior to the full development of
the Colonies under other rule, some individuals and some
groups had registered protest, first to the sanguinary nature
of penalties imposed on offenders and later to the degraded
state of prisons.   The fruition of this concern was the organization at Cincinnati, Ohio, in 1870, of the National
Prison Association, now the American Correctional Association, in whose original Declaration of Principles was one
of particular significance to this volume:

> Principle V: The prisoner's destiny should be placed,
> measurably, in his own hands; he must be put into
> circumstances where he will be able, through his own

exertions, to continually better his own condition.
A regulated self-interest must be brought into play,
and made constantly operative.

The principle cited gave, in effect, recognition to prior
efforts and formed a foundation at once philosophical and
pragmatic to further attempts to provide a place for the inmate to participate in both the program and the programming
of the prison.

Since the birth of the American Correctional Association in
1870, there has been a phenomenal increase in the population of the nation, and a sharp escalation in the number and
variety of types of institutions designed for the care and
treatment of offenders.   What has been described as the new
penology is astir in many of these facilities.   New concepts,
new directions, and new methods are creating a fresh atmosphere in which one can detect that most tantalizing
quintessence of progress--hope.   These facilities, these
activities, and this promise came not as a sudden revelation,
but resulted from the sustained efforts of many correctional
practitioners experimenting with many methods.   This volume is an accounting of the past, the present, and the potential of one of those methods--inmate participation in
administration, referred to first as inmate self-government
and later as advisory councils.

Throughout, the confined offender is referred to variously
as inmate, resident, student, ward, camper, or boy or
girl.   This is not an inconsistency.   Insofar as it was possible to do so, the language of the source has been used
here.

ACKNOWLEDGMENTS

The historical and current material for this work was obtained from a review of numerous books and periodicals in
the field of corrections and through the cooperation of the
men and women who direct and administer the adult, youth,
and juvenile correctional residential facilities in the fifty
states, the counties and cities contacted, the Federal Bureau

of Prisons, the District of Columbia, the Department of Defense, and the Department of Health, Education and Welfare. To these correctional colleagues, the author expresses his gratefulness for the quantity and quality of their responses to requests for information.

To Dr. Daniel Glaser, Professor of Sociology, University of Southern California, the author is deeply indebted for two contributions. First, for the encouragement, counsel, and active assistance given in the original research efforts and preparation of the manuscript of the original article and, second, for the Foreword to this volume. Dr. Glaser is a luminary in the galaxy of those practicing the science and art of corrections.

Special acknowledgment is made to Kenyon J. Scudder, career California correctional executive, who was the first superintendent of the California Institution for Men, at Chino; to Howard B. Gill, Director, Institute of Correctional Administration, American University, eminent correctional practitioner and academician; and to Austin H. MacCormick, Executive Director, The Osborne Association, Inc., whose accomplishments in the correctional effort are legion.

Mr. Scudder amplified the published account of the origin and development of the Chino Advisory Council, as did Mr. Gill with that of the Norfolk Prison Colony. Mr. Mac-Cormick made a critical review of draft portions of the manuscript dealing with the Mutual Welfare League at Auburn Prison, Sing Sing Prison, and the Naval Prison, providing new information and insights regarding the functioning of the League at each facility.

Although the author has already personally thanked him for the assistance rendered in researching the history of advisory councils in federal prisons, that thanks is repeated here to J. C. Taylor, friend and correctional executive colleague. Rising through the ranks of the Federal Bureau of Prisons to assistant director, Ches Taylor later charted the course on which the Commonwealth of his birth can reach modern correctional practice by his three-year period of service, 1969 to 1972, as Commissioner, Kentucky Department of Corrections.

In addition to former personnel of the Federal Bureau of Prisons Central Office--Mark S. Richmond, Assistant Director, retired; Louise L. MacKenzie, Librarian, retired; and

Jack H. Wise, now Warden, Federal Correctional Institution,
Seagoville, Texas--the author thanks the following for pro-
viding requested reference works: California State Library,
Sacramento; University of California, Los Angeles; Univer-
sity of California, Berkeley; Claremont Graduate School,
Claremont, California; Indiana State University, Terre Haute;
University of Massachusetts, Amherst; University of Michi-
gan, Ann Arbor; Cornell University, Ithaca, New York; the
Library of Congress; and the Kentucky Department of Li-
braries, Frankfort. At the latter, Mrs. Lucy Chapman,
Director of Information and Loan, was especially cooperative
and helpful.

In the course of researching this subject and in the preparation of drafts of several portions of the manuscript, assistance was given by two men who were then residents of a
correctional residential facility. To those men the author
reiterates his thanks and best regards.

The permission of the Office of the Chief of Naval Operations
to use the material regarding the United States Naval Prison
at Portsmouth, New Hampshire, is appreciated.

The original literature research and survey findings of the
author regarding self-government and advisory councils in
United States correctional institutions were published in the
Journal of Criminology, Criminal Law and Police Science,
vol. 55, no. 1, March 1964, under the title, "Inmate Self-
Government." The content of that article is used in this
volume by permission of the publisher, The Northwestern
University School of Law.

In 1966 and 1967, a survey was made of United States correctional institutions and agencies as listed in the 1966 edition of the Directory of Correctional Institutions and Agencies,
published by the American Correctional Association. No
contact was made with city and county correctional systems
or institutions, other than the cities of Detroit, New York,
and Philadelphia, and Westchester County, New York. This
was done because of literature references to or first-hand
knowledge of past or current programs relevant to the survey.
A literature reference indicating the possibility of a self-
government program having existed several decades ago at
the Essex County Penitentiary, Caldwell, New Jersey, was
followed up, but no record of the organization was found.

During the course of and subsequent to that survey, in which

285 replies were received to 412 inquiries and follow-ups
sent, research of the literature of corrections was continued.   Through the courtesy of Dr. E. Preston Sharp,
Executive Director, The American Correctional Association,
and Norman A. Carlson, now Director, Federal Bureau of
Prisons, copies of the indexes to the American Correctional
Association Proceedings for the years 1905-1934, 1935-1943,
and 1944-1946, were provided.   A selection was made of
those citations believed to be references to self-government
or advisory councils.   Photocopies of those portions of the
Proceedings referred to were then obtained from the American Correctional Association.   Much information was gained
which amplified accounts of self-government and advisory
council programs found elsewhere, and leads found to others
previously not known about.   An example of the latter is the
account of the Mutual Welfare League at the Kentucky State
Reformatory in Frankfort, Kentucky.   A reference to the
League was made in an address at the General Session of the
then American Prison Association on October 18, 1926, by
Austin H. MacCormick, at that time a professor at Bowdoin
College, Brunswick, Maine.   An account of the origin, purpose, and functions of the League was found in the Kentucky
State Archives.

Although an index of the Proceedings of the American Correctional Association for the years 1870-1904, was known to
have been published in 1906, no person or organization contacted by the author had ever seen it.   Just recently it was
found to be on file in the Library of Congress, referenced
as Senate Document No. 210.   A copy has been ordered, but
it is not available to review prior to publication of this volume.   Undoubtedly, the 1870-1904 Index will provide leads
to other past, and forgotten, experiences with self-government and advisory council programs.

Preparation of a manuscript based on the literature research
and the surveys made in 1960 and 1966-1967 was commenced
in the spring of 1967.   As the writing neared completion,
the author opted for early retirement from the Federal Bureau of Prisons to which he had devoted a twenty-seven year
span of his life.   The occurrence which precipitated that
decision was the proffer of the position of Warden, Penitentiary of New Mexico, at Santa Fe.

During the course of service in New Mexico as Warden and
as Secretary of Corrections of the newly created Department
of Corrections, and later as Deputy Commissioner, Kentucky

Department of Corrections, interspersed with and followed
by consulting contacts with state, county, and city correctional agencies and facilities, principally for the Law Enforcement Assistance Administration technical assistance
program administered by the American Correctional Association, and occasionally on personal contract, sufficient time
to properly complete the manuscript never seemed to be
available.

When the manuscript was finally completed, and tentatively
accepted for publication, it was readily apparent that an updating of the survey data was necessary.   The updating and
necessary rewriting has been interrupted by consultant con-
tracts, at one time for a period of four months when full-
time service was provided by the author to a correctional
facility in a large mid-western city.

The resurvey began in late 1972 and was completed in July
1973.   Inquiries and follow-ups totalled 234, to which 201
replies were received.   With each inquiry was sent an excerpt of the original manuscript as it pertained to the recipient, that account being based on information obtained in the
1960 and 1966-1967 surveys.   The 1972 edition of the Directory of Juvenile and Adult Correctional Institutions and
Agencies, published by the American Correctional Association
was used in the 1972-1973 survey.

The author especially recognizes and appreciates the assistance of his wife, Mary Elizabeth Baker, in researching,
rewriting, and proofreading, and her continuing attitude of
understanding throughout the preparation of this volume.

It is the author's belief that correctional practitioners
largely have defaulted on their obligation to assist the educator in determining the content of correctional studies,
and, in particular, have contributed little to the establishment of a sound historical identity for the field of corrections.   This volume is a step in that direction.

This is a history of the participation by confined of-fenders in the administration of United States correctional residential facilities from 1793 to 1973, presented to provide a proper perspective on what has long been regarded as a controversial issue.

In 1960 the author became interested in the past, present, and potential of inmate advisory councils in the administrative communication system of correctional residential facilities, with a focus at that time on the penitentiary. The literature on prisons was researched and a limited survey made by sending a questionnaire to fifty-two penitentiaries. Recipients were asked to give certain information as to the administration of their advisory councils if they "have or have had" such a group. The findings from the literature and the forty-four responses to the questionnaire were included in an article which appeared in the Journal of Criminal Law and Criminology in 1964.

Out of that experience grew the realization that a great body of information existed on both the history and the current state of advisory councils which had never been brought together for the benefit of correctional practitioners and students, and for the public at large. The knowledge most people had on the subject was limited, and opinionated. Apparently, there were few who took a neutral stance and both the pro and the con points of view were clouded by stereotypes not defensible on the basis of either reason or intellect.

It became readily apparent that of all the concepts in corrections, inmate self-government and advisory councils were most likely to arouse partisan feelings. Those in favor believed that the concept was a part of the "new penology," hence it was therapeutic in nature. Since we are nothing if we are not therapeutic, then we are in favor and we know

the concept will work if insidious forces do not undermine
it.

On the other hand, opponents maintained that the entire history of self-government and advisory councils proved
its unsoundness, since it had never lasted anywhere.   What
further proof of unworthiness was required?   Further, if
inmates were smart enough to govern themselves they would
not be in prison in the first place.

Since the greater number of persons working in the
correctional vineyard are rational thinkers, and all had de-
bated and resolved other issues arising from time to time,
it seemed odd that the same did not hold true for the concept of self-government and advisory councils.   The pros
and cons of the matter as then being expressed were essentially the same as those several decades ago.   A formulation of the reasons for the static quality of the debate was
made as follows:

First, there had been little thoughtful examination
of the concept and a paucity of fresh thinking.   Reasons for
or against apparently stemmed from the psychological truism
that we observe and remember selectively in accordance with
our developed expectancies.   Such selectivity tends to affirm
the correctness of the expectancy.

Second, it appeared that attitudes toward the concept
were based primarily on accounts of such arrangements as
they were advocated or practiced many years ago.   Apparently, there had been no organized attempts to apply theo-
retical studies of institutional processes or the results of
experimentation in inmate social organization to the concept.

Third, advocates of the concept tended to regard it as
a method or model of treatment which could be applied across
the board to all inmates in all institutions.

Fourth, in contrast to other concepts which had intermittently appeared on the correctional scene, there apparently had been no real application of scientific principles
in determining the efficacy and efficiency of the concept.

The last mentioned part of that original formulation
is being increasingly subject to challenge.   Hopefully, some-
day it will be no longer true in any sense, but as of now,
it remains a valid observation.   In fact, in the anatomy of

corrections, the determination of the efficacy and efficiency of most treatment programs remains the Achilles heel.

Much has occurred in the entire criminal justice system since the 1964 article was published. The report of the President's Commission on Law Enforcement and Administration of Justice, published in 1967, and the subsequent Task Force Reports made many recommendations for coping with the problem of crime in the nation. Of the recommendations made for the correctional system, ninety-six percent concerned improving treatment and rehabilitation efforts.

In 1968 the Law Enforcement Assistance Administration was created under the provisions of the Omnibus Crime Control and Safe Streets Act. The proportion of the millions of dollars allocated to the LEAA being used for corrections is increasing dramatically. While there yet remains a question as to the effectiveness of these massive expenditures, there can be no question that had the effort not been commenced the situation today would be desperate indeed. The effort has stimulated innovation which has generated new experiences as well as producing errors. What is vitally important, is that we are witness to the reception of new thought, the willingness to try new approaches, and above all, the emergence of the realization that corrections must move with the times and be willing to alter many of its traditions, particularly those regarding the relationship of the keeper and the kept.

Today, we can see an altering of the relationship between the individual and whichever institution of society, for whatever reason, has assumed some degree of control over his destiny. This alteration is taking place through several social movements whose collective thrust is that those who are to be affected have a legitimate interest in the actions taken by that social institution, and perforce the right to voice an opinion which will be given serious consideration in the formulation of philosophy as well as policy.

Movements by and in behalf of students, the mentally ill, welfare recipients, and consumers are examples of this striving for a new kind of relationship between the dispenser of largesse and the receiver. Again and again, in the swiftly swirling events of this decade in which Americans will embark on their third century, there are repeated demonstrations of the fact that policy and procedure produced in the

isolation of Washington, the state capitol, or the county or
city courthouse, are not always the best.   In order for any
agency of government to do even an adequate job of meeting
the needs of those it is to serve, and to promote the general
good of all the nation, there needs to be established and preserved a relationship of serious communication.

The correctional process is the manifestation of
society's assumption of control over the destiny of the offender.   The intent of the process is to assist the individual
to acquire modes of coping in his life style which do not
result in conflict with authority.   The individual must be
included in the dynamics, if the process is ever to become
successful.

Reason reveals to us that almost without exception
all offenders are engaged, either positively or negatively, in
the correctional process.   Wagner pointed out many years
ago that while the status of inmate participation in correctional institutions is controversial, and therefore uncertain,
one thing is definite--all institutions do have some form of
inmate participation whether planned or unplanned, and if
properly channelled, it can be an important constructive
force in the rehabilitation of offenders.   He defined inmate
participation primarily as free and easy avenues of communication between inmates and administration, with inmate
participation in both the planning and the operation of the
institution program as an almost natural corollary. [1]

Perhaps many of those who have seriously believed
that the administration controlled the direction and the destiny of the institution, have never fully comprehended the extent and the impact of offender influence on planning and
operations.   As the characteristics of those in confinement
change, to that extent the institution changes.   From that
stratum of society euphemistically designated as the disad-
vantaged, the places of confinement have traditionally received their clientele.   What the institution provided, or failed
to provide, was of little consequence to persons whose social
consciousness was undeveloped or thoroughly inhibited.   But
the man in confinement today is no longer the acquiescent
"good inmate" of yesterday.   The mainstream of the confined
population today contains in disproportionate numbers the
products of the urban scene, well aware of the life of abun-
dancy and affluence which surrounds them--they have seen
it on the tube and the screen, wanting what they want now,
and convinced that the continuing discontinuities of our social

order block their escape from the status they believe to be
the reason for their present situation. They have had it
with authority which seems to be blind or insensitive to the
individual who has no power or influence.

As the characteristics by which the confined population can be generally described have changed, likewise the
place of confinement. In some, the change has been evolu-
tionary. As the needs of the offender changed in response
to expectancies aroused by multitudinous social stimuli, the
institutional program shifted in accommodation. Perhaps
a school was added, or a new series of studies introduced--
black culture, for instance--a work release program, or a
furlough plan.

In other places of confinement, alas too many, offenders have brought about changes in program and practice
by revolution, as witnessed by disturbances, varyingly severe,
that send shockwaves throughout a state and in some instances
across the nation.

In either case, evolution or revolution, correctional
residential facilities have responded. Though in a variety
of ways, they have responded, just as those in power have
responded to the communication efforts of humans involved in
other social movements already mentioned.

In the correctional residential facility, the voice of
the inmate, prisoner, resident, ward, student, client--or
whatever designation has been adopted--is being raised, and
reason tells us that this will continue. Psychology tells
us that the provision of channels of communication so that
an individual can be assured of his being heard will provide
the kind of satisfactory emotional outlet that will make collective shouting unnecessary.

It has often been said that prisoners are people.
This so obvious a fact is too often overlooked. People want
and need to be heard, and need the satisfaction of knowing
that what they say will be given serious consideration. This
is important in dealing with others, either individually or
collectively. It assumes added importance in the confinement situation which purports to resocialize the offender
to the end that he will become a law-abiding, productive
member of society upon release. This goal cannot be
accomplished if his voice is stilled, his thoughts stifled, and
his opinion unsought or ignored.

The concept of inmate self-government grew out of the harshness of the old prison regime. It was an attempt to provide a framework within which the inmate could express some freedom of expression and choice. Certainly, such a concept was unique to the prevalent social patterns of the periods in which we find it first emerging, most often only briefly.

In a discussion of the sociology of self-government, Haynes stated that obviously persons in confinement know more about the working of the prison system than do others. The efficiency of the prison can be increased by utilizing that knowledge which inmates will transmit through a representative group of their own selection. The prison administration must accept the group seriously and grant it partnership in working for the betterment of all inmates. [2]

A man whose confinement experience spanned several decades reasoned that since prior to their confinement prison inmates were citizens of a democracy and when released will once more become citizens, the period of confinement should be the time for efforts to awaken and develop an interest in becoming self-reliant, responsible persons. As one method of fostering these desired qualities he suggested the introduction of as large a degree of self-government as is feasible. [3]

On the current scene there is no longer inmate self-government as proposed and attempted in some of the notable early experiences described herein. The features of those systems most acceptable to correctional administrators have been retained under an arrangement known as the advisory council regarded by some as one of the most satisfactory devices for encouraging confined offenders to think constructively about their own institutional environment and providing a means by which they may share responsibility with the staff for making the correctional confinement facility a better place in which to live.

J. E. Baker
Frankfort, Kentucky
September, 1973

---

1.   Wagner, Albert C.   "Inmate Participation in Correctional

Institutions." The Prison World, vol. 13, no. 5
(Sept-Oct. 1951), p. 9-11.
2. Haynes, Fred E. Criminology. 2nd ed. New York:
McGraw-Hill, 1935; pp. 335-356.
3. Leopold, Nathan. "What Is Wrong with the Prison
System." Nebraska Law Review, vol. 45, no. 33,
1966.

Part I

NOTABLE EARLY EXPERIENCES

Commentary

This first part is an account of self-government and advisory council programs originating prior to 1930 in United States institutions for the confinement of adult and youthful offenders and juvenile delinquents. Until 1930, prison administration as either science or art was at best in an embryonic state. Humane treatment of offenders was the concern of only a dedicated few.

. Life in the old prison was for the most part a deadly monotony under a stern and often brutal autocracy, excepting only the occasional administration whose chief characteristic was a condescending paternalism. There are few accounts of career administrators in the time before 1930 and even fewer accounts of occupational mobility. Usually, a guard remained a guard. Supervisory personnel were generally hired at that level. Wardens and their deputies were appointed as part of a political patronage system, in which most all personnel were as pawns.

Although the situation improved through the years, the 1966 and 1967 surveys made by the Joint Commission on Correctional Manpower and Training found widespread personnel recruitment and retention problems caused by low pay, heavy workloads, insufficient training and lack of merit system employment in the field of corrections.

Many of the early self-government and advisory council programs were both inadequately structured and improperly implemented. With few exceptions, all were superimposed on an untrained staff. The zeal of the originator of the program in most instances exceeded his correctional management ability. The programs were apparently too heavily dependent upon the originator since most rapidly expired when that person departed the scene.

However it cannot go unsaid that almost all of the
originators of those earlier programs were persons in advance of their time, innovators and experimenters, dynamic
and creative, sometimes flamboyant, and always impatient
with current conditions.   None had a trained or professional
staff recruited and developed under a merit system.   There
were no personnel development programs.   Salaries were
low, hours were long, tenure was insecure, and employee
benefits were unheard of.   All of these add up to extreme
conditions, which was usually the state of affairs in most
institutions.

Involvement in the disciplinary process appears to
have been a point of departure for the early programs of
inmate participation.   One need not ponder long the question
as to why.   Examine only briefly the accounts of early
prisons and the stark brutality of disciplinary practices
assaults the senses.   Revolting--yes, but they were the accepted methods of dealing with deviancy.   The untrained
personnel of the old prisons were ill-equipped to handle
discipline problems.   To several originators of the early
programs apparently this was the area in most urgent need
of change; also, this was an area offering the best prospects
for effecting a positive change.   There can be no denying
that any provision for inmate participation in any part of the
prison program was a dramatic if not downright audacious
idea.   Of all the features of self-government programs, inmate involvement in the handling of disciplinary matters was
the most visible; this prominence created the still lingering
impression that participation in disciplinary matters was the
whole of the self-government concept rather than merely a
minor part.

Only at Gill's Norfolk State Prison Colony in Massachusetts, the Sleighton Farm School for Girls in Pennsylvania,
the Clinton Farms in New Jersey, and the Long Lane School
in Connecticut, was staff support effectively enlisted.   In the
other institutions discussed in Part I, those employees most
affected, the line personnel, were often placed in situations
subordinating them to their charges.   Little comment is
necessary regarding the administrative crassness of this
arrangement.   Modern management recognizes the need for
interpretive communication in advance of putting a new procedure into effect.   The presence of untrained and incom-
petent personnel intensifies that need.   We can now only

speculate as to the many positive changes which might have
resulted had administrators of yesteryear focused their
efforts on staff development.

Walnut Street Jail

The earliest reference in correctional literature to
inmate self-government in American institutions was made
by the South Carolinian, Robert J. Turnbull. During his
visit to the Walnut Street Jail in Philadelphia in 1793,
Turnbull noted what he termed "a secondary and inferior
government among the criminals for their own convenience
and comfort." In his report he added: "One of their
principal regulations relative to cleanliness was, that no
one who found occasion should spit elsewhere but in the
chimney (that is, in the night rooms). The punishment
annexed to the person, who thought proper to infringe this
general rule, was simply an exclusion from the society and
conversation of his fellow convicts, and this is found to be
sufficient" [[1]notes at end of Part I].

New York House of Refuge

In the winter of 1815-16 a small group of men held
several meetings in New York City to discuss the treatment
of poverty and crime. From these discussions in the home
of Joseph Curtis and others came the Society for the Prevention of Pauperism which became the Society for the Reformation of Juvenile Delinquents. The Society founded the New
York House of Refuge which opened on January 1, 1825, with
Curtis as the first superintendent. [2]

Curtis maintained that the House of Refuge could not
be managed like a factory. Family life and the rule of a
loving but determined paterfamilias were chief factors in his
intensely personal administration. During the summer any
boy finishing his work by Saturday noon was permitted to go
for a swim in addition to an afternoon at liberty. Those
who behaved very well were allowed to visit parents and
friends in the city. Forgiveness was extended to any voluntarily returning runaway. He once stated: "Many things
may be done that to a casual observer may seem inadmissable,
but still, rightly managed, are productive of good. "[3]

In a brief time Curtis found considerable distance between ideals and realities.   To certain children, kindness
and verbal reprimands meant nothing.   An instance of this
caused him to substitute punishment for kindness; four days
later it was necessary to do so in an incident involving
another boy.   As time went on the security of the institution
proved to be one of Curtis' greatest problems.   Although he
found it contrary to his convictions, he increasingly adopted
severe modes of punishment.   However, it appeared that
nothing could prevent escapes.   Almost in desperation, Curtis decided that the children might be more likely to accept
a regime of punishment inflicted by themselves.   Consequently he set up a jury system, which he described in his Superintendent's Daily Journal on March 30, 1825:

> We believe that many of the boys are disposed to do
> the things that are right, and would do so were they
> not provoked by those who are restrained by fear on-
> ly.   We therefore, to enable them to get rid of such
> company, have organized a court and trial by juror;
> --the jurors consist of 5 to be elected by themselves,
> before whom ... charges of misconduct are to be
> stated, and they are to pass sentence. [4]

A break occurred between Curtis and the board of
managers because he refused to lash a boy who had voluntarily returned after running away.   Though Curtis' position
was deferred to, the resulting strained relations led to his
resignation on May 5, 1826.

Shortly after leaving the House of Refuge, Curtis became a partner in a jewel and pencil-case manufacturing
concern.   But his interest in the development of youth had
not waned.   He found fourteen apprentices, whose number
was subsequently increased to thirty, and collected them into a residence adjoining his own.   Characteristic of Curtis,
the school placed equal emphasis on social as well as vocational education.   Particular attention was given to social
interaction and the acquisition of basic education.   A sense
of independence was to be achieved not only through savings
--some accumulated as much as six hundred dollars--but also by each boy's contributing to the pay of the teachers employed.   The school ended when the firm failed following
disastrous financial investments in Virginia and North Carolina goldmining interests against which Curtis had counseled. [6]

Curtis' successor as superintendent of the New York
House of Refuge was Nathaniel C. Hart, a former school
teacher described as a tough-minded administrator and a
thorough disciplinarian.   He was superintendent for fourteen
years.   There is evidence that the jury system inaugurated
by Curtis continued for sometime.   It is mentioned in an
1827 listing of rules and regulations.   Additionally, the
"guard, " a detail of trusted inmates, kept watch along with
the regular staff.   However, the privilege of unsupervised
visits to parents and friends in the city had been discontinued.   An official report in January 1827 stated that those
trusted for such visits had "disgraced the Institution by gross
misconduct while absent. "   Records dated January 1844 refer to the selection of inmate monitors who safeguarded the
discipline of the institution. [7]

Boston House of Reformation

Another reformatory for delinquent children, the Boston House of Reformation, established in 1826, was the setting for an early experiment which was broader in scope and
lasted throughout the several years' tenure of its originator.
A young Episcopal minister, the Reverend E. M. P. Wells,
became superintendent of the institution in 1828, and promptly attracted considerable attention by his rather intensive
education programming.   Inmates were given a voting participation in the administration of the school.   Corporal punishments were entirely excluded.   Monitors were appointed
from among the youngsters at the beginning of each month
and the head monitor presided over the institution in the absence of the officers. [8]

Conceiving of his charges as citizens of a tiny republic, Wells made provisions for their participation in governing themselves.   In contrast to Curtis at the New York
House of Refuge who had resorted almost in desperation to
self-government via a jury system of the children themselves, Wells instituted self-government because of its experience value.   He viewed the institution as a laboratory to
serve the child, with emphasis on positive behavior.   The
similarity of this approach and the current total environment
or therapeutic community is startling, particularly since it
occurred almost a century and a half ago.

Gustave de Beaumont and Alexis de Tocqueville, two

young French prison commissioners on tour, commented on
the positive aspects of Wells' system.   They observed that
nobody in the institution could be punished for a fault not
provided for by divine law, or by those of the land, or of
the House itself. [9]

A book of conduct was kept in which each youngster
had his account of good and bad marks.   At a daily evening
assembly each was called upon to assign his own marks of
merit or demerit.   Such self-judgment was reportedly more
severe than if it had been made by others.   Violators of
moral law and other offenses were tried before a disciplinary court consisting of twelve inmate jurors and the superintendent.   A classification scheme provided three "bad"
grades and three "good" grades.   A schedule of promotions
from one grade to another and a system of progressively increasing privileges are interesting to note as an early form
of incentive program.

While his contemporaries had some reservations about
his program there was a consensus as to the outstanding nature and ability of Wells himself.   Disagreement with the
Boston Common Council after an official inspection visit in
1832 led to his resignation soon afterwards.

Wells than became superintendent of a South Boston
private school for the moral discipline of boys.   This institution was regarded as without precedent or equal in America.   With a capacity of forty and a tuition of $3.00 weekly,
the school admitted unruly boys and those for whom a special kind of curriculum seemed fitting.   Drawing on his experience at the House of Reformation, Wells instituted a
daily schedule which can be regarded as insurgent in an era
of dogmatic academic principles.   Through a maximum of
playtime, a broad academic curriculum, and an absence of
compulsory and supervised industrial training Wells evidently
sought to let each child find himself.   Lewis observed that
could Wells' scholastic and recreation methods be better
known, in all probability it would be determined that he was
a forerunner of Pestalozzi and Montessori. [10]

Massachusetts State Prison

The Massachusetts State Prison, Charlestown, opened
in 1805 and served as a maximum security institution until

it was officially closed in February 1956, when it was replaced by the Massachusetts Correctional Institution, South
Walpole.

Frederic Robinson became warden of the Massachusetts State Prison in 1843 and made many improvements in
prison life.   His views were remarkably modern even by
current standards.   He organized the Massachusetts State
Prison Society for Moral Improvement and Mutual Aid, with
himself as president and membership open to any inmate
willing to give a formal promise to lead an orderly and virtuous life and to take a pledge of total abstinence from liq-
uor.   Meeting fortnightly in the chapel a discussion was held
on some previously determined question.   A committee to
promote the objectives of the society was comprised of the
warden, the chaplain, who was vice-president, the prison
clerk as secretary, and six inmates chosen by a majority of
the members and approved by the warden.   Approximately
seventy-five percent of the inmates belonged to the society. 11

Gideon Haynes, who was appointed warden of the Massachusetts State Prison in 1858, wrote in 1869:12

> Mr. Robinson, in conformity with his ideas of prison
> discipline started a society among the convicts called
> 'The Massachusetts State Prison Society for Moral
> Improvement and Mutual Aid.' The meetings were
> held in the chapel.   The object as stated in the con-
> stitution, was, that 'every person, on becoming a
> member of this society, shall feel it to be his duty,
> and himself in honor pledged, to use all practicable
> means and helps for the improvement of his own mind
> and heart in knowledge and virtue, that by so doing
> it may be fitting himself for usefulness, respectabil-
> ity, and happiness, when he shall again enjoy the
> blessing of freedom and society; and furthermore,
> studiously to avoid everything which tends to corrupt,
> to debase, and to destroy; and thus to obtain the
> mastery over those passions and appetites, to whose
> influence and control so many owe their downfall and
> ruin.'
> The exercises at their meetings consisted of read-
> ing original or selected pieces, declamation, and dis-
> cussion upon various subjects, in which officers and
> prisoners joined indiscriminately, sometimes ending
> in scenes of doubtful propriety.
> Each member in good standing was presented, on

his discharge from prison, with quite an elaborate
diploma, signed by the president, vice-president, and
secretary of the society, 'recommending him to the
confidence, patronage, and the kind aid of his friends
and community at large. '

We have found no earlier references to any type of
self-government or advisory council group in American adult
institutions.   The Society for Moral Improvement and Mutual
Aid can be regarded as a noteworthy phenomenon in the
progress of American prison administration, since it is the
first recorded instance of an inmate being given a place,
however slight, in a formal communication with the administration of an adult institution.

There is no record of any other form of inmate council at the Massachusetts State Prison, Charlestown, until
1952.   Following the riot of that year an Inmate Council
was organized under an agreement referred to as the Inmate
Council Constitution.   Each work-shop could, by two-thirds
vote, elect one inmate to the Council.   The entire population
then elected six men from the Council to be councillors; the
remainder were designated as representatives.   The six
councillors elected a chairman to be the overall representative of the institution and the entire Council.   The only
qualification for Council membership was six months residency in the institution.   Term of office was six months.
Together with the editor of the inmate newspaper, who was
regarded as Council public relations officer, the councillors
met with the warden to review and discuss matters referred
by the full Council.   The Council chairman appointed a secretary who could be a non-member if there was no qualified
or voting member to fill the position.   He also appointed one
or more representatives to various committees approved by
the warden--Finance (Commissary), Sports, Entertainment,
Library, Kitchen, and Avocational.   The duties of committeemen were to observe and report in writing to the full
Council any complaints or suggestions inmates wished presented to the warden during the monthly meetings.   The
Council continued to function until the Charlestown institution
was abandoned. [13]

In 1956 all inmates were transferred to the new maximum security facility, the Massachusetts Correctional Institution, South Walpole.   The Inmate Advisory Council was
continued at the new location. [14]   Its intent and purpose according to the constitution was "to promote harmony and

insure cooperation through greater knowledge and understanding of the policy of the Administration ... and to help provide for the general welfare of all. " Provided he had six
months left to serve and had been at the institution six
months during which time he had not been confined to the
punishment unit, an inmate was eligible for election to a six
months term on the council of twenty-four members, comprised of three representatives from each medium security
housing unit and two from each of the maximum security
units. A plurality secret ballot vote by the Council determined which members would serve six months terms as
chairman, vice-chairman, and secretary. These three together with four others formed an Executive Committee
whose function was to recommend adoption or rejection of
reports made by other committees on finance, sports, entertainment, commissary, and avocational activities. Required
to meet twice a month and to conduct its deliberations according to Roberts' Rules of Order, the Council prepared an
agenda of items approved by a two-thirds majority vote for
meetings with the superintendent.

In the March 1969 issue of Mentor, the inmate publication founded in 1898, there was a front page black-bord-
ered box notice announcing that after considerable discussion
at a special session held on January 8, 1969, the members
of the Inmate Advisory Council voted to submit their resig-
nations effective forthwith. The account stated: "Reasons
for this action were multiple--most can be indexed under the
heading of 'non-cooperation' and that the Councilmen's usefulness as representatives of the Inmate body had ceased to
exist. Chairmanship, and all seats are now inactive, and
vacant. "

Detroit House of Correction

In his autobiography published in 1912, Zebulon R.
Brockway, the first superintendent of the Detroit House of
Correction which was established in 1861, reported an experiment in inmate self-government.[15] In discussing the case
of a life-term prisoner he stated:

> Now to relieve his despondency and unrest, also to
> extend an experiment in prison administration then
> afoot to utilize intelligent prisoners for their mutual

custodial and monitorial control, Brooks was assigned
to some duties usually performed by civilian officers.
He was entrusted with some inside prison keys and
given our general confidence.   He was entirely faith-
ful and remarkably efficient.   He seemed to recover
his normal mental tone and cheerfulness and he was
so engaged when I resigned my office and left the institution.   Later he relapsed into melancholia, became a permanent hospital patient, and died.

The experiment of engaging prisoners in monitorial
and mechanical supervision and in educating their fellow prisoners, as it was conducted at the Detroit
House of Correction during my Superintendency, was
ennobling to the prisoners who were so assigned, and
at one stage of the experiment it seemed feasible to
establish in such a municipal prison (at least in the
details of its administration) a system of almost complete self-government.   So much confidence did this
measure evoke that on an occasion when a majority
of all the citizen officers conspired to force my com-
pliance with an unreasonable demand by refusing further service, with the intent of closing the manufacturing activities of the establishment as the alternative, at the usual turn-out noon hour I ordered that
the six hundred prisoners be sent from their cells to
the factories in the enclosure, there to be guarded
and directed by the fellow prisoner monitors selected
and designated for such service.   But this was not
put to the test because the striking officers relented
and returned to their duty.

The promotion of prisoners to semi-official relations and duties, a practice that worked so well at
Detroit and afterwards at the Elmira Reformatory,
was very different from the use of "trusties" in common jails and prisons.   The duties were less servile
and the institutional social status of the prisoners
thus engaged was much more elevated.   It is an important and sound principle of reformatory prison science, as was attested by Maconochie at Norfolk Island, although it is disesteemed by many wardens.
The inception of the practice in my prison experience
is closely associated in memory with the service of
Brooks, Stewart, McKay, and others of the longer
sentenced United States prisoners who were confined
with the common class of misdemeanants in the Detroit House of Correction, but who were more intelligent. [15]

Helfman has advanced the thought that no doubt Brockway felt that the civic opinion of the day would brand as
sugar coating and coddling any deviation from the orthodox
"watch dog" supervision of inmates and so made no public
utterances at the time on the worthwhileness of his experiments. [16]

In 1926 Jesse O. Stutsman reported that about five
years previously while superintendent of the Detroit House of
Correction he conducted an experiment in self-government. [17]
At that time the population was a mixture of city, county,
state, and federal inmates, first offenders and recidivists of
all ages serving both misdemeanor and felony sentences.
The experiment originated as a plan to instill in the inmates
responsibility for their own conduct during entertainments
and movies which were held during evening hours when no
more than five officers were present to supervise.   Until
then the number of entertainments was sharply limited since
it had not been regarded as advisable to allow men out of
their cells unless a large number of officers were present.

Eighteen men were elected by popular vote to be responsible for the deportment of the entire population.   This
Central Council was later enlarged to thirty-six when the
population doubled.   The system was in force for three
years, working well with no serious violations despite an
original dubious staff attitude.

Reportedly the good deportment of the men was engendered by knowing that added privileges had their genesis
in this self-government arrangement in which the group sponsored its own conduct.   The Central Council drew up a constitution, approved by the superintendent and adopted by unanimous vote of all inmates.   Objectives were stated as:

1.   To promote the general welfare of all inmates.
2.   To maintain a harmonious feeling between inmates
and officials.
3.   To assist in the formation of constructive rules
for the direction of the inmates.
4.   To see that all accused inmates have a fair and
impartial hearing and that every inmate has the opportunity
for the highest possible physical, mental and moral development.
5.   To cooperate with the officials to bring production
of the shops to the highest quality of efficiency.

During the three years of the system, population turnover necessitated frequent reinterpretations of its purposes
and conditions. Although Stutsman admitted the experiment
was no acme of success, he cited several "features of ex-
cellence. " For that institution and that particular time many
constructive ends were attained whose accomplishment in any
other manner might not have been possible. During the
spring through fall months, a group of twenty men was selected each week for an outing at the prison farm located
thirty miles outside of Detroit. With an inmate as driver,
these men travelled in large open trucks. Return to the
prison was usually after dark. No man attempted to escape
and no depredations were committed along the way. However, it is reported that three of the most trusted members
of the Central Council escaped (evidently from within the
prison). This breach of trust was greatly disapproved by
the rest of the men.

Although undertaking many additional duties, members
of the Central Council were not excused from regular work
assignments nor granted special privileges. The focus of
Council members' activities was on better conditions for
all. No destructive criticism was permitted, the objective
of the system being to give the men opportunity to make
suggestions and perform services for the benefit of the entire institution.

At their own suggestion, the men organized a Production Committee of inmate foremen whose weekly meetings
resulted in closer inspection of finished products, better
methods of repairing and replacing broken machinery, and
a hundred percent increase in factory production. The Central Council also financed and directed the editing and publication of a periodical dedicated to informing the public on
modern prison methods and to educating inmates.

Superintendent Stutsman retained the authority to cen-
sor all actions or to disband the entire organization. In all
instances he fully interpreted his rulings. Discontinuance of
the Central Council occurred when all long-term prisoners
were transferred to the state prisons. The average length
of sentence was about thirty days among the misdemeanant
population remaining, being insufficient time to provide continuity of Council membership.

In 1928 the Detroit House of Correction was moved to
farmland near the town of Plymouth, Michigan. Most of the

records were lost or destroyed in the moving so that explor-
ation for other experiments similar to those reported by
Brockway and Stutsman seems not to be possible. [18]

Assuming office in April 1972, the present superintendent of the Detroit House of Correction, initiated an informal inmate council in both the women's and men's facilities. The experience with both groups led to the adoption
of a formal constitution and by-laws in the men's facility in
November 1972, with similar work in progress at that time
in the women's facility. [19]

The purpose of the Resident Advisory Council is the
maintenance and promotion of a better understanding between
residents, administration, and society. The Council's powers are limited to recommendations concerning the welfare
of the inmate body, with emphasis that members should not
attempt to interfere in daily functions, particularly custodial
matters. The Social Service Office supervises all nominations and elections. Any resident of thirty days or longer
may be nominated by the residents of his dormitory as a
representative or alternate representative. If screening by
the Disciplinary Board reveals that he has had no major
disciplinary reports in the month preceding the screening,
the nominee is allowed one week to campaign in support of
his election, at the end of which a secret ballot election is
held. The Record Office clerk is secretary to the Council.
Two members elected by the Council provide a liaison with
the superintendent during the period between monthly meetings, which are held to discuss an agenda prepared a week
earlier at a Council-member-only meeting. Tenure is limited to two consecutive four-month terms of office, with
provision for removal for disciplinary reasons by the superintendent, or recall by a two-thirds vote of the Council and
approval by the superintendent, for non-feasance or unex-
cused absence from meetings. [20]

Elmira Reformatory

Zebulon R. Brockway was appointed as the first superintendent of the Elmira Reformatory, Elmira, New York, in
1876, and remained in that position until he resigned in
1900. In his autobiography published in 1912, Brockway described a system of martial control instituted in 1888:

The reformatory became like a garrison of a thousand prisoner soldiers; more of the prisoners were utilized in the details of management, and prisoners to the number of nearly a hundred were given some military rank. They were assigned to participate in governing by service as monitors, instructors, inspectors, patrolmen, record clerks, etc. The military control was, at one time, so completely by the prisoners that on one occasion at the evening dress parade of the regiment, with a thousand men in line (no citizen but myself was present to observe it), the whole command from colonel to corporal was composed of prisoners.

The court martial and the civil court procedure were both used for the trial of offenders against rules and regulations. The courts were a mixed composition of citizens, employees, and selected prisoners. Juries were impaneled, sometimes prisoner counsel was allowed, and always full stenographic reports of the trials were made and preserved and the right of appeal was conferred. The courts served well for a time, but they became too cumbersome, so that later the trials were held before a permanently assigned examining judge from whose decisions appeals were allowed to the general superintendent, thence to the board of managers. Appeals for clemency to the general superintendent, upon whom alone devolved the duty of imposing penalties, were frequently made, but rarely an appeal for a new trial; and never except in one instance was an appeal for a new trial or review of judgment made beyond the general superintendent to the board of managers. [21]

Michigan State Prison

Hiram F. Hatch was warden of the Michigan State Prison from 1885 to 1891. His belief in the rehabilitation of amenable delinquents was in sharp contrast to the prevailing practices of the day. In 1888 he approved an organization for social betterment among the 457 inmates. [22] In an unsupervised meeting an inmate committee drew up a constitution, naming the organization The Mutual Aid League of the M. S. P. This constitution set forth the ideals of the group:

The objects of this league shall be: by social inter-
course to improve ourselves, and to aid in the moral,
intellectual, physical and financial advancement of
our fellowmen.   To inculcate a higher appreciation
of the value and sacred obligations of American citizenship, and the necessity of unconditional loyalty to
the Federal and State government, as exemplified by
a strict maintenance of the laws by them promulgated.
To resist and oppose corruption and dishonesty in all
forms and places and to promote honesty and efficiency in the discharge of all labor, tasks and duties
assigned.   To respect and aid by personal discipline,
in the maintenance of all rules and regulations necessary to the discipline and good order of the prison.

Meetings were held monthly with the warden as presiding officer.   Reports indicate he did this alone without
guards.   In line with the by-laws of the organization, Warden
Hatch appointed nine members as an executive board who
met with him weekly.   The organization provided a means
of communication between staff and inmates and was expected to assist in the orientation of new arrivals.

Warden Hatch received considerable criticism from
contemporaries, which he answered by referring to a favorable record in the maintenance of prison discipline.   The
program was dropped with his resignation on February 3,
1891.

The George Junior Republic

The Junior Republic movement has particular importance in a study of self-government in institutions.   Two of
the later strong advocates for inmate self-government were
associates of the founder.   They were Thomas Mott Osborne,
a member of the Board of Directors, and Calvin Derrick,
General Superintendent of the National Association of Junior
Republics.

William Reuben George (1866-1936), New York City
manufacturer, became interested in the problem of slum
children.   Beginning in the summer of 1890 he took approximately fifty teen-agers to the Dryden, New York, area of
his boyhood for a two-week outing.   Railroad fares were

paid by the New York Tribune's Fresh Air Fund and food
was furnished by farmers in the vicinity.   The following
summer George took an annual lease of a forty-acre farm
near Freeville, New York.   Nearby churches began donating
food and supplies.

Prior to the fifth summer George decided to introduce
the idea that everything must be paid for by work.   The
idea was at first resisted, but eventually it prevailed.   In
previous summers George had dealt with the problem of discipline by having offenders tried before a jury of their fel-
lows.   Impressed with the results, he decided to combine
the principles of both self-support and self-government.   He
set up a small-scale model, both politically and economical-
ly, of the larger society to which the children would soon
belong and thus was launched the Junior Republic in 1895.23

As a model village, the Republic was composed of
boys and girls sixteen to twenty-one years of age.   The Republic had a president, vice-president, cabinet, judges,
courts, and a prison.   Town meetings for legislative purposes were provided.   The community had its own currency
and various economic enterprises--a farm, carpentry shop,
printing shop and others, all offering employment for wages.
During the late 1890's the Republic was established on a
year-round basis, and a school became an important part of
its facilities.

While for the most part the residents continued to
come from the New York slums, as the fame of the Junior
Republic spread it received some youthful offenders who
might otherwise have been sent to reform school.   Contemporary accounts reported high morale and suggested that the
George Junior Republic was notably successful in channeling
the energies and loyalties of potential delinquents to constructive ends.

While the George Junior Republic acquired a wide
reputation prior to World War I, and other republics were
organized in five states, the experiment did not prove successful on a national scale.   A Junior Republic is still in
operation at Freeville, New York.

Auburn Prison--Women's Division

The records of the Women's Prison Association of
New York for the year 1903 contain the comments of Alice
L. Woodbridge, Prison Visitor, following a visit to the
State Prison for Women at Auburn:

> The Superintendent, Mrs. Welshe, has organized a
> society among the prisoners. This is known as the
> 'Society of the Red Badge of Merit, ' and women who
> break no rules for six months are eligible as mem-
> bers. When a rule is broken by a member, she is
> suspended for six months. This has had a wonderful
> effect upon the prisoners. The society meets once a
> month, and some kind of entertainment is provided.
> A badge made of common white cloth bound with red
> and bearing the letters 'S. R. B. M. ' is worn by them
> but it is easily defaced and a more substantial one
> is needed. As this society has proved its efficiency
> as a means of discipline, the prison department
> should supply a proper badge for it. Twenty-five dol-
> lars would purchase a sufficient number of substantial
> badges to last for two years.
> For some unaccountable reason, the women em-
> ployed as matrons in Auburn State Prison are not
> subjected to State Civil Service examination. In all
> other prisons and jails where women are employed,
> a Civil Service examination is required; and if effi-
> cient and intelligent supervision is needed anywhere,
> it is needed in a State Prison. Without it, the posi-
> tion is open to all sorts of abuses. [24]

In November 1913, Madeline Zabriskie Doty, a member of the New York State Commission on Prison Reform,
together with Elizabeth C. Watson, voluntarily spent a week
in confinement at Auburn Prison--Women's Division. Their
identity was unknown to either staff or inmates. Both were
committed on the evening of November 13, as Maggie Martin
and Lizzie Watson. Supposedly each had been sentenced to
serve eighteen to thirty months for forgery. Their joint report revealed rather extreme conditions, and resulted in
some improvements. [25]

Some months later, Miss Doty received letters from
the inmates indicating that the matrons were not fully in accord with the changes. After she learned there was a new
head matron, Miss Doty visited the prison and met with the

inmates.   Out of their discussions came the idea to organize
a group to provide a channel for inmate communication to
the head matron.   The latter agreed to accord the group the
same recognition given to employees.   The new organization
was called the Daily Endeavor League; its color emblem a
blue bow. 26

A charter of organization was drawn, providing for a
president and representative of each housing unit to be
chosen by the inmates.   All inmates were to be members
of the League and even though suspended for abuse, good behavior could make a new enrollment possible.   Participation
in the League turned the interest of the women toward the
improvement of conditions from their prior sole concern
with personal woes.   A reign of good behavior resulted in
the women's being allowed outside their cells on Sunday after-
noons for a recreation hour.   Correspondence and visiting
rules were liberalized.   The head matron proposed and held
a Valentine Day party, lasting from four to nine p. m.

Soon, however, the matrons began reasoning that
should the good behavior of the inmates continue, fewer
matrons would be needed and this could result in a staff reduction of perhaps fifty percent.   The situation deteriorated,
and despite a work-training plan introduced by Miss Doty,
staff antagonism to the League caused the head matron to
reverse her original favorable stance.   There then ensued
an incident which marked the end of the League.   A woman
suspended by the group for poor conduct was befriended by
the staff, putting the League in a position of ridicule and,
in the opinion of Miss Doty, placing a premium on bad conduct.   A few days later the head matron declared herself
president of the League and directed the representatives to
report misbehavior to her and the staff.   Returning to the
prison, Miss Doty called an assembly of all inmates, announcing that she believed self-government with the officials
in command was a farce and that there could be no tolera-
tion of an organization whose representatives must become
informers.   A unanimous vote to disband the League was
made.

The Women's Division of the Auburn Prison was
merged with the Westfield State Farm at Bedford Hills, New
York in 1933.   The facility is now designated as the Bedford
Hills Correctional Facility.

Sleighton Farm School for Girls

Sleighton Farm School is a residential treatment center for girls between the ages of 12 and 18 who have been
committed by the county juvenile courts.   The School is located six miles southwest of Media, Pennsylvania.   It is a
private institution, owned and operated by a non-profit cor-
poration and governed by a nineteen-member Board of Managers, of which four are court appointed.   The Commonwealth
of Pennsylvania, by legislative act, gives an appropriation to
the School, which is matched by the committing counties for
the girls whom they refer.   This school may be the second
oldest private institution accepting troubled youngsters in the
United States.   Originally called the Philadelphia House of
Refuge, it began operation on December 8, 1828.   In the
early 1890's the boys' section was moved to Glen Mills and
in 1910 the girls' section moved to its present location.   The
two schools were incorporated under the name of Glen Mills
Schools, but on April 17, 1931, the girls' section was given
its present designation.

Superintendent Martha Platt Falconer took office in
1906 and established in 1910 a dynamic system of student
government designed to place responsibility upon the girls
for the maintenance of good morale and to make possible a
large measure of freedom and self-expression. [27]   The program was operating under the same concept and with basically the same procedures in 1967, and was referred to as
Cottage Government. [28]

The purpose of student participation in government in
the five Honor Cottages was to help the girl to develop inner
controls so that she could become an acceptable citizen, first
in her Honor Cottage, then in the school as a whole, and
next in the community.   Additionally, each girl was given the
opportunity to develop leadership, gain ability to help others,
and experience the satisfaction of cooperative work with
adults.

After undergoing a period of orientation in the reception cottage, a girl moved into an honor cottage of her own
choice where she was accorded junior citizenship status.
Upon completing a six-weeks' period of demonstrated mature
behavior she could be voted citizenship privileges by other
girls in that status.   If during the ensuing eight weeks she
was regarded as making progress in her personal development

and interpersonal relationships she attained Leader standing.
Following a like period she was eligible for election to a
Cottage Council.   Council girls were largely responsible for
morale in the cottage and the behavior of its residents.   In
weekly Council meetings they also assisted the housemothers
and the student government director in making decisions regarding the discipline of other girls.   The decision might be
to talk with the girl involved and attempt to help her to improve, advise her that a recurrence of the unacceptable behavior could result in a restriction of movie attendance or
participation in some other activity, or the actual imposition
of a restriction.   In extreme situations the offender could be
removed from the Honor Cottage temporarily, or permanently, and placed in another type of living unit.

        During the nineteen-sixties there began a slow but ob-
vious change in the characteristics of the population.   A
greater number of more disturbed and harder-to-reach youngsters, from all strata of society, rather than principally
from the ranks of the underprivileged, were referred by the
courts.   These more sophisticated and educationally ambit-
ious individuals, many the products of the drug culture, required a more intensive treatment program than had hitherto
existed.   Additional psychiatrists, social workers, and other
professionally trained personnel were added to the staff.
The original concept of student government was expanded to
develop consultants among the girls in matters of clothing
and other needs where adolescent taste is important.   As
they develop in insight and maturity the girls are assigned
as junior staff and assist in group therapy.   The fact that
runaway attempts are minimal is attributed to this involvement in their own treatment process.   The focus of school
efforts is increasingly on helping the girls to gain greater
independence and to assume greater responsibility as they
move through the program.   A Graduate Student Unit has
been established for those who attend off-campus programs
of vocational and business training and academic classes at
the secondary and college levels.   It is hoped that a half-way
house can be developed within the year.[29]

Preston School of Industry

        Calvin Derrick utilized the pioneering work of William
Reuben George who founded the George Junior Republic, when

appointed superintendent of the Preston School of Industry,
Ione, California, in October 1912.   He outlined and formu-
lated a program using inmate self-government as the key-
stone of its arch.   It is significant to note that the Ione
program represents the first acknowledgment and endorsement of inmate self-government by any state.   At the in-
auguration of the second president of the self-government
group, Governor Hiram Johnson of California went to the
school and placed the stamp of his official approval upon the
program. 30

Prior to inaugurating the self-government program
Derrick requested that the Department of Sociology of the
University of California send out a questionnaire on the subject to various correctional institutions.   His conclusions,
based on the receipt of over one hundred replies, were:

1.   Few people in correctional institutions thoroughly
believed in the principles of democracy and their application
to populations in custody.
2.   Almost all correctional institution personnel were
ignorant of the manner in which these principles should or
could be applied.
3.   The rank and file of institution people were so
prejudiced against the plan that they could not be induced to
examine it with an open mind.

Perhaps Derrick's philosophy concerning self-government can best be expressed by his statement: "The principles of self-government are the principles of democracy.
If democracy is right, then self-government is right.   It is
not, therefore, a question of principles; it is a question of
the intelligent application of principles to a given set of
conditions. "

The Ione concept of the application of self-government
was characterized by two ideas:

1.   Self-government is not an end, but a means to a
very definite purpose.   While the prosecution of one inmate
by another is not the main object of self-government, it
does serve a definite purpose and affords splendid training
in a variety of ways.
2.   Since the home, school, church, and city have
each in turn failed to make the boy fit into the established
and approved pattern of civilization, we cannot place him in
an institution which forces a much higher and more nearly
perfect social order on him.

The sole purpose of this system of self-government was to furnish a medium in which the boys might develop a civilization of their own with as many degrees and gradations as necessary to meet their needs and interests, the ideal being to come as close as possible to standards of civilization.

As an introduction, boys were granted two hours a day of self-government under staff supervision. The institution was operated as a quasi-military organization, the population being divided into companies. Each company was given a brief and faulty constitution. Two experimented with a military government, but a civil form of government was developed by all after some fourteen months of operation. Differences of opinion concerning interpretation of the constitution gave rise to political parties. Confusion resulting from the differing laws of the various companies brought about a House of Congress. Disagreement as to which laws should be retained or abolished caused the formation of a commission to codify civil and penal procedure and finally a body of uniform law. A prison was built to enforce the mandates of the courts. With prisoners to care for, it was necessary to provide work for them. A commissioner of labor was appointed to administer a work program of certain rough, unskilled labor. An orientation program was organized with the provision that its completion by newly admitted boys was a prerequisite to eligibility as a voter.

There were twenty-two marshals and deputy marshals responsible for an honor system operated among some 350 boys. These boy marshals had as much liberty and as much responsibility concerning the custody of the boys in their companies as did the staff within the grounds. Approximately ten percent of the population were found unfit for participation in the self-government program and were controlled by employees.

It is understood that Derrick was granted a leave of absence effective July 1, 1916, to become assistant warden to Thomas Mott Osborne, then warden of Sing Sing Prison, Ossining, New York, and that the self-government program at the Preston School of Industry was discontinued the following year. No information has been obtained whether or not he took the Sing Sing Prison position (Warden Osborne resigned on October 16, 1916), but it has been verified that Derrick was superintendent of the Westchester County Penitentiary, Valhalla, New York, from 1917 to 1921, and

established a self-government group known as the Effort
League, which is later recounted.

At the present time, each of the eight living units in
the Preston School of Industry is designed to serve the
specific needs of groupings such as drug users, recalcitrants,
and parole violators.   Ward participation is provided in a
variety of opportunities ranging from scheduled large group
meetings attended by the superintendent and assistant superintendent, to well organized student government in the drug
program.   Other formal communication is achieved in small
groups.   Wards assigned to the Food Service elect representatives who meet weekly with the Food manager and his
staff to discuss assignee-related problems. [31]

New Jersey State Reformatory

The New Jersey State Reformatory at Rahway was
opened in 1901.   In 1948 it became an adult institution and
is now known as the New Jersey State Prison.

Dr. Frank Moore became superintendent in 1909,
bringing to the position many years of experience in school
administration.   He made many program changes based on a
policy that life in the reformatory should approximate that
outside to the end that a releasee might better be able to
adjust himself to a normal existence.   He conducted programs of public education by arranging for illustrated lectures to be given in all counties of the state upon the methods of reformation employed at Rahway.

In 1913 Dr. Moore established a tentative form of
inmate self-government which he described in his annual report of 1914:

> One of the new features of the year has been the
> adoption of a plan of self-government.   During the
> summer just passed there was organized a Council
> composed of thirty of the inmates elected by the in-
> mates themselves.   The duty of this Council is to
> assist in the discipline of the institution.   They give
> particular attention to the keeping of order on the
> tiers, and to suppressing conversation with regard to
> crime and to preventing profanity.   They have elected

their own president and secretary, and meet twice a
week.   All new inmates after they have been ad-
dressed by the superintendent are taken into the
Council meeting and given advice by the president of
the Council as to how they may best conduct themselves while in the reformatory and as to what is the
spirit of the inmates and the desire of the Council to
lend them help whenever it can.   The power has been
given to the Council not to administer punishment in
any way, but to deprive inmates whose influence is
harmful from the privileges of the yard and from entertainments. 32

In his annual report of 1915, Superintendent Moore reported:

We gave the plan a trial for one year and then put
the question to a vote of the inmates as to whether
or not they desired to have the plan continued another
year.   A feeling had grown that there had been more
or less unfairness by 'The Council. '   Politics to
some extent had entered from time to time in the
selection of the councilmen, so that the two plans of
being governed by council or officers of the institution
were now put squarely before the young men for a
decision as to which system of government they preferred.   The result of their vote was overwhelmingly
in favor of being governed by the officers rather than
inmates.   This vote shows that the young man who
has been unable to control himself aright realizes that
he is incapable of controlling others.   He sees that it
is best for him to be under proper control.   When
that control is fair and administered with a spirit of
sincerity and kindness, he feels it is for his good and
willingly yields to it.   Especially will he do this, if
he feels that he can look up to those who are governing him.   But he will rebel, if those who assume to
be his superiors are only his equals, who take advantage of their position to secure special privileges,
violate rules or play favorites.   Realizing these facts
after giving the question sober consideration the inmates of the Reformatory felt that it was better for
them that the institution should return to the original
plan of being governed by the appointed authority of
the institution and hence the council disbanded. 33

Wines commented on Superintendent Moore's report:

Lack of familiarity with governmental procedure would seem to be as strong a reason for continuing self-government as for abandoning it. Then, too, the inmate officers at Rahway who assumed to be 'superior' and took advantage of their position to secure special privileges might have been quickly dealt with by the other inmates, one would think, if these had been sufficiently induced to regard self-government as their venture--as something that they could make or mar as they chose.... One suspects that possibly the remedy ... was an arrangement for the 'recall' of arrogant and recalcitrant officials by the inmates themselves.

Superintendent Moore's explanation did not appeal to the members of the New Jersey Prison Inquiry Commission [1917] as final. Referring to the fact that this experiment was said to have developed 'ward politics,' the commission pointed out in its report that 'that is an incident not unknown to self-government outside prison walls, and if it is a greater menace in correctional institutions than in the wards of a city, it is, on the other hand, more easily dealt with.' Of all correctional institutions, it went on, Rahways seems, 'both in the character of its population and in the strong and efficient government that it possesses, to be the one best adapted to work out such an experiment safely and successfully.' It finally suggested that 'another trial might wisely be made' before the method was wholly abandoned. 34

Auburn Prison

Thomas Mott Osborne of Auburn, New York, had long been interested in the problems of prison management and in prisoner resocialization. As a member of the Board of Directors, George Junior Republic, he had learned first-hand of the self-government program iniated by William Reuben George. His belief that the principles of self-government could be utilized as a remedy for the evils of the prison system was expressed in his address to the National Prison Association in 1906:

The prison system endeavors to make men industrious by driving them to work; to make them virtuous by

removing temptation; to make them respect law by
forcing them to obey edicts of an autocrat; to make
them far-sighted by allowing them no chance to exercise foresight; to give them individual initiative by
treating them in large groups; in short to prepare
them again for society by placing them in conditions
as unlike real society as they could well be made. . . .
    Outside the walls a man must choose between work
and idleness--between honesty and crime. Why not
let him teach himself these lessons before he comes
out? Such things are best learned by experience.
Some can acquire their lesson in life by the experience of others; but most men are in prison for the
very reason that they cannot do that. But everyone
who is not an absolute fool can learn by experience,
and the bulk of men in prison certainly are not
fools. . . . [35]

Late in 1913, Osborne spent a voluntary one week
term of confinement in Auburn Prison under the pseudonym
of Tom Brown. Out of this grew the plan for establishing
an inmate self-government program whose stated purpose and
objective was to alter concepts of confinement then practiced
routinely in the majority of penal institutions. A cardinal
principle was that the prisoners must work out their own
plan, rather than have an outside plan presented to them.
Osborne noted: "This was real, vital democracy; this was
solving the problem in the genuine American spirit. "[36]

The first name proposed for the organization was
Good Conduct League, followed by the Tom Brown League.
The latter was rejected by Osborne as being too personal.
Finally, Mutual Welfare League was agreed upon as the of-
ficial designation. There then followed several meetings to
implement the plan of self-government. [37]

On December 26, 1913 a free election was held in the
institution to choose a committee of forty-nine to determine
the exact nature and organization of the League. The first
meeting of the elected Committee was held on December 28,
and a chairman was selected. It was unanimously decided
to make League membership available to all, with bad conduct as the sole reason for expulsion. In addition, a sub-
committee of twelve members was selected to formulate by-
laws. The League objective was stated as: "The promotion
in every way of the true interests and welfare of the men
confined in prison. " The motto "Do Good--Make Good" was

adopted.   Emblematic of Hope and Truth, green and white
were chosen as League Colors.   It was agreed that there be
a Board of Delegates of forty-nine members, elected for a
six-month term, to serve as the governing body of the organization.   Election of the Board of Delegates took place
on January 15, 1914, and the members were installed in office on January 18.

On February 11, 1914, the Board of Delegates met in
order that the inmate sergeant-at-arms could give instruc-
tions for conduct during the first general meeting of the
League.   The first general meeting of the Mutual Welfare
League, featuring a piano and violin recital, was held on
February 12, 1914.

It is significant to note that Warden Rattigan, of Auburn, with the approval of the New York State Superintendent
of Prisons, proposed to hand over all infractions of discipline to the League except in five instances: assault on an
officer, deadly assault upon another inmate, refusal to work,
strike, and attempt to escape.

Prisoner cooperation was the foundation of the League.
Its operations were based on the premise that the prison
could be treated as a community.   Tannenbaum espoused
this by his comment: "Prisoners possessed among themselves a public opinion that if properly harnessed could be
made effective in the enforcement of public policy and the
development of public morale, which would make discipline
both easier upon the Warden and more effective with the
men. "38

The Mutual Welfare League continued to function at
the Auburn Prison until 1929, but its original purpose and
procedures were deflected throughout the years.   (See the
report from the 1926 edition of the Handbook of American
Prisons on page 54.)

In 1966, the then warden at Sing Sing Prison, basing
his comments on his service since 1926 with the New York
State Department of Corrections, stated that the Mutual Welfare League was deeply involved in the riots of 1929 at the
Auburn Prison and ceased operations thereafter.   Leadership
apparently had fallen into the hands of inmates who should
not have been elected to represent others as they had actually strong-armed their way into leadership. 39

Sing Sing Prison

In 1914, during his very brief administration, Warden
McCormick succeeded in "opening up Sing Sing. " He introduced a system of regulated leisure, allowing prisoners
freedom of the yard on Saturday afternoon and all day Sunday.   The dire predictions of chaos by others were not fulfilled.   He also formed the first inmate self-government organization at Sing Sing known as the Golden Rule Brotherhood,
whose design was similar to the Mutual Welfare League at
Auburn Prison. [40]

Thomas Mott Osborne became warden of Sing Sing
Prison, Ossining, New York, on December 1, 1914.   He
immediately organized a Mutual Welfare League which was
described in Wines' book:

> At Sing Sing, the Secretary of the League was relieved
> of all other prison duties and gave his full time to
> this work.   An office was fitted up for him next to
> that of the principal keeper, and here he kept his
> records, interviewed his callers and dictated his
> correspondence.   He was one of the busiest men in
> prison.
>   The real instruments of self-government at Sing
> Sing were the Committees.   It was these that effec-
> tively expressed the wishes of the prisoners and took
> initiative in getting things done.   The Warden's day
> was filled with appointments with Committee Chair-
> men who wanted assistance or advice.   The Chair-
> men quickly came to realize that a great deal of
> power lay in their hands if they knew how to wield
> it.   Not only were they the trustees of the wishes of
> their fellow-inmates, but the prison officials came to
> regard them as responsible makers of institution
> policy.   Some of them became adept in the art of
> getting what they wanted without appearing to ask for
> much.   Aside from the specific things they accom-
> plished, their activity was beneficial in two ways:
> (1) It taught them some of the difficulties of adminis-
> tration, thus enabling them to pass that knowledge
> back to their constituents; and (2) It enabled the pris-
> on authorities, by means of the understanding they
> promoted, to rely upon cooperation where before they
> would have received only suspicion and distrust. [41]

Barnes commented on the program:

> A number of influences combined to bring Mr. Os-
> borne's regime to a premature end at Sing Sing.
> Among these may be mentioned Mr. Osborne's failure
> to comprehend that his system was applicable only to
> non-defective convicts, and that it must be preceded
> by an adequate system of clinical observation, classi-
> fication and promotion of convicts; his own unyielding
> and uncompromising attitude, so characteristic of the
> ardent reformer on the defensive; the opposition of
> the keepers and guards who had been trained wholly
> in the savage methods of the conventional repressive
> penology; the bitter enmity of grafting contractors
> who found Mr. Osborne as little susceptible to dis-
> honesty as to conventionality; the opposition of politi-
> cal rivals among the most notorious 'rounders' of the
> machine politicians; and the jealousy of leading penol-
> ogists of a more conventional and conservative cast. [42]

In his book, Twenty Thousand Years in Sing Sing,
Lewis E. Lawes, who became warden there in 1920, described the Mutual Welfare League as then being part and
parcel of the administration. League officers were permitted
out of their cells long after midnight, and were assigned to
the visiting room where they had unrestricted contact with
outsiders. Also, they were in charge of all tours of the
prison, an activity popular with out-of-town groups in 1920,
and had full control of the store, making their own purchases, and banking and disbursing League funds with practically no supervision. The League's Executive Board appointed its sergeant-at-arms who selected his own deputies.
In addition to functioning as monitors in the mess hall, they
had charge of the recreation field, the chapel, and all athletic events and entertainment. It was their right and duty
to report any prisoner for violation of rules or for delin-
quencies to the League Court. Before this group of seven
judges the accuser and accused presented the facts. Sadly,
not always being of the highest calibre, the judges often
failed to examine facts impartially. Instances of double
jeopardy were reported. Men disciplined by the Warden's
Court were often held answerable for the same offense to
the League Court. [43]

Lawes believed that the Mutual Welfare League was a
worthwhile organization but that it had been badly administered. The membership was divided into two camps whose

energies were concentrated on coralling votes. The better
element remained aloof from the League, as a consequence
of which it became the plaything of the less desirable men.
On election day, apprehensively anticipated by the staff, the
first-aid clinic was kept busy.

Within a brief time, Lawes abolished the League's
Court, as well as party politics. He clearly defined the
sphere of influence of the League in its relation to the prison administration. With the disappearance of partisanship,
the type of men capable of exerting a good influence on others came to the fore. Lawes was of the opinion that the
term self-government in prison was a much abused and
greatly misconstrued term and that the true meaning of the
term was the government of self.

Although Lawes cited Thomas Mott Osborne as being
outstanding among prison administrators, he did not hesitate
to point out what he believed to be mistakes made by Osborne in his dealings with the Mutual Welfare League.
Lawes commented:

> I believe that prisoners should be allowed a measure
> of self-expression, a voice in the kind and character
> of their social and recreational activities. These,
> however, must at all times be subject to administra-
> tive supervision and censorship. The defect of Mr.
> Osborne's administration was in the overlapping of
> prisoner self-government with the Warden's responsi-
> bility as an administrator. His intense desire to
> raise the prisoner to a normal place led him to sur-
> render his prerogatives. He became an advisor in-
> stead of a leader and ruler. The swing of the pen-
> dulum from severity to liberality was too wide. It
> resulted in chaos. Mr. Osborne was not given the
> opportunity to correct this fault. His term of office
> ended too soon. [44]

In the 1926 Handbook of American Prisons, editors
Austin H. MacCormick and Paul W. Garrett stated that the
following comments were equally true both of the prison at
Sing Sing and at Auburn:

> While the League has, in all the different and varying
> conditions, never entirely ceased to be a factor in the
> administration of the prison, it has, unfortunately,
> ceased to be much more than an aid to prison

management. The tendency is for the prison authorities to use the League as a convenient aid to secure
easy prison administration: they do not guide and
direct it so that it accomplishes its fundamental purpose of developing the right social viewpoint to replace the criminal viewpoint of individual selfishness.
They use the League chiefly to serve the prison management rather than use both the League and the administration to serve society. To accomplish the
fundamental and larger purpose requires a type of
leadership, at once imaginative and constructive,
which has not been given. [45]

The Mutual Welfare League is no longer in existence,
having faded away in 1950. [46]

New Jersey Correctional Institution for Women

Opened in 1913, the Correctional Institution for Wom-
en, Clinton, was originally known as Clinton Farms and later as the New Jersey Reformatory for Women.

From 1914 until January 1973, student government,
the core of programming, grew progressively less able to
meet the needs of a changing population. In response to a
request by inmates, a staff-inmate committee recently revised the system in the hope of providing a mutual relationship which will increase problem solving at the cottage level
and open up channels of communication between inmates and
administrative staff. The system is based upon the use of
General Inmate Representatives (GIR's) elected by secret ballot for a term of six months. Since these women not only
represent their cottages at meetings with administration but
also are expected to assist staff in mediating and counselling
with inmates, final approval of GIR's is given by the Classification Committee. Any staff member may meet at any
time with their GIR's and a monthly meeting is held with the
administrative staff and one GIR from each cottage to discuss problems affecting the entire population. [47]

Reports received in 1967 provided the following information regarding the Student Government Program from its
inception in 1914. [48]

Student government was brought to the then Clinton Farms by Superintendent May Caughey from the Sleighton Farm School for Girls in Pennsylvania, where the theory had been introduced by Superintendent Martha P. Falconer in 1910.   The insufficient physical accommodations of the institution and the small staff complement permitted no more than minimum security so that some form of student government honor system was necessitated.

The continued use of self-government meant a constant refining of its procedures and purposes.   However, the basic philosophy that responsibility for one's own progress makes a most effective rehabilitative tool was not changed.   Student officers were elected by each cottage. An Honor/Group was made up of residents with a three months' clear conduct record who were recommended by their peers.   An Honor Pledge was used as a symbol of acceptance of the effort that constitutes resocialization.   The original requirement for "reporting anyone I believe to be planning to run away," was later deleted in consistency with a de-emphasis of implied authority of one inmate over another.   The governing advisory group in 1914 consisted of an executive group called the Council of Commissioners and Improvement Committee, composed of representatives from each cottage.   It was later renamed the Improvement Committee.   Its functions were advisory and sanctions suggested required approval by the superintendent.   In 1961 the duty of orienting the new girls to the rules of the institution was added as a function.

In 1948 overcrowding was regarded as the cause of numerous runaways.   The staff consulted with the population on methods both to prevent and to discipline runaways, and to consider methods of rewarding cottages having no runaways.   This is a good example of staff and student government integration.   Group responsibility key-noted this cooperative effort which aided the institution during a crisis.

Several instances were advanced as to why student government had lasted at Clinton Farms:

1.   It is functional.
2.   It allows for open lines of communication.
3.   The charisma of the superintendents.
4.   The unity and cooperation of the staff.
5.   Since it was an original part of the institution administration it has never posed a threat to the administration.

The identification is now traditional.

    6.   Student government allows for flexibility in dealing with institutional and individual crises.

    7.   No outside political pressures to disband the form have been exerted.

Two instances of the spread of student government from Clinton Farms to other institutions are documented. Dr. Mary B. Harris, who was superintendent in 1918, became superintendent in 1927 of the Federal Reformatory for Women at Alderson, West Virginia; and Miss Grace Robson, who became head of a juvenile girls institution in North Carolina, instituted student government in those institutions.

Connecticut State Reformatory

The October 1, 1914, report of the Board of Directors, Connecticut Reformatory, Cheshire, Connecticut, states:

> Recently a Welfare League has been established by the inmates, founded on a somewhat similar institution at Auburn, New York, and along the lines of the George Junior Republic, its object being to encourage the boys, not only to assist each other, but in certain minor matters to govern and police themselves, under the general supervision of the Superintendent of the institution. The features of this League are of such recent establishment that little can be said at the present time of its success.... 49

In September 1915, C. H. Johnson who was assistant warden at Sing Sing Prison, New York, under Warden Osborne, became superintendent at the Connecticut Reformatory. The League was abandoned in May 1916, according to Superintendent Johnson's report:

> The reason for the dissatisfaction in the organization was that it lent itself readily to so much misrule and dishonesty that the inmates were tired of it. The young men in the reformatory were, to a large extent, foreigners from the industrial sections of the cities of the State. Many of them knew but little of the English language, some of them practically nothing. There were very few who knew anything about

forms of government, and their ideas in such matters
were extremely vague. When it came to the election
of officials, the more clever inmates were able by
threats, bribery and other similar means to secure
their own election, and the more ignorant inmates
had but a vague idea of what it was all about. In
judicial matters it was extremely difficult to find in
such a population inmates who had a mind which lent
itself to judicial procedure and which could weigh
evidence for or against the institutional offender.
The result was that the judges were invariably those
who had been selected by the inmate population because it was expected that they would be helpful to
possible offenders in time of need. All kinds of adjustments were attempted to overcome these conditions, which were inherent in the nature of the population of the institution, but without success. ... It
was finally decided at a gathering of the inmates that
the management of the institution should be placed
with the Superintendent and the officers appointed by
law.

There was then begun the development of a method
of military instruction. It was found that the young
men who came to the institution had done practically
as they pleased most of their lives, had no respect
for authority and had very little idea of obeying any-
body when they were told to do so. Their physical
carriage was just about as slouchy as their mental
condition and social attitude. A military battalion
was organized, inmate officers were selected on the
grounds of merit and ability and not on the basis of
purchased popularity, and beneficial results were
quite noticeable in the physical appearance and attitudes of the inmates. It was quite evident that what
the inmates needed was not more freedom, of which
they had had an excess in their life, but direction
and instruction in self-control and obedience to law
and order. 50

Westchester County Penitentiary

Calvin Derrick was superintendent of the Westchester
County penitentiary from 1917 until 1921. His philosophy of
self-government as he had expressed it at the Preston

School of Industry, Ione, California, was enunciated again
when he approved an inmate meeting on September 17, 1917,
to discuss forming an organization.   Temporary officers
were chosen and successive meetings resulted in the adoption of a constitution and by-laws on October 12.   Known as
the Effort League, the group had as officers a president,
vice-president, judge, secretary, sergeant-at-arms, and a
public defender.   These officers formed a League Cabinet
which met periodically with the administration. [51]

As given in the constitution, the aims of the Effort
League were:

1.   To discipline ourselves.
2.   To cooperate with the Warden of this institution
in the enforcement of all rules.
3.   To educate ourselves by lectures, debates, and
by whatever other means, making for uplift, we are capable
of securing.
4.   To promote our welfare by the improvement of
conditions and by whatever material aid we can and are
privileged to contribute.
5.   To entertain ourselves by clean and healthy
sports and amusements.

The warden was an honorary president and the associate wardens were honorary members.   An officer was appointed by the warden to serve as League ambassador.   The
initiation ceremony was quite impressive according to a contemporary account:

> It usually takes place during a Saturday evening so-
> cial meeting.   The new men, who have previously
> been instructed by a reception committee as to the
> League and its purposes, are called before the Presi-
> dent, the Judge and the other members of the Cabi-
> net.   The President speaks a few words of welcome
> and the Judge, after a short talk on the responsibil-
> ities and privileges of membership and the meaning
> and reality of the pledge, administers the latter.
> The new men in turn sign the constitution, the entire
> membership standing and singing 'America' mean-
> while, after which the newly-made members file be-
> fore the Cabinet for a hearty hand-shake and personal
> greeting. [51]

The Effort League sought to extend its influence and

aid to every member after his release.   Those returning to
the community were encouraged to contact the League for
any readjustment assistance.   The League sponsored cash
donations and volunteer work for the Red Cross.   It organized an evening school program whose principal purpose was
social rather than academic education.   Supervision was
given to the cleaning of living and work areas by the appointment of a League inspector who made daily sanitation
inspections.

An Inmate's Court for the Establishment of Good Relationship, regarded as the most important feature of the
self-government work, was presided over by an inmate judge
who, with two other members, heard all cases referred for
trivial infractions of the rules, such as failure to have a
clean cell or lack of attention to work.   The Court had no
punitive powers.   Its effect lay in the ability of the members
to motivate cooperation by counsel and advice.   Failing this,
the Court could expel the offender from the League.

In his annual report for the period January 1, 1917,
through December 31, 1918, Superintendent Derrick stated:

At the beginning of the year the matter of discipline
was practically all in the hands of the institution
officials.   They were wholly responsible for the
maintenance of good order and the proper behavior
of the inmate population.   In many cases the results
were not all that were to be desired.   How to handle
some of the problems arising was a question not always easy of solution without resorting to older and
harsher methods, which we would not under any circumstances consider.   After many official confer-
ences, and having in mind the growing influence of
the Effort League and its possibilities for good, we
determined to grant to the inmates the opportunity for
governing themselves by assuming some of these
disciplinary responsibilities.   At first in a limited
way, then, as our confidence increased, in larger
measure.   We found this method most successful.
Minor cases were referred to the Inmates' Court,
and as time went on, more important matters, until
practically all complaints, both inmate and official,
were handed over to this court, where they were
handled in a most judicial and satisfactory manner,
not only to the official force but also to the offending
inmates.   In this way our disciplinary problems were

reduced to a minimum, and we had very few cases where it was necessary to in any way take matters into our own hands.

On January 1, 1918, the Effort League of the Westchester County Penitentiary and Workhouse had been in existence just two and one-half months. It had demonstrated its right to continue, but while its ideals were worthy ones not much had been accomplished in a practical way. Nothing had been forced upon it, in fact nothing has ever been done at any time that savored of coercion, but the men, and particularly the members of the League Cabinet, realizing something of the possibilities of such an organization and its power for good to the inmate population, worked earnestly to advance the League's power and influence. The way was not always plain, either to the inmates or the officials, but one principle always prevailed, viz: every privilege must be earned by the men through their assumption of some work or responsibility connected therewith. The men instead of avoiding these added burdens, voluntarily sought them, and when received made serious efforts to prove that they were worthy and could carry them out like men. A number of examples may be cited.

In the beginning, the Inmates' Court had no punitive powers. All that could be done when an offender was brought before it was to endeavor by reasoning with him, by counsel and reprimand, to bring about a better understanding and to smooth out the difficulties. This plan was soon found to be wholly insufficient. Larger powers, powers involving fitting punishments and the power of enforcing its decrees, were needed, with the support of the administration behind it. To that end a penal code, prepared by the League Judge and unanimously adopted by the members, was brought to the Warden for his approval which was readily given. It meant much more work for the Court, and consistent, loyal support from the membership. But from that time the Court became an increasingly important factor in the inmate life. More and more the confidence of the officials was won and held, until, as has been stated, practically every complaint was referred to this Court, and not a decision has ever been overruled by the Warden. 51

In October 1918 it was announced that a contract had been signed by officials of Westchester County and the federal government to use the Penitentiary as a barracks in connection with General Hospital No. 38. The courts ceased committing offenders to the Penitentiary on October 8, 1918. By mid-November, the population had rapidly reduced.

On September 19, 1919, the institution reverted to Westchester County jurisdiction. Twenty-two prisoners being boarded in other institutions were transferred to the Penitentiary ten days later and the admission of newly sentenced offenders commenced. The Effort League was reinstated on October 1, 1919, by unanimous vote of the inmates.

The report of the Department of Corrections, Westchester County, for the period beginning January 1, 1921, through December 31, 1923, confirms the Effort League as still active and continuing to function in a highly satisfactory manner, handling matters of discipline through the Inmate Court, orienting new arrivals to their obligations to the League, explaining to them how good-time was earned and the significance of the Credit System. The League had been empowered to appoint inmates as foremen of inmate work groups, with the approval of the warden.

In his 1926 book, Jesse O. Stutsman, who had been superintendent of the Detroit House of Correction in the early nineteen-twenties, referred to the initiation of an Effort League at the Westchester County Penitentiary by the then Superintendent Warren E. McClellan. He was no doubt referring to the League as it operated in the 1921-1923 period. [52] The population was then comprised of males serving terms ranging from ten days to a maximum of one year. A system of four grades was established providing for the earning of a certain number of credits daily by cooperating in work and by perfect group or individual conduct. The higher the grade the greater the credit earning potential. Payment for work was tied to the credits earned as was time served within certain limits.

Each work group was given credits based upon evaluations of its deportment, and to some extent the group was held responsible for the diligence and conduct of its members. The purpose of group credits was to instill a sense of value for cooperative effort. The rationale was that the average prisoner, being selfish and individualistic, needed to learn respect for the rights of others if he was ever to properly relate himself to the community.

A committee of the Effort League interpreted to each new arrival its purposes, regulations, and benefits of membership. After a ten-day trial period membership could be attained if the applicant proved himself worthy. About ninety percent of the population so qualified. League officers were a president, vice-president, judge of the inner court, sergeant-at-arms, public defender, and secretary. Elected by popular vote to a four-months' term, the officers comprised a cabinet which acted as a link between the population and the administration.

In addition to being responsible for practically all conduct and order within the institution, the League had extensive powers of recommendation to the warden. These included recommendations for trusty assignments and gang foremen. Reportedly men in non-supervised situations were deterred from escape by loyalty to the League. The superintendent reported that many times the League had requested a more secure assignment for an individual it suspected of planning escape.

On the complaint of another inmate or of any prison official, a man could be brought before the prisoner's court. A description of the court, then still regarded as one of the most important parts of the League's machinery, reads:

> It has been found necessary to limit the severity of the court's sentences, and the maximum sentence has been placed at expulsion from the League, together with five days in a cell on limited diet. Expulsion from the League means that the offender is turned over to the Warden for discipline ... separated from the other prisoners and loses all privileges.... The probation system, which was put into operation by the Effort League about three years ago, has proved very successful. First offenders are usually placed on probation for five or ten days and must report regularly to the probation officer assigned to their cases by the judge of the inmate court. 52

Derrick left the Westchester County Penitentiary in 1921. The League continued to operate until the early 1930's when it reportedly deteriorated into "kangaroo courts" and died out. It was reestablished in May 1938 under a new constitution which was revised in May 1950. No disciplinary function was given to this new group. In 1966 it was reported that exploratory work was then in process with

the Men's Council, started in 1965, under the guidance of a
psychiatric team unit in a 135-bed living unit opened in January 1965, as a therapeutic community. The by-laws of the
group stated its objective was "to set up an orderly and
systematic method of communication with the staff, and other interested individuals and groups."[53]

The League is still in existence but lacks both formal
organization and recognition from the administration. In
1966 and early 1967, an Inmate Council, which in operation
proved to be faulty by not providing a true representation of
the population, was disbanded. Administration communication with inmate groups currently is through liaison committees.[54]

U. S. Naval Prison, Portsmouth, N. H.

In January 1917, Thomas Mott Osborne underwent
twelve days' voluntary confinement at the U. S. Naval Prison
in the Navy Yard at Portsmouth, New Hampshire, the first
five days being spent on the Southery, the prison's receiving
ship.   His mission, undertaken at the request of Secretary
of the Navy Daniels, was to study the operation of the prison and the treatment of the prisoners.   In his report to
Secretary Daniels, Osborne was severely critical.   While
the Southery was described as being well administered,
clean, and conducive to instilling proper attitudes and creating good morale, the prison itself he indicated as having a
degrading influence which was breeding criminals.   He advocated abolishing the Naval Prison and establishing in its
stead a detention school whose program would place emphasis on education, training, and work.   Although this proposal was not adopted in its entirety, its underlying principles were accepted, as were Osborne's additional recommendations that restoration to duty or discharge from service be given at such time as was believed appropriate by a
board of rehabilitation whose membership would consist of
two officers, an educator, and a psychiatrist.[55]

During his period of voluntary confinement, Osborne
had been accompanied by a former inmate of Sing Sing Prison and Austin MacCormick, then a young instructor at Bowdoin College and destined to become one of the world's leading figures in corrections.   The three were listed as

deserters, but their true identity and the fact that none of
them had been in the Navy was an open-secret. Osborne
used the alias of Tom Brown as he had in 1913 when serving a week of voluntary confinement at the Auburn Prison;
MacCormick's assumed name was John Austin, and the former inmate used his true name.

During the summer of 1917, after the entry of the
United States into World War I, Osborne and MacCormick
were commissioned in the U.S. Naval Reserve Force and
assigned to the Naval Prison. With the rank of Lieutenant
Commander, Osborne was commandant of the Prison. En-
sign MacCormick was the executive officer and second in
command.

The Survey, a national magazine, in its issue dated
August 18, 1917, reported:

> Mr. Osborne, it is understood, has been given a free
> hand by Secretary Daniels to apply his own theories
> of prison administration. Self-government will be in-
> troduced as soon as practicable. The inmates of a
> naval prison are in some respects better qualified to
> succeed with self-government than those in a large
> civil prison ... general level of intelligence of the
> prison is apt to be higher. The majority ... have
> not really committed criminal acts and the percentage
> of so-called habitual offenders is small.... In ac-
> cepting his appointment as commandant, Mr. Osborne
> declared that young men sent to the naval prison
> should be returned to the navy as fit for the service
> as possible, and that he would endeavor to make this
> object the aim of his administration.[56]

The Naval Prison underwent a sudden and innovative
change following Osborne's arrival. A Mutual Welfare
League was organized, and adopted as its motto "Trust and
be trusted," and as its colors, green and white signifying
hope and truth. Its newspaper, The Mutual Welfare News,
was published weekly. Following the established policies of
the League the Marine sentries were relieved of all inside
guard duties, but continued to guard the perimeter. They
were replaced by League members. The League also had
the responsibility of enforcing prison regulations through its
police and court system. A Judiciary Committee of five
prisoners was given the power to investigate and hear all
charges of rules violations and to recommend punishments to

the commandant. Prisoners could appeal their decisions to
the commandant or his designated representatives. The
practices of shaving heads and the use of yellow numbers
and "red legs" on the inmates' clothing were discarded. [57]

Prisoners responded to the efforts to raise their
morale. A Welfare League Dramatic Company presented
plays and minstrels in the City of Portsmouth to raise money
for the Red Cross, and on August 29, 1919, fifty men travelled in two trucks to York Harbor for that purpose. [58]

While education, recreation, trust, and an opportunity
to exercise the duties and responsibilities of citizenship in
the Mutual Welfare League were important factors in building morale and increasing the likelihood of success in civilian
life after release, the Osborne administration's most significant contribution, at a time when the country was at war,
was to develop the prisoners' desire to be restored to duty
in the Navy and to prepare them for return. During the
War and during the years immediately after its end, over
five thousand prisoners convicted by general courts-martial,
and usually sentenced to end their confinement with a dis-
honorable discharge, were restored to duty in the Navy,
Marine Corps, and Coast Guard. While the exact figure is
not known, the great majority of those restored had successful records. This success in restoring prisoners to duty
furnished a precedent for the restoration program of the
Army in World War II, under which forty-two thousand prisoners were restored to duty. More than ninety percent of
those restored did not again become general courts-martial
prisoners. [59]

The success of the restoration program at the Naval
Prison under Commandant Osborne was not entirely due to
the high morale developed in the prison body. Under Navy
and Marine officers and non-commissioned officers, some
of whom were former prisoners who had been restored and
kept at the prison as instructors, an extensive and intensive
training program was carried on, and restored men went
back to duty with added technical knowledge and skills as
well as a determination to "make good. " Work of great
value to the war effort was also performed. Prisoners
volunteered to unload ships coming into the Navy Yard.
Gangs worked in shifts around the clock, and the Portsmouth
Navy Yard was credited with clearing cargo ships faster than
any other Eastern port. Some of these volunteers were men
who, because of the nature of their offenses, were not eligible for restoration to duty. [60]

It was inevitable, of course, that traditionalists would frown on Osborne's methods. Charges of lax discipline and immoral conditions among the prisoners were eventually made which resulted in the appointment by Secretary of the Navy Daniels of a special inquiry board. The distinguished membership of that board, Assistant Secretary of the Navy Franklin Delano Roosevelt, Rear Admiral H. O. Dunn, and Rear Admiral A. S. Halstead, found the charges untrue, stating:

> The board found the sanitary and physical conditions to be very good.
> The board found the general situation in regard to the guarding of prisoners and their well-being to be satisfactory. The question of dual control has been adjusted satisfactorily by the executive action of the commandant. The result of the guarding of prisoners by prisoners on the prison side of the deadline is proven to be justified by the result obtained, only eight prisoners out of a total of sixty-six hundred having succeeded in making good their escape over a period of more than two years....
> In particular no facts were developed to indicate conditions of lax discipline or immorality existing in the Naval Prison, or that the prisoners in any way constitute a menace to the safety of the Navy Yard, of the inhabitants or property in the communities of Kittery, Portsmouth, or surrounding territory. [61]

After the end of World War I, the number of prisoners decreased from more than two thousand to fewer than a thousand. Osborne resigned as commandant, returning to civilian life on March 17, 1920. He was succeeded at Portsmouth by Commodore A. V. Wadhams, USN; and MacCormick, then a lieutenant (senior grade) was recalled from sea duty to serve again as executive officer. Wadhams was impressed with the Mutual Welfare League. He became a firm advocate of its principles and continued the organization in its entirety until reassigned July 5, 1921. MacCormick had returned to civilian life in May 1921. Commodore Wadham's pamphlet describing the League states:

> Among the recreational activities of the prisoners may be counted the Farragut Club, which is just like any Y. M. C. A. hut having a gymnasium replete with all kinds of athletic gear, and containing a large recreational room where men may, during their

leisure hours come and enjoy themselves. We have
also a library, which contains some four thousand
volumes, fiction and non-fiction, which is one of the
most important factors in the educational activities
of this institution.   There are also two other activities or branches of the Mutual Welfare League, which
deserve mention. One is the Tom Brown Club, a
literary club, named after its founder Thomas Mott
Osborne (Tom Brown being the name adopted by him
when he first went into prison work) which holds its
meeting every Sunday night.   Before it are presented
talks by prominent men of affairs as well as debates
and literary discussion by the prisoners themselves.
There is also a Bible Study Club, which is presided
over by the Chaplain, who every Saturday night deli-
vers a heart-to-heart talk on Christian life and endeavor, sometimes illustrating it by lantern slides.

A campaign of education is carried on continually
through the machinery of the League.   The Commanding Officer is constantly in touch with the
League's activities, for he reviews for approval or
disapproval the minutes of all the meetings of the
Board of Delegates and the Executive Committee.
The League Chief-Sergeant-at-Arms makes report from
time to time to the Commanding Officer of all offenders for violations of orders and rules and also of
the general state of discipline; and the Commanding
Officer transmits these reports to the Judiciary Committee for investigation.

The systematic supervision and administration
stated above and the wise guardianship of the League
by the Commanding Officer and his aides, without
undue interference in the essentials of self-government, is in essence the modus operandi of the Commanding Officer in his relation to the prisoners.

... [T]he greatest factor is the growth of self-respect, pride in the institution and a sense of loyalty
to those over them which has developed under the
League.   The men do their work conscientiously, not
from fear of punishment, but because they take pride
in seeing it well done.   They maintain excellent discipline, not because offenses will bring punishment
upon themselves, but because bad conduct will de-
stroy what they feel is their own personal project,
the League. 62

Under Osborne and Wadhams the Naval Prison had

been a Naval command.   After Wadhams left, it again became a Marine command.   Commodore Wadham's successor
did not share his views of the Mutual Welfare League.   He
felt that under the system shrewd inmates managed to gain
control of the League and manipulated it to their own advantage.   He also believed that inmates did not have the
scientific attitude or technique necessary for dealing with
violations of regulations and were likely to be more cruel
and less judicious in their treatment of difficult prisoners
than were the prison officials themselves.   Under the Welfare
League system the prison populace had enjoyed considerable
freedom.   Living quarters had lacked the traditional bars
and dull drabness of most prisons.   The cell block with a
capacity of 320 men was practically empty.   To house the
increased number of prisoners, 2600 at its peak, during
World War I, open barracks housing about 2000 prisoners
were constructed inside the wire fence.   The cell block had
been used for new prisoners and those under punishment.
After dissolving the League, the new Commandant filled the
cell block and divided the remaining men into two battalions
of ten companies each.   The suddenness of this drastic
change in policy naturally had a depressing effect upon morale and this was sharply reflected in a decided rise in the
incidence of rules violations. [63]

The Naval Prison, however, has since been com-
manded by a series of Marine officers who, while not operating under the Mutual Welfare League plan, have accepted
and followed the basic philosophy and policies of modern
corrections. [64]

The Long Lane School

The Long Lane School at Middletown, Connecticut,
opened in 1869, as a training school for delinquent girls.
Information was received in 1966 that the facility had a self-
government program dating to 1917, which had changed from
time to time in concert with turnover in students and staff.
Each cottage had its own council which could suggest action
to be taken upon staff reported incidents of misconduct.
Staff made the final decision as to the kind and extent of
penalties, usually some degree of privilege loss. [65]

After three months at the school, a new girl could be

admitted to the responsibilities of citizenship in student government by vote of her peers, if they believed she had
learned and practiced the seven ideals of the school: self-
control, self-respect, loyalty, honor, obedience, appreciation, and courtesy.   On becoming a citizen the girl pledged:
"I pledge my loyalty to the United States of America and to
Long Lane School.   On my honor I will assume responsibility as a citizen to promote an interest in the welfare of others and do everything in my power to uphold the ideals for
which self-government at Long Lane School stands. "   The
school motto was "Not Self-But All"; colors were yellow and
white; the school flower was the daisy; and the 121st Psalm
had been chosen as reflecting the purpose and hope of the
group.

For current information regarding the Long Lane
School see under Connecticut in Part II.

U. S. Disciplinary Barracks, Governors Island, N. Y.

In his annual report for the fiscal year beginning July
1, 1918, and ending June 30, 1919, Colonel John E. Hunt,
commandant of the Atlantic Branch, U. S. Disciplinary Barracks, Governors Island, New York, gave credit to the cooperation of the inmate Honor Association for the maintenance of proper discipline. [66]   Formed in November 1918, at
Colonel Hunt's suggestion, the Association proved its value
when the population increased considerably and it was necessary to occupy additional quarters.   Proper discipline was
maintained with no increase in the staff complement due to
the assistance of the members of the Honor Association.

Disciplinary infractions decreased as a result of the
Honor Association's influence.   A disciplinary board of inmates conducted a trial under staff supervision and meted
out punishment to any man reported by Association members.
Those men reported by staff were tried by the staff disciplinary board.

Colonel Hunt's remarks on the philosophy underlying
the utilization of inmate organizations show keen insight for
the time:

It seems to me that such an experiment although it

has proved successful here cannot be inaugurated at
any time and under all conditions. It requires for
its successful operation, a group of earnest prisoners and a sympathetic advance by the administration.
Its operation needs careful watching lest the group of
earnest workers be replaced by a less trustworthy
element. It is purely a measure for local administration and its continuance or dissolution must be
solely in the hands of the local authorities. When
such an association works with the end in view that
in whatever way it benefits the institution it benefits
its own individual members, it will prove successful,
but if members use the association for purely selfish
ends it is doomed to failure and may become a positive menace.

It appears to me that the value of a properly conducted association aside from the immediate local
benefits mentioned above has a wider application. It
teaches members in a very concrete way, the necessity for and benefits derived from a social order,
and I believe it cannot but have its educational effect
on some when they again assume their places in organized society.

Kentucky State Reformatory

The Kentucky State Reformatory at Frankfort was in
existence from 1797 until 1937, when heavy floods forced
evacuation to nearby temporary quarters with subsequent
transfer of all prisoners to the not then completed new State
Reformatory at LaGrange, some fifty miles northwest.

A Mutual Welfare League, organized at the Frankfort
institution in 1920, had as its objective "the promotion in
every way of the true interests and welfare of the men confined in prison." At one time reportedly ninety percent of
the institution population were members. Reports as late
as 1931 mention the League as still active. [67]

Activities of the League were entirely of a charitable
nature, and were not connected with the management or operation of the institution. The organization received no financial or other support from the State except occasional
investigations by parole agents in the course of other duties.

Membership, open to any prisoner, was divided into three classes:

1.   Active members--those paying monthly dues, the amount paid being determined by the amount of compensation received by the member.   For instance: members receiving as much as ten cents a day were assessed twenty-five cents a month, while those receiving less than ten cents paid twelve cents a month.
2.   Inactive members--described as those who through unfortunate conditions for which they were not to blame were not able to pay dues.
3.   Honorary members--those who merited membership by reason of charitable deeds.

The League derived income from the profits of several enterprises--a mercantile store, a printing shop, and various recreational activities.   Charitable work included aid to dependent families which was initiated in 1921, burial of deceased members, if no other funds were available; and the furnishing of such extras as fruit or milk for hospitalized members.

The aid to dependent families program was known as the Department of Dependent Welfare.   Any member of the Mutual Welfare League could apply for aid to his dependents, including wife, children, parents, and siblings, by completing an application form which called for certain identifying data, the amount of money remitted in the past by the member to the dependent, and the listing of four references acquainted with the dependent.   Investigation was then made, often by a parole agent.   Occasional contributions were made to the Salvation Army, the Eastern Kentucky Flood Relief, and similar causes.

Management of the Mutual Welfare League was exercised by a Board of Directors composed of nine prisoners selected for a one-year term.   The prison chief clerk was the custodian of all funds,   Activities proposed for League undertaking were subject to the approval of the superintendent.

On January 11, 1929, a conference was held at the invitation of Governor Sampson between members of the State Board of Charities and Corrections and a group of educators and social and religious leaders of the Commonwealth to discuss the establishment of schools of citizenship

and moral training in Kentucky penal institutions.   Five of
the community group members were appointed as a Committee of Laymen which filed its report and recommendations
on April 24, 1929, a portion of which concerned the Mutual
Welfare League:[68]

> We believe that the Mutual Welfare League offers
> large opportunities for moral training.   Among the
> present avenues for citizenship training through the
> activities of the League there are: (1) The Mutual
> Welfare League Courier.   This paper gives an oppor-
> tunity for self-expression and for the prisoners to
> correlate the problems of the institution with those
> of the outside world.   (2) Commissary.   This affords
> the satisfaction of certain individual wants and might
> also serve as a practical problem in economic rela-
> tionship.   (3) Social Service.   This consists in rais-
> ing money, contributing to needy families and paying
> the expenses of prisoner and guard on visits to sick
> relatives.   (4) Education.   This consists in the pay-
> ment of fifteen cents a day to teachers of night
> school and the contribution of one-half fee for any
> correspondence course taken by any inmate.
> An analysis of the Mutual Welfare League shows
> that it is well planned for the field of work alloted
> to it.   There is much conflicting opinion as to wheth-
> er or not greater responsibility can be given the
> prisoners, the weight of opinion seeming to indicate
> that an honor system in a modified form such as
> exists at the Reformatory, coupled with an organiza-
> tion like the League, works for the most good.   There
> is a question as to whether the League might not be
> consulted with regard to changes in school curriculum
> since it virtually pays for instruction.   Furthermore,
> the recommendation of the United States Children's
> Bureau might be restated, for in it seems to lie the
> possibility of valuable training in social relations and
> the problems arising out of these relations.   The
> recommendation is as follows: 'Employment by the
> State Board of Charities and Corrections of a suffi-
> cient number of trained family case workers to in-
> vestigate all families of newly committed prisoners
> in order to assist them in the readjustments made
> necessary by the imprisonment of the father, and
> give such friendly supervision as may be necessary.
> This work should be coordinated with the parole work,
> for which it will be an excellent foundation, preparing

the family and the community for the prisoner's return.   The case workers should also render assistance
to the Mutual Welfare League in the investigation and
supervision of cases. ' It also seems to the committee that the privileges of the league should be extended to women prisoners.

New Castle Correctional Institution

        An Honor Court was in operation at the New Castle
Correctional Institution, Wilmington, Delaware, from 1921
to 1931, under the administrations of two wardens.   Factors
cited as contributing to its demise were the release of inmates competent to carry out the purposes of the organization, declining administrative interest, and the nonavailabil-
ity of suitable staff supervision. [69]   The institution was replaced in April 1971 by the Delaware Correctional Center at
Smyrna.

        Haynes described the Wilmington Honor Court as com-
posed of eight members and dealing with all matters of discipline, recreation, entertainment, and welfare of the inmates.   The Court made rules and selected the three judges
before whom offenders were given a hearing.   The approval
of the warden was required on all penalties.   There was no
regular term for the members of the Court.   Whenever a
vacancy occurred, an election was held, but members were
subject to recall at any time.   Inmates replaced guards to
the extent that only two guards during the day and one at
night were required for the custody of four hundred men.
Conceding that the reduction of guards may have been carried too far, Haynes nonetheless felt it was a striking demonstration that a prison can be conducted practically without
guards, without serious internal disturbances and without an
unusual number of escapees, raising the question whether a
very considerable part of the cost of the employment of
guards is necessary. [70]

Massachusetts State Prison Colony

        The State Prison Colony, Norfolk, was opened in
1931.   Currently it is designated as Massachusetts

Correctional Institution. During the period 1927-1934, Howard B. Gill, the first superintendent of the State Prison
Colony, Norfolk, inaugurated a program of individual and
group treatment of inmates called the Norfolk Plan. Mr.
Gill described the Plan in an article published in 1931 and
in a letter to the author in 1966.[71]

The Norfolk Plan utilized balanced programs in the
following five broad areas:

1.   Normalcy--affecting the inter-personal relationship between officials and inmates, the nature of structures
in the institution, all institutional activities, rules and regulations, and the general overall climate of the institution.
2.   Small Group Principle--applied to living quarters,
dining, bathing, industries, leisure time activities including
hobbies, athletics, entertainment, visiting, religious services, education, medical care.
3.   Inmate-Staff Organization--based on joint participation of officials and inmates through joint action and joint
responsibility for all institution activities except discipline,
parole, finances, and similar official administrative matters.
4.   Community Contacts--bringing the community into
the prison and taking the prisoners, as much as possible,
into the community.
5.   Individual and Group Treatment--through individual problem-solving in five main areas, namely situational,
medical, psychological, anti-social (ethical), and custodial,
and through group discussions in meetings of the Inmate
Council, fifteen standing joint committees, and weekly House
Meetings.

It soon became evident that under the Norfolk Plan
only a select population of the more tractable, adult, "normal" prisoners who would cooperate on a basis of mutual
trust could make up the prison population. At first this
precluded escape risks while the inmates were housed in an
open camp. Later, however, upon completion of the walled
enclosure, such inmates could be included provided other
criteria for normalcy, cooperation, and ultimate adjustment
were met. Inmates and officials regarded each other with
courtesy and respect. Except in the Receiving Building,
housing was in normal rooms, not cells. There were only
two prison rules--no escapes and no contraband. All regulations affecting routine operations were regarded merely as
procedural matters. There were no limitations on

correspondence or visiting.   The typical prison uniform was
replaced with ordinary clothing.   Only watch officers (tower
guards, gate keepers, patrol) wore uniforms.   Inmates had
freedom of movement within the walled enclosure.   There
were no marching formations.   The test of any suggestion
was, "Is it normal?"

The small group principle applied not only to housing
inmates in groups of fifty men under the direction of two
house officers acting as resident caseworkers, but also to
all other activities.   For example, there were fourteen
play spaces including four large athletic fields.   The auditorium was purposely designed to hold no more than half the
population.   The chapel provided only approximately one
hundred seats.   Four-man tables were used in each of the
dining rooms, each of which in turn was limited to fifty
inmates.   Each dining room had its own small service
kitchen where all except main dishes (meats, vegetables,
desserts) could be cooked for small order service.   The
central bathhouse, typical of prisons at that time, was replaced by ordinary toilets and baths on each of the three
floors of each house of fifty men.   Access to these toilets
and baths could be had at any time.

The third phase of the plan, an inmate-staff organization, was built around an Inmate Council, which developed
as a direct outgrowth of the group system of housing and
supervision, and the need to foster inmate responsibility because of limitations in numbers of staff.   Together the staff
and this council, through a system of joint committees, were
responsible for the conduct of all institutional activities except as noted above.   This was neither an honor system nor
an inmate self-government program, and this was a basic
essential in the success of the Norfolk Plan.

The Norfolk Plan of joint participation and joint responsibility of many inmates and many staff members was
in sharp contrast to the advisory councils in many prisons
where a small inmate committee worked with a single staff
member, for instance the warden or associate warden.   One
of the outstanding features of the Norfolk Plan in its most
successful phase was the involvement of some thirty or more
staff members and some sixty or more inmates who made
up the joint committees.

In an address before the Conference on the Treatment
of Criminal Delinquency at Cambridge, Massachusetts, December 4, 1930, Gill reported:

This is not to be confused with the strictly penal administration of the Colony which is in the hands of the Superintendent and his assistants. Also in contrast to inmate organizations in some institutions which are founded on the principle of self-government in the hands of inmates only, this community operates on the principle of joint responsibility in which both officers and inmates take part.

The Council consists of fifteen inmates, three nominated and elected by the inmates from each of the five houses (referring to inmate living quarters) for a term of three months. The three councilmen from each house and the house officers act as a house committee which meets weekly, and a weekly meeting is also held in each house with all members and the house officer present. Questions affecting the welfare of the house or the institution are discussed at these meetings. Such questions are then carried by the council-men to the weekly staff meeting. The Council elects its own chairman and secretary and appoints its own committees on construction, education and library, entertainment, athletics, food, maintenance, store, etc. The Staff also has its chairman and committees on construction, education and library, entertainment, athletics, food, maintenance, store, etc.

Questions relating to any of these fields of activity are taken up in weekly joint meetings of the respective committees and by them referred also to the weekly meetings of the Council and the Staff. The Staff and the Council meet weekly with the Superintendent who refers any action taken in the meeting to the other for confirmation. The Council has advisory powers only and final action always rests with the Staff; suggestions may originate in either body, however, and are referred to both before final action. However, in the thirty months in which the plan has been in operation, the two have failed to agree finally on only one decision. The plan does not always give the 'best men' the leadership--frequently otherwise, and it has been interesting to note what responsibility does for these others. That the plan has not run into difficulties frequently encountered by inmate self-government organizations where control has soon passed into the hands of the bold and unscrupulous, is due to the very important and sincere part played in it by the officers, who (contrary to the usual circumstances)

are wholeheartedly a part of it and who act as a
proper balance wheel. ...

In general the plan has worked, although it is
neither an 'honor system' nor 'self-government, ' because it is founded frankly on a basis of results for
both Staff and men.... Neither officers nor men
give up their independence or their responsibilities,
and each continually checks the other to insure square
dealing; but both agree that cooperation works better
than opposition where men must work and eat and
live together, whatever the circumstances.

Mr. Gill has summarized some of the more obvious
advantages of the inmate-staff organization under the Norfolk
Plan as originally operated.

The joint committees, for example, furnished the
most effective means of communication between staff
and prisoners. A valuable fringe benefit of these
committees also was the release of tensions which
are inevitable in any institution. In both committee
and house meetings grievances were aired and resolved before minor problems became major crises.
There has never been a riot at Norfolk in its entire
forty years' history. It was once the proud boast
that there had been only three fights among inmates
in one three year period--a remarkable record for
any institution. Due to the cooperation between inmates and official personnel all activities within the
institution were enhanced. At one time construction
work doubled its production as a result, winning a
special commendation from the Commissioner of Correction, Sanford Bates.

Naturally, the sense of responsibility engendered
by inmate participation tempered by Staff cooperation
developed a kind of civic pride and interest among
many prisoners who may never before have experi-
enced any such feelings. Cooperation with responsible
officials sometimes gave criminals for the first time
the notion that they too could belong to the side of
law and order. To other prisoners it gave opportunity to express much that was sound in their personalities. Instead of developing leaders among the worst
prisoners, the Plan brought out the better element in
the prison population because such prisoners through
cooperation with the Staff could secure the most benefits for all prisoners.

While group treatment had not then become the
vogue in prisons, at Norfolk individualized treatment
was paralleled by something called 'Socialized Treatment.' Such socialized treatment was naturally developed in the joint committees of the Norfolk Plan.
There the influence of law-abiding officers on prisoners, and vice-versa, had its therapeutic effect.
While present day 'group discussions' had not been
introduced in correctional work, the informal discussions in council or committee meetings at Norfolk
often had the same effect.

The May 1, 1964, issue of the inmate newspaper,
The Colony, contains the remarks made by Mr. Gill earlier
that year at a meeting of the Norfolk Protestant Fellowship
and mentions the recent placement in the administration
building of a placque inscribed:

In Recognition of the Establishment
at Norfolk, Massachusetts, of the first
COMMUNITY PRISON FOR MEN
in the United States under the leadership of:
HOWARD B. GILL
Superintendent, 1927-1934

An Inmate Council was organized in February 1937
under a constitution, revised periodically thereafter, which
provided for the secret ballot election of two representatives
from each housing unit to serve a six-month term. [72]   The
superintendent and the community service director were
designated as ex-officio members.   Several standing committees were established.   A Financial and Store Committee
of five, with the community service director as an ex-officio
member, was charged with responsibility for the conduct of
the Inmate Store and the making of recommendations regarding any appropriations involving the expenditure of store
profits.

The constitution also established the Cooperative Aid
Society of Norfolk whose purpose was stated as being to provide financial aid to any inmate, or his family, when the
need was imperative and could not be obtained from the usual
sources, or when such aid was necessary to forestall a definite approaching need; to finance transportation for family
members, or surrogates, to visit inmates who had not had
a visit for a lengthy period because of the visitor's indigen-
cy.   A five-member Board of Directors composed of three

inmates elected by the Inmate Council and two staff members, the institution treasurer and the family welfare director, guided the Society. The staff members were designated, respectively, as treasurer and secretary. Fifteen
percent of the net profits of the Store was committed to finance this assistance.

Article V of the constitution, entitled Inmate Joint
Responsibility for Escapes, stated that in return for community privileges granted to the inmates, the inmate body at
large assumed a joint responsibility with the staff for orderly and efficient institution operations, especially in regard
to escapes. In the event of escape by an inmate entitled to
Council privileges, it was stipulated that the inmate body
would forfeit Council privileges for a period not to exceed
one week.

Information was received in 1966 that the Inmate
Council still functioned with its actions subject to staff veto.
Three factors were cited as contributing to the decline in
some of the actual practices of joint participation attained
by Superintendent Gill: the larger number of inmates, a
dilution of the criteria for selection of those to be sent to
the institution, and changing leadership. At that time the
opinion was expressed that inmates were not as likely to
accept much responsibility for escapes. It was reported
that at times they had defaulted on other obligations to maintain orderly and efficient operation of the institution, notably
kitchen work. [73]

Illinois State Penitentiary

In the summer of 1929, Major Henry C. Hill was
appointed warden of the Illinois State Penitentiary at Joliet,
and of its branch at Statesville. The following autumn he
introduced into both prisons the idea of electing a grievance
committee composed of two representatives from each cell
house. The committee was to meet with him periodically
to present requests or complaints referred to it by other
inmates. However, after two or three meetings the plan
was disbanded. Disagreement among the committee members and a lack of sound suggestions contributed to the warden's decision that the idea was not productive. [74]

SOURCES

1.   Turnbull, Robert J.   As quoted in: The Cradle of the
      Penitentiary, by Negley K. Teeters; The Pennsyl-
      vania Prison Society, 1955; p. 46.
2.   Sedgwick, C. M. Memoir of Joseph Curtis. New
      York: Harper & Bros. , 1858; p. 66.
3.   Lewis, O. F. "Inmate Self-Government a Century
      Ago. " The Delinquent, vol. 8, no. 1 (January
      1918), p. 9-15.
4.   Pickett, Robert Stanley.   "The New York House of
      Refuge: A Case Study of Nineteenth Century Hu-
      manitarian Reform, 1825-27. " Unpublished doctoral
      dissertation, Syracuse University, 1963; p. 112.
5.   Lewis, O. F. Op. cit.
6.   Sedgwick, C. M. Op. cit. , pp. 107-135.
7.   Pickett, Robert Stanley. Op. cit. , pp. 135, 170-71,
      259.
8.   Lewis, O. F. Op. cit.
9.   Pierson, George Wilson. Tocqueville and Beaumont
      in America. New York: Oxford University Press,
      1938; pp. 435-36.
10.   Lewis, O. F. Op. cit.
11.   Lewis, O. F. The Development of American Prisons
      and Prison Customs, 1776-1845. Prison Associa-
      tion of New York, 1922; pp. 169-70.
12.   Haynes, Gideon. Pictures from Prison Life. Boston:
      Lee and Shepard, 1869; pp. 62-63.
13.   Letter from then Supt. Palmer C. Scafati, Massachu-
      setts Correctional Institution, South Walpole,
      Mass. , February 9, 1967.
14.   Letter from then Supt. Palmer C. Scafati, September
      30, 1966.
15.   Brockway, Zebulon R. Fifty Years of Prison Service:
      An Autobiography. New York: Charities Publica-
      tion Committee, 1912; pp. 96-97.
16.   Helfman, Harold M. "Antecedents of Thomas Mott
      Osborne's 'Mutual Welfare League' in Michigan. "
      Journal of Criminal Law and Criminology, vol. 40
      (May-April 1949-50), pp. 597-600.
17.   Stutsman, Jesse O. Curing the Criminal. New York:
      Macmillan, 1926; pp. 215-219.
18.   Letter from then Supt. W. H. Bannan, Detroit House
      of Correction, Plymouth, September 6, 1966.
19.   Letter from Supt. John M. Amberger, Detroit House
      of Correction, December 7, 1972.

20. Constitution and By-Laws, Resident Advisory Council,
     Men's Division, Detroit House of Correction, Ply-
     mouth, November 1972.
21. Brockway, Zebulon R. Op. cit., pp. 302-3.
22. Helfman, Harold M. Op. cit.
23. American Council of Learned Studies. Dictionary of
     American Biography, vol. XXII. New York:
     Scribner's, 1958; pp. 226-27.
24. Letter from Executive Director Carolyn M. Thompson,
     The Women's Prison Association of New York, New
     York City, May 9, 1967.
25. Doty, Madeline Zabriskie. "Maggie Martin, 933."
     Century Magazine, October 1914, pp. 843-857.
26. Doty, Madeline Zabriskie. "Maggie Martin's Friends."
     Century Magazine, April 1915, pp. 875-883.
27. Letter from then Supt. Myrtle E. Gray, Sleighton
     Farm School for Girls, Darling, Pennsylvania,
     March 22, 1967.
28. Memorandum re Honor Cottage Standings, Sleighton
     Farm School for Girls, March 1966; and Brochure,
     1966, p. 5.
29. Letter from Supt. Adeline F. Tabourin, Sleighton
     Farm School for Girls, January 8, 1973.
30. Derrick, Calvin. "Self-Government." The Survey,
     September 1, 1917, pp. 473-478.
31. Letter and Reports from Director Allen F. Breed,
     Dept. of The Youth Authority, Sacramento, Califor-
     nia, January 25, 1973.
32. Barnes, Harry Elmer. A History of the Penal, Re-
     formatory and Correctional Institutions of the State
     of New Jersey. Trenton, N.J.: MacCrellish and
     Quigley Co., 1918; p. 293.
33. Wines, Frederick Howard. Punishment and Reforma-
     tion: A Study of the Penitentiary System. Revised
     by Winthrop D. Lane. New York: Thomas Y.
     Crowell, 1923; pp. 408-409.
34. Ibid., pp. 409-410.
35. Osborne, Thomas Mott. Society and Prisons. New
     Haven, Conn.: Yale University Press, 1916; p.
     164.
36. Ibid.
37. Ibid.
38. Tannenbaum, Frank. Crime and the Community. Bos-
     ton: The Athenian Press, Ginn & Company, 1938;
     p. 416.
39. Letter from then Warden W. L. Denno, Sing Sing Pris-
     on, Ossining, New York, September 20, 1966.

40. Lawes, Lewis E. Twenty Thousand Years in Sing
       Sing. New York: Ray Long & Richard E. Smith,
       1932; pp. 104-5.
41. Wines, Frederick Howard. Op. cit., pp. 397-98.
42. Barnes, Harry Elmer. The Evolution of Penology in
       Pennsylvania. Indianapolis: Bobbs-Merrill Co.,
       1927; p. 426.
43. Lawes, Lewis E. Op. cit., pp. 112-120.
44. Ibid., pp. 105 and 107.
45. MacCormick, Austin H., and Garrett, Paul W., eds.
       Handbook of American Prisons. Prepared by Na-
       tional Society of Penal Information, Inc. New
       York: G. P. Putnam, 1926; pp. 450-51.
46. Denno, W. L. Op. cit.
47. Letter and Reports from Director Albert C. Wagner,
       Division of Correction and Parole, Trenton, New
       Jersey, March 5, 1973.
48. Quarles, Mary Ann. "A Comparative Study of the Re-
       lation of the Treatment Program at the New Jersey
       Reformatory for Women for the Fifty Year Period,
       1910 to 1960, to Concepts of Penology." Unpub-
       lished doctoral Dissertation, pp. 187-222; Brochure,
       "The Functioning of the New Jersey Reformatory
       for Women," July 1, 1966, pp. 10-13.
49. Letter from then Supt. Robert T. Grey, Connecticut
       Reformatory, Cheshire, Connecticut, September 19,
       1966.
50. Wines, Frederick Howard. Op. cit., p. 407-8.
51. Letter from Commissioner Louis P. Kurtis, Dept. of
       Public Welfare, County of Westchester, White
       Plains, New York, December 13, 1966; First An-
       nual Report, Commissioner of Charities and Cor-
       rections, Westchester County, January 1 to Decem-
       ber 31, 1917; Second Annual Report, Westchester
       County Penitentiary and Workhouse, January 1 to
       December 31, 1918; Reports of Dept. of Correc-
       tions, Westchester County, September 1 to Decem-
       ber 31, 1919, and January 1, 1921 to December 31,
       1923.
52. Stutsman, Jesse O. Op. cit., p. 219-222.
53. Letter from then Warden William J. O'Brien, West-
       chester County Penitentiary, Valhalla, New York,
       November 29, 1966; Constitution and By-Laws, Ef-
       fort League, Rev. May 1, 1950; By-Laws, The
       Men's Council, September 1965 and July 1966.
54. Letter from Commissioner Roberts J. Wright, Dept. of

Correction, Westchester County, Valhalla, New
York, November 29, 1972.

55. Verge, Robert J. A History of the U. S. Naval Prison
     at Portsmouth, New Hampshire. Portsmouth, N. H. :
     U. S. Naval Print Shop, 1946, p. 16-18.

56. The Survey, August 18, 1917.

57. Op. cit.

58. The Mutual Welfare News, Naval Prison, Portsmouth,
     New Hampshire, September 14, 1919.

59. Correspondence from Austin H. MacCormick, Executive
     Director, The Osborne Association, Inc. , New York
     City, January 24, 1973.

60. Ibid.

61. The Survey, March 27, 1920.

62. Verge, Robert J. Op. cit. , pp. 20-21.

63. Ibid. , pp. 22-23.

64. Correspondence from Austin H. MacCormick, op. cit.

65. Letter from then Supt. Ethel D. Mecum, Long Lane
     School, Middletown, Connecticut, October 7, 1966.

66. Annual Report, Atlantic Branch, U. S. Disciplinary
     Barracks, Governors Island, New York, June 30,
     1919; pp. 16-17.

67. Report of Board of Prison Commissioners, Kentucky
     Public Documents, 1927-1929, pp. 48-49; Report
     for Biennial Period ending June 30, 1931, pp. 96-
     98.

68. Ibid. , pp. 51-55.

69. Letter from then Commissioner William Nardini, Ph. D. ,
     Dept. of Correction, Smyrna, Delaware, October
     13, 1966.

70. Haynes, Fred E. Criminology. 2d ed. New York:
     McGraw-Hill, 1935; Chapter XII.

71. Gill, Howard B. "The Norfolk State Prison Colony at
     Massachusetts. " Journal of Criminal Law and
     Criminology, vol. 22 (1931), pp. 107-112; Corres-
     pondence from Howard B. Gill, Director, Institute
     of Correctional Administration, American University,
     Washington, D. C. , October 4, 1966.

72. Constitution and By-Laws, Inmate Council, Massachu-
     setts Correctional Institution, Norfolk, Mass. , as
     amended and compiled January 1962.

73. Letter from Director of Treatment Raymond W. Bren-
     nan, Massachusetts Correctional Institution, Norfolk,
     August 12, 1966.

74. From Nathan F. Leopold, Jr. Life Plus 99 Years.
     New York: Doubleday, 1958; pp. 232-33.

Part II

THE STATES

Commentary

There is no common correctional system administration model in the United States. In some states, all correctional residential facilities are under a single department, or division of a department. In most states, the facilities for juvenile delinquents are administered by a Youth Service, or similarly named governmental entity, which may be a division of a larger organization.

In New Hampshire there is no central administration of either adult or juvenile delinquent facilities. In Alabama, the State Board of Corrections administers the facilities for adult and youthful felony offenders, but each of the schools for juvenile delinquents is operated under a separate board of trustees. In Mississippi and Nevada, there is a central agency to administer the facilities for juvenile delinquents, but none for the adult institutions.

While the states have little in common in correctional administration organization, most share a past history of and a current experience with programs designed to include the offender in the operational dynamics of correctional residential facilities. However, all too frequently a practitioner may be totally unaware of either the past or the present in this regard in his own state or in some instances, in his own institution. For example, during the course of the surveys made in 1966-1967 and 1972-1973, occasionally the first response received from a state or an institution administration was that no self-government or advisory council program had ever existed. With leads provided to them, these same respondents were often able to find the details of prior programs.

The foregoing gives rise to the question of just how
much valuable information about other programs lies buried
in forgotten files.   How much and what kinds of experiences
have been relegated to oblivion as corrections has coped with
its problems on a crisis-oriented basis?   It has been said
that of all American enterprises, corrections apparently has
been the least dependent on organized facts, either past or
present.   The validity of this observation is the result of
several factors, of which two seem to be major.

First, corrections has always been and largely remains a mix of facilities and programs whose operations
are administratively fragmented among many governmental
levels.   This mix has been in a continual state of flux, as
society has struggled to define its attitude toward the ever
growing problem of what to do about those who offend the
social order.

Second, the turnover of personnel in corrections has
been of such magnitude that continuity of programs and the
establishment of a rational data system on which to base
planning, monitoring, and evaluation has been nigh impossible in most jurisdictions.

The already mentioned 1967 report of the President's
Commission on Law Enforcement and Administration of Justice, and the subsequent creation in 1968 of the Law Enforcement Assistance Administration under the provisions of
the Omnibus Crime Control and Safe Streets Act, have done
much toward mobilizing public and legislative support for
improvement and innovation in correctional services.   Only
an informed public can be an interested public.   And only
an interested public can resolve the paradox in the handling
of offenders, establish realistic objectives for corrections,
and provide the means to insure the realization of these objectives.

There has been considerable progress made in the
past half-decade to alleviate, if not resolve, the problems
of recruitment and retention as revealed by the Joint Commission on Correctional Manpower and Training.   The availability of federal funds not only for college and university
programs designed to prepare students for careers in corrections but also for intensive in-service training programs
makes possible the hope that in the foreseeable future correctional institutions are not as likely to be staffed by persons with little knowledge of or commitment to correctional

work. It is likely that the number of persons with a professional education or a professional attitude (or both, since
one usually nurtures the other) will soon rise dramatically
in the field of prison management and correctional work.

Many professionals already in the field are examining
the development of ideas and attitudes embodied in the philosophy and procedures of corrections as a preliminary to
fully comprehending current practice. Hopefully, this examination will be accelerated and its dimensions expanded as
the ranks of the professional corrections worker grow.

And, perhaps, the information in this Part II will
facilitate the efforts of both the professional practitioner and
the student of corrections in examining the past regarding
self-government and advisory councils, to become aware of
the present, and to ponder the potentials.

ALABAMA

State Board of Corrections

The State Board of Corrections administers six institutions for adult and youthful felony offenders. Additionally,
the Board shares jurisdiction with the State Highway Department of fourteen road camps. No current information has
been received regarding inmate advisory councils, but in
1966 it was reported there was no current program involving
inmates in institution administration.[1]

Juvenile Facilities

Each of the three facilities for juvenile delinquents is
administered by a separate board of trustees. There is no
student council at the Alabama Boys' Industrial School, Birmingham. However, in each cottage, "lieutenants" assist in
the supervision of other boys. All boys are encouraged to
make suggestions regarding procedure and program.[2]

In 1971 and through early 1972, at the Alabama Industrial School, Mt. Meigs, a pre-release program was developed under a Law Enforcement Assistance Administration
grant. A feature of the program was the development of a
self-governing housing unit. The group process was the

methodology of choice of the trained staff that implemented the program. The dynamics of resident turnover soon resulted in the orientation of new arrivals in the unit by those already there. Rules of self-governing behavior emerged as the groups acquired expertise. Additional efforts are currently underway to involve students in self-governing behavior. [3]

At the State Training School for Girls, Birmingham, planning was commenced in the latter part of 1971 to initiate treatment through modern programs. This required much study, considerable planning, and intensive staff training. The latter has included extensive leadership training in behavior modification and sensitivity training to impress staff with the need for change and how to cope with change. The students are now involved in policy changes, program planning, and campus government. In November 1972, announcement was made of a plan to elect in each of the four cottages a Cottage Council to be composed of a president, vice-president, secretary, cottage recreation leader, and a representative to a Campus Council Committee. The latter group is to include the president and representative of each Cottage Council as interim members until an election is held. [4]

ALASKA

Division of Corrections

All facilities for adult and youthful felony and misdemeanor offenders and juvenile delinquents are administered by the Division of Corrections, Department of Health and Welfare.

The situation regarding inmate advisory councils has changed several times during the past few years. Currently, inmate councils are permitted in all institutions, but are not required. The most active group is the Council at the Adult Conservation Camp, Palmer, a minimum security facility. A member of the Council may sit in on a disciplinary committee hearing if requested to do so by the inmate charged with a rule violation. [5] This Council was organized in 1964. The five democratically selected representatives-at-large met monthly with staff members to discuss matters of mutual concern. It was regarded as a well functioning organization whose existence provided a meaningful experience for both inmates and staff. [6]

In a 1966-1967 survey it was found that Alaska was
then the only state requiring by administrative order the establishment of an inmate council in each of its jails.   A
representative from each major living area of the jail was
selected by the inmates under officer supervision to serve
for one month.   Men in segregation and those who had received a misconduct report in the preceding two weeks could
not be selected.   Total representation could not be more
than three nor less than two.   The group met weekly with a
staff committee composed of the superintendent or his designee, an officer selected at large by the jail staff through
balloting, and a member of the local probation staff selected
by the jail commander with the approval of the chief probation officer.   It was required that replies to all questions
and problems presented by the Council be made no later than
one week after the meeting.   Several features of the "Policy
Memorandum" on council procedure are interesting and
worthy of note since each was an affirmation of the administration's interest and sincerity:

> (1)   One Councilman is permitted to confer with each
> segregation inmate for a period not to exceed five
> minutes unless a time extension is granted by the
> Jail Superintendent, subject only to visual supervision.
> (2)   Preferably Council meetings are to be held be-
> tween nine and eleven a. m. in a suitable room or
> office, at which coffee is to be available to contribute
> to an informal, relaxed atmosphere.
> (3)   Meetings are to be held despite no items of busi-
> ness to be presented by the Council.   The staff is
> charged with utilizing the time to promote a better
> understanding of matters in general.
> (4)   If he believes the meetings are not being held
> properly, any representative, either staff or inmate,
> may send a letter explaining the problem to the Di-
> rector, Youth and Adult Authority. [7]

Exceptions to the policy were permitted at the Ketchi-
kan and Nome State Jails at the extreme ends of the state.
At these facilities the superintendent contacted the inmates
several times a month regarding any complaints they might
have.   A complex population of sixty-five percent unsen-
tenced prisoners, disciplinary transfers from the Adult Conservation Camp, and a high turnover at the Anchorage State
Jail reportedly made for considerable difficulty in maintaining a balanced council there. [8]

ARIZONA

Department of Corrections

The Department of Corrections administers two institutions for adult and youthful felony offenders and four facilities for juvenile delinquents.   There are no inmate advisory
councils.   The administration looks with disfavor upon the
establishment of such groups in extremely large institutional
settings.   However, in three Community Correctional Centers now in operation, each populated usually by twelve offenders in their early teens, a family-style participation in
the development of behavior standards and the planning of
outside activities is regarded as having been successful. 9

ARKANSAS

Department of Correction

The Department of Correction administers the three
Arkansas institutions for adult and youthful offenders, the
Arkansas State Penitentiary, Grady, the Tucker Intermediate
Reformatory, Tucker, and the Women's Reformatory, Grady.

Each of the institutions has an inmate council whose
members are elected to represent their living quarters.
These councils make recommendations for expenditures from
the Inmate Welfare Funds, sponsor projects promoting the
welfare of inmates, and present to the staffs problems of
general concern together with suggested solutions. 10

The constitution and by-laws of the Inmate Council at
the Arkansas State Penitentiary provide for the election of
two representatives and one alternate from each living unit
to serve a six-month term of office, with tenure limited to
two terms.   Candidates must have been at the institution for
at least two months and have a niminum of six months' time
remaining prior to expected release.   Additionally, candidates must not have been subjected to major disciplinary action during the three months preceding election, and shall
be in not less than Class II status.   The meritorious good-
time statute of 1971 provides for a system of grading for
the purpose of determining the number of days sentence
credit to be allowed monthly to each inmate.   All newly
classified inmates are placed in Class II.   A chairman,

vice-chairman, and treasurer, elected within the membership, constitute an Executive Committee. Two meetings of
the Council are held each month. One meeting is a closed
session. At the other, the superintendent or the commissioner of correction is in attendance. Special meetings may
be called by the Executive Committee with administration
approval. Additional members may be appointed by the
chairman subject to approval by the Executive Committee.
A permanent Finance Committee composed of two appointed
members and the treasurer, the latter serving as chairman,
make monthly and semi-annual financial reports. Special
committees, each chaired by a Council member, are appointed to carry out specific projects and tasks.

Juvenile Services

The Juvenile Services of the Social and Rehabilitative
Services administers the three facilities for juvenile delinquents. According to information received in June 1967,
there was no advisory council nor had there ever been one
at the four facilities then in operation.[11] No current information has been received.

CALIFORNIA

Department of Corrections

The Department of Corrections administers twelve
institutions for adult and youthful felony offenders. An update of 1966 information furnished by the Department of Corrections Central Office and the institutions was recently obtained from all sources except the California State Prison,
San Quentin, the California Conservation Center, Susanville,
the Sierra Conservation Center, Jamestown, and the California Institution for Women, Frontera.

Inmate councils have been utilized in the Department
of Corrections Institutions as a means of direct communication between inmates and staff. Department officials stress
that the councils do not have administrative or executive
authority.[12]

An Inmate Activities Manual issued in July 1963, de-
fines an inmate council as "... a group of inmates elected

by the general population to represent the inmate body in an
advisory capacity to the Warden or Superintendent.   Institution heads are authorized to organize inmate advisory councils
cils limited to discussing the welfare of the inmate body as
a whole.   No individual gripes or grievances may be presented.   Councils are permitted no disciplinary or administrative functions.   Councils may not discuss individuals,
either staff or inmate.   Members must be selected by free
election, eligibility requirements being discretionary with each
institution.   Certain categories of inmate are excluded and
the head of the institution may exclude anyone who has been
a recent or chronic disciplinary problem.

        The California State Prison, San Quentin, established
in 1852, is the oldest and largest of the correctional institutions in the state.   Information was received in 1966 that
an Inmate Advisory Council then in operation was organized
in 1944.   Prior to that time there had been a less structured group.   The administration expressed the opinion that
a council system works well in certain areas, such as serving of equivalent kinds of food at particular meals, but did
not believe the real inmate leaders become involved, the
example being cited that Council members sometimes were
not even aware of portending major disturbances.   Conversely, however, it was admitted that Council efforts in resolving many minor grievances no doubt reduce the potential for
serious discontent resulting from an accumulation of petty
gripes. [13]

        The California State Prison at Folsom, Represa, re-
ceived its first group of prisoners by transfer from San
Quentin in July 1880.   A maximum security institution, Fol-
som is programmed for recidivists, management problems,
and severe escape risks.   An Inmate Advisory Council there
became active in 1956 under a constitution and by-laws developed in September 1955 and since revised on several occasions, the last being in August 1972.   The group, now
known as the Men's Advisory Council, is composed of twenty
members elected to represent their housing units.   A chairman, vice-chairman, and secretary are elected within the
membership.   Meetings are held bi-weekly without staff
representation present, and with the warden and other staff
members as the need arises.   Minutes of all meetings are
widely disseminated within the institution.   The Council
sponsors charity drives and assists with the selection of
movies and radio programs. [14]

The California Correctional Institution, Tehachapi, was reopened on January 3, 1955. (Constructed originally as an institution for female prisoners, the facility was so operated until serious earthquake damage forced evacuation in August 1952.) The initial program was designed to care for parole violators and recidivists who could be managed in a minimum security setting. Late in 1957, a shortage of minimum custody men gave rise to plans for additional security features necessary for conversion to a medium security institution. However, required group counseling for medium security men was substituted for the proposed additional physical security features. This approach was in line with the underlying philosophy at Tehachapi and has proven quite successful.

The community living program, patterned somewhat after Dr. Maxwell Jones' therapeutic community concept, has an Inmate Advisory Council as one of its features. The Council was organized soon after the institution opened in 1955, and functions in accordance with the Department of Corrections Inmate Activities Manual. In August 1967, a 640-bed Medium Security Unit was opened and now houses all medium security inmates. This Unit currently has an Inmate Advisory Council as does the Minimum Security Unit. [15]

The California Institution for Men, Chino, was opened in 1941. Approximately six months later, when the population numbered 170, problems affecting general morale began to arise and Superintendent Kenyon J. Scudder believed it would be helpful to discuss the matters with representatives of the men. An Advisory Council of ten members representing the housing units was elected by secret ballot. A constitution and by-laws provided weekly meetings with the superintendent during which no discussion of staff or other inmates was permitted. Various committees assisted in planning and organizing special holiday events, and regular athletic and recreational programs. Term of office was six months. Council officers were a president, secretary, and an Executive Committee of three or four. The superintendent met alone with the Council as he believed doing so was conducive to freer discussion. Further, it was a means of his "feeling the pulse of the institution." During Superintendent Scudder's fifteen years at Chino it was necessary on only two occasions to administratively remove a member who tried to use the Council for personal advancement. [16]

Superintendent Scudder has consistently emphasized his belief that councils should be of an advisory nature only, and that this can be assured by a carefully drawn constitution, and that a principal purpose of a council is to bring attention to those problems whose impact on the men is unknown to the administration and thus potentially harmful. As an example of the latter, he has related an incident which occurred at Chino some years ago:

> Periodically the subject of coffee came up at a meeting. Any correctional administrator knows the value of good coffee. The men wanted to know why the taste of the coffee varied so from week to week. We asked the Chief Steward to discuss this with the Council. He told the Council that we had the best equipment for making coffee and the coffee was the same as that for personnel. It was a case of the man on the coffee assignment simply not doing his job. The Chief Steward thanked the Council for calling the matter to his attention, then took the opporturnity to discuss ration procedures. The reaction of the Council was good, especially the next morning when the coffee was pronounced excellent. [17]

Early in 1966 the Chino Advisory Council was discontinued, having reportedly lost the confidence of the responsible inmates. The cause of this was attributed to the nomination of poorly qualified persons--for instance, a clownish individual--and the seeking of membership by militant individuals. The Council was replaced with a procedure under which a representative from each housing unit met with the superintendent once a month. Reportedly, these meetings seemed to accomplish the same objectives as did the Council. [18]

The Chino institution is now a complex of four facilities, encompassing the Southern Reception Guidance Center, a Medium Security Unit which functions as a reception center for the complex, a Minimum Security Unit which is an academic and vocational education center, and a new four hundred man unit which will probably be designated as Reception Guidance Center--East. Recently, a Men's Advisory Council was organized. An inmate committee, with a staff advisor, is preparing a constitution and by-laws, the format of which is expected to follow along previous lines to allow for maximum inmate representation to the administrative staff. [19]

The Correctional Training Facility at Soledad is a
medium security correctional complex originally consisting
of three distinct facilities. An Inmate Advisory Council was
established as each facility was opened: South Facility in
January 1948; Central Facility in July 1952; and North Facility on December 1, 1958. South Facility was closed on
January 3, 1970. The Councils in North and Central Facilities are still in operation. [20]

Any inmate who has been nominated by three others
may become a nominee for a twelve-month term of office
as a representative of his housing unit, providing he has
been at the Facility a minimum of six months, has at least
ten months to serve, and his record of adjustment warrants
approval by the administration. Elections are by secret ballot. There are ten permanent committees, including an
Executive Committee composed of the chairman, vice-chairman, secretary, and sergeant-at-arms, which meets with
the administration at the call of the latter. [21]

The Deuel Vocational Institution, Tracy, was moved
to its present location in July 1953, following use of a
temporary site on the desert near Lancaster. Information
previously obtained was recently reviewed by the present administration. [22] An inmate Advisory Council has been active
there since March 1958. The constitution provides for secret ballot election of three representatives from each housing unit to serve terms of six months. The chairman,
vice-chairman, secretary, and sergeant-at-arms compose an
Executive Committee which meets monthly with the administration to discuss topics referred from meetings of the full
council membership. [23]

The California Medical Facility at Vacaville is regarded as the psychiatric unit of the Department of Corrections. In addition, it serves as a reception and guidance
center for all newly committed felons for the 47 northern
counties. The capacity is 1911 which includes facilities for
472 in the reception center. All ages are represented, with
a minimum of age eighteen, the most prevalent group being
those twenty-five to thirty-five years old. All are classified
under three general categories: patient, worker, and administrative. A Men's Advisory Council was established under a constitution and by-laws adopted on September 9, 1963,
and revised periodically since. Its objectives include encouragement to inmates to be interested and actively participate in the advancement of the institution by contributing

advice and suggestions for the improvement of the conditions
under which they live.   An Executive Committee meets
monthly with the superintendent and his executive staff. [24]

The California Men's Colony, San Luis Obispo, is
composed of two facilities--West, opened in 1954, and East,
opened in 1961.   The following information, obtained in
1966, was reviewed recently and returned without change by
the present administration. [25]   An inmate advisory council
is active in each facility under an institution general order
which provides guidelines for the formation of groups, and
stresses the development of those habits and skills of membership most likely to be transferrable to community organizations, such as Alcoholics Anonymous.   A constitution and
by-laws set forth the procedures of each council.

A Resident Advisory Council was organized shortly
after the opening of the West Facility in 1954 and has operated successfully since.   Meetings are held on the housing
unit level and all decisions requiring administrative action
are forwarded by an officer who monitors the meeting.

An Inmate Advisory Council was organized in the
East Facility soon after its opening in 1961.   The facility is
divided into four quads and Council meetings are held on
that level.   The Council was abandoned for approximately a
year when it was determined to have been a factor behind a
food demonstration.   It was reestablished, however, and has
since been reported as operating satisfactorily.

The California Conservation Center, Susanville,
opened in February 1963.   An Inmate Advisory Council was
organized soon afterwards.   Emphasis was placed on the advisory nature of its functions.   According to a 1966 report,
no serious incidents or problems had been encountered and
the administration had had no occasion to consider discon-
tinuing the group.   Non-involvement in disciplinary action for
a ninety-day period was the membership eligibility requirement given in the constitution and by-laws, with representation by housing units, four members for each. [26]

The Inmate Advisory Council at the Southern Conservation Center, Chino, was organized in 1963 when the facility
was the Chino Branch of the California Rehabilitation Center.
Officially established on August 1, 1964, to assist the superintendent in determining inmate reaction and the welfare of
the inmate body as a whole, the Council reportedly has

served these purposes very well. Guidelines for operation
are given in an institution administrative order. The constitution provides for the secret ballot election every ninety
days of one representative. Eligibility for membership is
limited to those free from disciplinary action during the
month prior to election. [27] This camp is now designated
Unit D, Medium Security Facility, California Institution for
Men, Chino.

The Sierra Conservation Center, Jamestown, opened
on July 15, 1965, organized an Inmate Advisory Council in
both its minimum and its medium custody units on April 1,
1966. The constitution and by-laws of the minimum custody
unit (Calaveras) provided for the secret ballot election of
one representative from each housing unit to a six months'
term. No qualifications of conduct or length of time served
were noted. Six standing committees were authorized, including an Executive Committee composed of the Council
officers, the chairman, vice-chairman, executive secretary,
vice-secretary, and sergeant-at-arms. Presumably the
medium custody unit Council operated under a similar constitution. [28]

The California Rehabilitation Center, located near
Corona, is not technically a penal institution. Although
operated by the Department of Corrections, it is an institution for the control, treatment, and rehabilitation of the
civilly committed narcotic addict.

A Resident Central Committee was organized in May
1964. It operates under a constitution which provides for
the secret ballot election of two representatives from each
living unit to terms of four months. An Executive Committee, consisting of the chairman, secretary, sergeant-at-
arms, and two other Central Committee members, meets
periodically with the administration to accomplish the principal objective of the organization, stated as being "to improve relations and foster better communications and understanding between residents and staff at all levels; to keep
staff and residents advised of their respective problems so
these problems may be dealt with in an appropriate manner."

In the Women's Section at the Patton State Hospital,
San Bernardino, one representative and an alternate are
elected from each living unit to serve a six months' term of
office. The total council membership is ten. Meetings are
held every other week with the program administrator. [29]

The California Institution for Women, Frontera, was established when legislation in 1929 provided for the removal of women from the State Prison at San Quentin. A site was selected at Tehachapi and four buildings to house one hundred and fifty persons were completed and dedicated in May 1932. Legal difficulties delayed occupancy until September 1933 when the institution formally opened as a unit of San Quentin. The remoteness of the Tehachapi location caused eventual relocation in 1952, hastened by a severe earthquake, to the present site. The institution provides care for all types of felony commitments and may admit referrals from the Youth Authority. The vigorous program designed to engage the inmate in purposeful activity at all times prompted one of the women to utter a remark which became a catch phrase: "I haven't got time to do my time."

Although the records are not precise, it appears that the Frontera Resident Advisory Council was organized when the institution was in its original location. It continued actively until the summer of 1964 when numerous housing reassignments made impossible the continuation of a representative elective group. In lieu of the Council a Liaison Committee was formed whose members were recommended by cottage supervisors and confirmed by the superintendent. While each cottage had active representation there was a feeling among the women that members did not actually represent the inmate body, but had attained membership by winning recognition of the cottage supervisors. The administration could discern no difference in operation between this group and the Resident Advisory Council, and in January 1966 the latter was reactivated.

Projects carried out by the Resident Advisory Council were cited as possibly being the greatest value of its existence. Enumerated as disadvantages in Council operations were: the length of time required for the group to acquire cohesiveness, estimated to be six months, which is the term of office, and the likelihood of disproportionate representation of the more vocal and demanding inmates. The latter was not considered to be totally disadvantageous since it did provide an opportunity for the superintendent to deal firsthand with the demands. It had been found that quite often members of a pressure group became fairly good representatives in the course of their six months in office. 30

Department of the Youth Authority

The Department of the Youth Authority administers
fourteen facilities for felons, misdemeanants, and commitments from juvenile and criminal courts under the Youth
Authority Act. Current information regarding student councils in each facility was provided by the Department director. [31]

Due to the short time spent by wards at the Northern
California Reception Center-Clinic, Sacramento, it is impractical to attempt to organize an ongoing advisory council.
However, eight to ten wards meet periodically with a Citizens Advisory Council to discuss ward recreation and program needs, and to develop volunteer services.

There is no formal student council at the Southern
Reception Center-Clinic, Norwalk, because wards are there
usually less than thirty days. As an alternative, weekly
meetings are held in each living unit to discuss and resolve
problems pertaining to unit operation. Any individual dis-
satisfied with answers received at these meetings may request to see the superintendent. A grievance procedure is
being developed in order to establish a permanent channel of
ward-policymakers communication.

In 1966 it was reported that each student was assigned
to one of eight small groups. A representative of each
group and the resident newspaper editor made up the membership of a Cottage Council which had been in operation for
more than a year. The Council examined various problems
of community living, solicited suggestions from the groups,
made recommendations on means to effect constructive
changes, supervised a bi-monthly rating system in which
groups rated each of the members as to how they were doing in program basic areas, and counseled boys who presented serious behavioral or attitudinal problems. Committees on entertainment, activities, crafts, and the newspaper
were active and could seek Council assistance. [32]

The Ventura School, Camarillo, has been a co-educational facility since October 1970, housing girls twelve to twenty-
two years of age, and boys seventeen to twenty-four years
of age. The facility was first opened in 1891, moving to its
present location in 1962. A Reception Center-Clinic, for
girls only, was added in 1964.

A Student Advisory Committee holds an hour meeting each week with the superintendent, assistant superintendent, and the supervisors of the Treatment Teams to talk informally about anything regarding the institution which has impact on the wards.   Additionally, a group of officers and student body members hold monthly discussions with the supervisor of education regarding educational facilities and curriculum.   A Recreation Committee of two representatives from each living unit meets with two social workers to develop ongoing as well as holiday recreation projects and events.   The Protestant chaplain meets monthly with an advisory committee of students.

A 1966 report told of a Student Advisory Committee then in operation, whose members were chosen by a Progress Evaluation Committee.   A minimum of two months' residence in the institution was an eligibility requirement. The six-month average length of stay obviated the necessity for a time limit on membership.   Removal could occur if a girl's attitude or behavior deteriorated.   If she did not participate in the meetings, the superintendent might ask that she be replaced, although this had been done only twice in four years.   The Committee met weekly with the superintendent at which time other staff members might attend in relation to the problems presented.   Topics discussed might include food, recreation projects, clothing, personal care items, policies on progress evaluation, and parole referrals. [33]

Community meetings are held as required by each living unit, and attended by all wards and cottage Treatment Team members available, at the Fred C. Nelles School for Boys, Whittier.   The Treatment Teams are given a large degree of autonomy by the School administration, which is reflected in the differential of structure and purpose of the community meetings in the various living units.

Information obtained in 1966 on the Nelles School also reflected considerable autonomy in the activities of each cottage.   At that time each cottage had a five-boy Recreation Committee responsible for suggesting program and activities modifications.   Members were chosen from those who had been residing in the cottage for at least sixty days and whose conduct and attitude were regarded as being among the best. The purchase of a tug-of-war rope was mentioned as an example of an accepted suggestion. [34]

The Los Guilucos School, Santa Rosa, was opened in 1943, as a school for girls, became co-educational during 1970-71, and was closed in June 1973. During the co-educational period, a Student Advisory Committee met once a month with the superintendent. The purpose of the group was to provide an opportunity for articulate, participating students to review their experiences at the School and to suggest changes which if made would in their opinion ensure more effective programs.

Weekly Community Meetings, also held at the Santa Rosa facility, are described as having been the primary vehicle for the conveyance of student opinion and suggestions for program changes. The meetings were attended by the Treatment Team Supervisor who subsequently held discussions with his staff on student suggestions, and presented proposed program changes at weekly meetings of the administrative staff.

In 1966 there was a Girls' Advisory Committee, composed of two representatives of each cottage, that met weekly with the superintendent and assistant superintendent to discuss topics referred by the various cottages. Length of time in the program and general leadership ability were the criteria for the selection of representatives. [35]

The Youth Training School, Ontario, opened in 1960, has had a formal Student Council since 1970. The twelve to fifteen members, elected by students and staff, represent their cottages at twice-a-month meetings with the superintendent and six of his administrative staff, seeking clarification of policies and procedures, registering group grievances, and recommending program and policy changes. The superintendent maintains a positive posture relative to the group and often seeks reactions to pending decisions that would affect housing unit social activities. The Council also participates in housing unit meetings. Additionally, there is a twelve-member Food Advisory Council which meets with the food administrator each month.

The Mt. Bullion Youth Conservation Camp, Mariposa, has a Student Council which meets each week with a senior youth counselor. Selection of a representative is made by each work crew. Work crews frequently discuss camp program problems during "tail-gate" counseling sessions. Community counseling sessions are held on alternate weeks.

A Camp Council of six representatives selected at
large by the population will be reactivated in the near future
at the Pine Grove Youth Conservation Camp, Pine Grove.
The group will meet with the superintendent each week to
discuss anything of concern to the membership.

At the Ben Lomond Youth Conservation Camp, Santa
Cruz, the senior youth counselor supervises the Advisory
Council whose members are chosen on the bases of demonstrated positive leadership ability and interest in the program.   The principal function of the Council is to provide a
means of communication between wards and staff.   An open-
door policy permits wards to talk to administrative staff
members at any time they believe their assigned counselor
cannot help them.   This program was reported as being in
operation in 1966, then being designated as the Ward Council. [36]

A four-member Ward Council meets regularly with
the superintendent to discuss suggestions for program improvement and to maintain open lines of communication between wards and administration at the Washington Ridge
Youth Conservation Camp, Nevada City.

The Northern California Youth Center, Stockton, is
a complex of three facilities, each with an approximate
capacity of four hundred:

O. H. Close School for Boys.   There is no formal
student council.   Ad hoc committees from each living unit
meet as needs indicate.   Community meetings, five days
each week, are held in the living units.   These meetings
are attended by seven Treatment Team members--team
supervisor, a social worker, three teachers, and two youth
counselors.   Discussions dealing with any operational problem of each unit and any inter-personal problems between
wards and staff and between the wards themselves, are conducted in a democratic atmosphere.   This facility opened in
1966 and the program described herein was reported as being in operation the same year. [37]

Karl Holton School for Boys.   The School has no formal student council.   However, community meetings held in
all fifty-bed living units daily attended by the Treatment
Team supervisor, social worker, teachers, and youth counselors, deal with unit operational problems, program planning, and interpersonal relationship problems between the

wards and staff.   In addition to the community meetings,
the Ethnic Studies Program has a Ward Advisory Committee
which is comprised of the various minority groups who advise staff on curriculum content in this area.   Each fifty-
bed unit also has a Student Recreation Committee which
works with a staff member to plan and develop recreation
for the unit.   All units have an Orientation Committee of
wards and one staff member to develop and conduct ongoing
orientation programs for all new wards.

        DeWitt Nelson Training Center.   A trainee Advisory
Council meets twice a month with the superintendent for two
or three hours.   The five dormitories each elect three
members to the Council whose duties include:

        1.   Orienting new arrivals and assisting staff in ac-
quainting them with rules, regulations, and programs.
        2.   Acting in an advisory capacity to the superinten-
dent in disseminating ward benefit funds.
        3.   Acting as spokesmen for their ethnic groups.
        4.   Advising what items of value should be placed on
the canteen list.
        5.   Assisting as leaders in preparation of school-
wide activities.
        6.   Acting as a sounding board directly to the super-
intendent, giving him feedback on the overall morale of the
ward population.

        The Paso Robles School for Boys, Pasa Robles, was
opened in 1947 and closed effective October 1972.   Information received in 1966 indicated that while there was no cen-
trally organized ward-staff advisory council, the program of
the School was designed to encourage operation of the nine
living units as semi-autonomous therapeutic communities.
There were student government activities of varying degree
in each unit.   Four of the cottages had popularly elected
committees working closely with staff in ongoing programs. [38]

        The past and the current scene regarding student
councils at the Preston School of Industry, Ione, were reviewed in Part I.

                        COLORADO

        The Colorado Department of Institutions has jurisdic-
tion over all institutions for adult and youthful felony

offenders and juvenile delinquents.

Division of Corrections

The Division of Corrections administers two institutions, each with subsidiary units, for adult and youthful felony offenders. An Inmate Advisory Council that meets regularly and has had quite an influential voice in the administration, making a number of contributions, is reported as having been initiated at one of the institutions. The process of electing members to a similar group in the other institution is underway. Information as to which institution the references pertained was not obtained. However, information obtained in a previous survey, as given in the following paragraph, was confirmed as being essentially valid for the present. [39]

At the State Penitentiary, Canon City, in 1966, a number of groups were reported as having fairly complete control of their activities under the supervision of sponsors. Cited as examples were Alcoholics Anonymous and the Dale Carnegie Alumni Group. The latter had developed a crime prevention program working with schools, churches, and various community groups. Its main function was to evangelize the "crime does not pay" message to teenagers and to impress parents with the importance of taking an active interest in the affairs of their children. [40]

Division of Youth Services

There are no student councils at any of the six facilities administered by the Division of Youth Services for juvenile delinquents and children in need of supervision. However, residents participate in discussions on cottage administration and in decision making during daily housing unit meetings at the Mount View Girls' School, Denver, and the Lookout Mountain School for Boys, Golden. Regular boy/staff meetings and occasional marathon meetings are held at the Lathrop Park Youth Camp, Walsenburg, and the Golden Gate Youth Camp, Golden. [41]

Several years ago an attempt to form a student council among the high school age group at the Mount View Girls' School was cancelled after various girls ganged up on others to coerce votes during the election campaign. [42]

CONNECTICUT

Department of Correction

The Connecticut Department of Correction administers
four institutions and one conservation camp for felony and
misdemeanor offenders.   The following information regarding
the Connecticut Correctional Institution, Somers, and the
Connecticut Correctional Institution, Niantic, obtained in
1966 and 1967, was reviewed by the current administration
of the Department in latter 1972.   The only change made
was the notation that Warden Reincke of the Somers institution had resigned in 1969.

The first prison in the Colony of Connecticut was an
abandoned copper mine, opened at Granby in 1773 and named
Newgate Prison.   Its use was discontinued on September 28,
1827, when the Connecticut State Prison at Wethersfield
opened.   In 1963, the latter was replaced by the Connecticut
Correctional Institution, near Somers.

The warden at the Connecticut State prison until 1969
stated in 1966 that from information available it would appear that in the late 1950's an inmate committee was functioning, but was not apparently officially sponsored or recognized. [43]   The warden from September 1956 until December 1961 took office following an inmate uprising which
necessitated calling out the National Guard to put down.
He found a self-appointed inmate committee which, if not the
focal point of inmate unrest, had succeeded in gaining a
great deal of public and official recognition through its ability to verbalize feelings of discontent and unrest.   The
group gradually dissolved when recognition was denied it.
Selected inmate committees were used thereafter for a variety of special purposes but no central council was organized. [44]

The Connecticut State Farm and Prison for Women
at Niantic, now designated as Connecticut Correctional Institution, was first opened in 1917 as a farm.   Although no
records are available, it is known that a type of self-government was used in the early twenties.   Its discontinuance
has been conjectured as due to a change in staff.   Currently
the Honor Cottage is self-governing and its fifteen to twenty-
two residents are carefully screened by the administration.
The latter also determines policy and guidelines on behavior
and operational procedures.   A staff member is on duty at

all times but it is seldom necessary for her to become involved in discipline or management.   The residents elect
officers, for three-month terms, who may request additional
privileges on behalf of the others.   Residents may also voice
disapproval of the administration's choice of girls for the
Honor Cottage.   Some time ago the request of another Cottage group of twenty-eight girls for some self-management
was approved.   This plan appeared to hold promise but expired after about three months when the leaders were released. [45]

No information has been received regarding the cur-
rent situation with reference to advisory councils at the
Connecticut Correctional Institution, Enfield, the Connecticut
Conservation Camp, Portland, and the Connecticut Correc-
tional Institution, Cheshire.   An account of the Welfare
League at the latter institution, then known as the Connecti-
cut State Reformatory, from 1914 to 1916, was given in
Part I.

Department of Children and Youth Services

The Department of Children and Youth Services has
jurisdiction over three facilities for youthful delinquents.
The self-government program at the Long Lane School for
Girls, Middletown, was described in Part I.   In the 1966-
1967 survey, no information regarding advisory councils at
the Connecticut School for Boys, Meriden, was received.
However, current information indicates that students there
have been involved in this kind of communication group activity for sometime.

In 1973 the Connecticut School for Boys and the Long
Lane School for Girls were merged, with all students being
housed at the latter institution which now bears its original
designation as Long Lane School.   A Constitution dated July
1973 contains the School statement of purpose, establishes
a preference for the use of positive reinforcement, and in
general provides a structure for the general program, which
includes student participation through a Student Council. [46]

Each of the cottages elects two representatives and
one alternate to serve for one month as members of the
Student Council.   At weekly meetings of the Counseling
Team, comprised of all staff members working in a cottage,
the Student Council representatives are voting members on

all matters having to do with cottage rules. Meeting every
two weeks with the superintendent, the Council may introduce any topic and have the option of inviting any staff member to explain any matters not fully understood.

Additionally, Student Council representatives--three
girls and three boys--serve on a Commissioner's Council.
These six meet with the commissioner twice a month in the
central office in Hartford to provide feedback regarding conditions at the institution.

DELAWARE

The Department of Health and Social Services exer-
cises administrative jurisdiction over all facilities for adult
offenders and juvenile delinquents.

Division of Adult Corrections

The Honor Court in operation at the New Castle Correctional Institution from 1921 to 1931 was reviewed in Part
I.   That institution was closed in April 1971.   Currently
there are no inmate advisory councils in the three institutions administered by the Division of Adult Corrections.
However,. the administration provides support to and assists
in the organization and functioning of various ad hoc committees elected by housing units to be concerned with a
specific purpose in matters of food, recreational programs,
library services, rules and regulations, commissary, and
special events.   Currently, work is progressing on the
adoption of a Bill of Rights for prisoners based on that of
the United Nations. [47]

Division of Juvenile Corrections

The Division of Juvenile Corrections provides residential care for juvenile delinquents in five facilities, including two detention homes.   Information received in 1966 and
1967, indicated that an informally organized Planning Committee, which elected its own officers, had been in existence
for about ten years at the Woods Haven-Kruse School for
Girls, Claymont.   The group was composed of five representatives from each of the two cottages, and reportedly was

self-perpetuating in that incumbents elected the new members as vacancies occurred.   The criteria of ability to show
positive leadership and demonstrated good citizenship were
used in this selection process.   In addition to a role in coordinating social events, the group was a means of frank
and open discussion with staff.   In particular, the airing of
program weaknesses and the need for special services to
individual girls were cited as benefits of this communication.   A staff coordinator was assigned by the administration
from the clinical personnel. [48]   No current information has
been received.

        A Student Council was organized at the Ferris School
for Boys, Wilmington, in October 1969, under a written
procedure that provided for the secret ballot election of two
representatives from each cottage to serve three-month
terms of office.   The group, which elects from the membership a president, vice-president, and secretary, meets
weekly with either the superintendent, the assistant superintendent, or a designate.   Any topic may be discussed except that no verbal attack may be made upon any boy or
staff member.   All planning and programming decided by
the Council must be consistent with the purpose, goals, and
regulations of the School. [49]

                              FLORIDA

        The Department of Health and Rehabilitative Services
has jurisdiction over all facilities for adult and youthful offenders and juvenile delinquents.

Division of Corrections

        The Division of Corrections administers nine major
institutions, twenty-five Community Centers, and fourteen
road prisons.   All of the latter and six of the institutions
have never had inmate advisory councils.   The Glades Correctional Institution, Belle Glade, had a Dormitory Council
some twelve or thirteen years ago.   The reason for its discontinuance is not known.   The Florida State Prison and the
Union Correctional Institution, both at Raiford, had inmate
councils for a period of time in 1971. [50]

Division of Youth Services

The Division of Youth Services has not issued directives on the implementation, purpose, and operation of student councils, but it does suggest that each facility under its
administration organize such a group.   Each of the training
schools has organized a student council on both the junior
and senior campus level, whose members are elected to
represent their cottage of residence. 51

Agenda topics at weekly staff-council meetings may
pertain to suggestions for policy or program changes and
improvements, maintenance problems, leisure time activities, dress codes, and inter-scholastic athletics.   Program
and staff grievances are also aired.   Community relationships are fostered by council participation in parades and
pageants and assisting in clean-ups and giving help at other
gatherings or activities.   Liaison with the other Division of
Youth Services facilities is maintained through inter-school
council meetings.

The Student Council at the Arthur G. Dozier School
for Boys, Marianna, was organized over six years ago.
Students prepared a constitution and by-laws.   The Council
planned many school activities and was said to be responsible for presenting educational programs monthly to the
entire student body.   Members of the Council were described
as those students who had distinguished themselves in the
program.   In recognition of their efforts, and to motivate
others to emulation, they were given additional privileges
and permitted to wear a special insignia. 52

GEORGIA

Department of Offender Rehabilitation

Institutions for adult and youthful felony offenders are
administered by the Department of Offender Rehabilitation.
At present there are no inmate advisory councils.   However,
offenders at the Georgia Diagnostic and Classification Center, Jackson, decide on a quarter-year basis which recreational programs will be implemented. 53

Department of Human Resources

None of the ten Youth Development Centers for juveniles, under the Georgia Department of Human Resources,
has an advisory council. [54]

HAWAII

Corrections Division

All facilities for adult and youthful felony offenders
and juvenile delinquents are administered by the Corrections
Division of the Department of Social Services and Housing.
The account herein, based principally on information received in 1966, was sent to the administrator of the Corrections Division for review with a request for update information. It was returned with a notation that no changes are
indicated at present. However, the Corrections Division
Manual as it pertains to inmate advisory councils is under
study and due for some major amending.

The establishment of advisory councils is regarded
by the Corrections Division as being a good institution management technique to facilitate staff-inmate communication.
Directive No. 71 of the administrator describes the purpose,
policies, and procedures of ward/inmate advisory councils. [55]
A constitution and by-laws drawn up by the inmates, reviewed by the facility superintendent, and approved by the
administrator govern council activities. The superintendent
attends the weekly meetings of the council members who are
elected as representatives of their housing units. The term
of office is limited to six months. Discussions concerning
individuals, either inmate or staff, are not allowed. Prior
to the establishment of a council the facility superintendent
must interpret its purpose and objectives to both inmates
and staff, stressing the advisory nature of the group. No
authority over other inmates may be given to council members. All communication between the council and staff must
be through the superintendent.

A Grand Council at the Hawaii State Prison, Honolulu,
was organized around 1955. In 1962 a Ward Advisory Council was formed at the Hawaii Youth Correctional Facility,
Honolulu. [56] In 1956 the warden of the Hawaii State Prison
reported on various activities of the Inmate Council there.

For four years a committee had been responsible for developing and recording a fifteen-minute program of entertainment, discussion, and prison information which was broadcast regularly over a local radio station.   In addition, a
welfare committee raised funds to aid inmates and parolees
in time of need; a teen-age committee sponsored a community settlement swimming team, and another committee
studied delinquency in the light of its own experiences, preparing radio programs and news articles.   A public relations committee was credited with having played an important part in an effective community relations program.   The
Inmate Council of the Kulani Honor Camp at Hilo had a blood
donor program under which they had agreed to supply blood
to two young anemic boys. [57]

IDAHO

State Board of Correction

The Idaho State Penitentiary, Boise, is the state
facility for adult and youthful felony offenders.   A five-member Inmate Advisory Council was organized on October 8,
1969, and operates under the provisions of a constitution
and by-laws whose preamble cites the purposes of the organization as the maintenance of high morale, the encouragement of participation in programs designed for personal accomplishment, and the propagation of inmate-administration
cooperation and understanding. [58]

Elections are held in January and July.   Any inmate
who has been in continuous residence for six months may
be elected to a six months' term, with tenure limited to
two consecutive terms, to serve at large.   The Council
elects its own officers, with each member filling one of the
following offices: chairman, vice-chairman, secretary-reporter, parliamentarian, and sergeant-at-arms.   Unsupervised meetings are held the first and third weeks of each
month, in a location chosen by the Council, to prepare an
agenda of no more than four major topics, each representative of a broad segment of the institution community, for
discussion at a monthly meeting with the director.   If it is
believed they can more effectively present a proposal, one
or two non-members may be asked by the Council to attend
this meeting.   A councilman may be removed from office by
a majority vote of the population provided he is given a

written notice of the charges against him.   Standing committees may be appointed by the Council.

        A member of the Inmate Advisory Council attends
meetings of the Adjustment Committee, Incentive Pay Board,
and other staff committees, his role being described as
basically that of a consultant.   This arrangement has improved inmate-staff relationships.

State Board of Education

        The State Youth Training Center, Saint Anthony, is
the state facility for juvenile delinquents.   The Student
Council is involved in many aspects of facility government
and behavior policies.   A dress code and student possession
of money on campus are cited as results of Council initiative. [59]

ILLINOIS

        The Department of Corrections has jurisdiction over all
facilities for adult and youth offenders and juvenile delinquents.

Adult Division

        The Adult Division administers nine facilities for
males over the age of seventeen and females over eighteen.
The Illinois State Farm, Vandalia, receives only misdemeanants.   The State Reformatory for Women, Dwight, receives both felons and misdemeanants.   An attempt by Warden Hill to form an inmate grievance committee at the Illinois State Penitentiary, Joliet, was recounted in Part I.
No current data has been received regarding the status of
advisory councils in the nine institutions administered by the
Adult Division.   Information was obtained in 1966 that although there were no advisory councils, the formation of
such groups as a part of social education had not been entirely excluded from future planning. [60]

Juvenile Division

        The Juvenile Division administers sixteen facilities,

of which eight are forestry camps and schools.   Currently,
it is reported that student councils or similar groups, are
active in seven facilities. [61]   A Student Council at Hanna
City State Boys' School, Hanna City, meets weekly as teams
with dormitory staff.   A monthly meeting is also held with
the superintendent and administrative staff.   At the Illinois
Industrial School for Boys, Sheridan, an Administrative Call
Line of key staff visit each housing unit weekly to discuss
the delivery of services.   Everyone is heard and all problems and suggestions are discussed.

Although the short length of time students are in residence before assignment to an institution precludes the establishment of a formalized student council at the Reception
and Diagnostic Center for Boys, Joliet, informal student input is provided in the Gemini program, and it is planned
that students participate in procedure and program policy-
making in a Bridge Learning Center currently being developed.

Four separate program units operate independently
but share the general facilities at the Illinois State Training
School for Boys, St. Charles.   All four programs have a
student council in each cottage, meeting together as a student government.   The councils are regarded as productive
avenues in the decision-making process.   The Illinois State
Training School for Girls, Geneva, now operates as a co-
educational facility.   A Student Involvement Committee,
representing all cottages, meets with the superintendent and
key administrative staff to develop program, projects, and
activities, as well as to participate in the planning and implementation of rules.

The Dupage State Boy's School, Naperville, has group
therapy programs, such as guided group interaction, the
dynamics of which provide student input relative to daily
living practices.   Preparole groups meet weekly with the
administration to make recommendations pertaining to cottage
life and program problems.   A Student Involvement Council
plays an integral role at the Valley View School for Boys,
St. Charles, in parole plans, token economy, reinforcement
implementation, as well as reviewing rules on dress codes,
dietary plans, and social activities.

No information was provided regarding the Jubilee
Lodge, Brimfield, a thirty-six person facility which opened
in 1972, or the eight school camps under the office of

Forestry Camps and Schools, Springfield. In 1967 it was reported that a Student Advisory Committee was in operation at the Pere Marquette School Camps, Grafton. All nominees were required to make a speech setting forth their qualifications, after which open elections were held. Committeemen met with a staff member and were free to make recommendations on all subjects. [62]

INDIANA

All facilities for adult and youth offenders and for juvenile delinquents are under the jurisdiction of the Department of Correction.

Adult Authority

The Indiana Adult Authority administers five institutions, including a reception and diagnostic center. Early in 1957 inmates at the Indiana State Prison, Michigan City, petitioned the warden to approve an inmate council. However, the warden questioned the request which was subsequently formally disapproved by the Commissioner of Correction. [63]

An Inmate Advisory Council was organized at the Indiana State Prison in June 1969 with a membership of approximately forty. Upon taking office in August of that year, the present warden initiated a reorganization under which two Councils function, one representing the main institution and the other representing the two prison farms and a trusty dormitory. To be eligible to run in the annual January election, an individual must obtain fifty signatures endorsing his candidacy. The twelve members serve until released from the institution. An agenda, prepared and submitted to the warden for his approval and additions, is discussed at periodic meetings which are taped for evening broadcast over the radio system. The Council officers--president, vice-president, secretary, and committee chairmen--work full-time in an office provided by the administration. The committee chairmen are permitted to visit their areas of responsibility during working hours to talk with inmates and to gather information for Council meetings. The hospital, food service, and recreation are mentioned as service areas represented by council committees. Council accomplishments include the restructuring of diets, lowering the cost of certain food items sold in the commissary, and selection of recreational item purchases.   Effectiveness of the Council is questioned as it is felt that those persons attracted to membership are not representative of the institution population. 64

Sometime prior to 1935, a Cadet System was established at the Indiana Reformatory, Pendleton.   Cadets were assigned to supervise groups of inmates as they marched to and from work areas and to assist in the cleaning and keeping of order in living quarters.   When it was no longer felt to be a viable approach, the system was abolished in 1964.

While superintendent from May 1961 to February 1966, John Buck organized a Coordinating Committee of one representative from each inmate group, such as Alcoholics Anonymous and Jaycees, to assist in planning special programs.   He found the participation of the group to be most helpful.   Between 1967 and 1968 a group calling itself Inmate Committee for Better Relations came into existence. This group ostensibly meant to foster wholesome relations between staff and inmates.   It defeated itself, however, by attempting to control job assignments and to set itself up as an official control force.   Lack of administrative guidelines and controls added to the ineffectiveness of the group.   The approach used by the group created new gulfs between staff and inmates and widened those already existent.   During 1966 to 1968 there was sporadic discussion concerning the efficacy of inmate advisory groups.

In 1969, after discussion with both staff and inmates, Superintendent George Phend initiated action to develop an Inmate Council.   The group meets regularly and has the guidance of an assigned staff advisor.   In January 1970 a general election was held by the inmate population.   A Council of 48 men was elected to represent the population, subsequently electing their own officers.   The Council has proven itself to be an effective communications medium for both staff and inmates.   A number of projects proposed by the Council have been adopted--e.g., merit visits for inmates and more privacy during visits.   The three-year operation of the Council has been enhanced by the practice of openness in discussions, promptness in investigating grievances, and observance of adequate controls relative to the function of the Council.   Council representatives are included in most discussions where the inmates are directly

involved. Mutual openness between staff and inmates, the
controlled, progressive delegation of responsibility to the
inmates themselves, and the general acceptance of this responsibility by the inmates are cited as constituting a triad
of reasons contributing to the acceptance and effectiveness
of the Council. [65]

The annual population turnover of four to five thousand
misdemeanor offenders at the Indiana State Farm, Green-
castle, has inhibited the organization of an inmate advisory
council. [66] At the Indiana Women's Prison, Indianapolis,
an Inmate Council, composed of two elected members from
each of the five cottages, was organized in October 1968.
Meetings are held on call with the superintendent to present
problems and discuss solutions, with other staff members
attending should the topic pertain to their areas of responsibility. [67] There is no inmate council nor plans for one in
the immediate future at the Reception-Diagnostic Center,
Plainfield. This is a very short-term facility. [68]

Youth Authority

The Indiana Youth Authority administers eight facilities for youthful offenders and juvenile delinquents. The
Student Council established on July 1, 1969, at the Indiana
Boys' School, Plainfield, is a member of the Indiana Association of Student Councils. Each cottage at this minimum
security facility elects a member to the Council. A president, vice-president, secretary, and assistant secretary are
elected by the membership. The purpose of the group is to
sustain a spirit of confidence and trust between the young
men and the administration by providing for open communication. At the monthly meetings, any topic applicable to
life at the School may be discussed. Several changes in
policy are cited as originating through Student Council suggestion. All pertain to increased privileges. [69] Six years
ago a Student Council was organized at the Indiana Girls'
School, Indianapolis. Each cottage elects one girl to serve
a one-month term on the Council, which meets weekly with
the superintendent to discuss grievances and suggest changes.
The group is described as being advisory in nature. [70]

The Indiana Youth Center, Plainfield, has an Inmate
Council whose constitution provides for the popular vote
election of one Councilman and two alternates to represent
each housing unit for a six-months' period, providing the

candidate has been at the facility for at least sixty days and the date of his release is six months or more distant. A president, vice-president, and recorder-secretary are elected within the membership. Meetings of the Council are held weekly. On alternate weeks, staff advisors meet with the group to review actions. No resolution may be forwarded to the administration without advisor consent. The superintendent is given a monthly report on the progress of the Council.[71]

No information was received from the Indiana Youth Rehabilitation Facility and the Rockville Training Center, both located at Rockville, nor from the youth camps located at Henryville, Medaryville, and Albion.

IOWA

The Department of Social Services has jurisdiction over all facilities for adult and youth offenders and juvenile delinquents.

Bureau of Adult Correction Services

The Bureau of Adult Correction Services administers six institutions for adult and youth offenders. Current information received makes no mention of inmate advisory councils at the Riverview Release Center, Newton, or the Iowa Security Medical Facility, Oakdale. The establishment of an advisory council at the former is no doubt neither feasible nor warranted in view of the community orientation of the program. The population of the Oakdale facility is composed of persons committed for evaluation by the courts, mentally ill offenders, and dangerous patients from mental health institutions.

While there is no central inmate advisory council at the Iowa State Penitentiary, Fort Madison, three groups operate under staff sponsorship and procedures defined by practice or written constitution. There are: the Lainett Alcoholics Anonymous Group founded in 1948; a Gavel Club (Toastmasters International), organized on November 10, 1965; and the Pen City Jaycees, active since May 5, 1966.[72] In 1940 there was an unsuccessful experience with an inmate committee which helped operate an honor dormitory for a time.[73]

An Inmate Council was organized in 1956 at the
Men's Reformatory, Anamosa.   It ceased to exist in 1962,
but was reorganized in 1964, and functioned under a constitution and by-laws which provided for the election of work-
area representatives who met bi-monthly with a staff sponsor. [74]

A current description of the Men's Reformatory Inmate Council makes no mention of a constitution, by-laws,
or staff sponsor, but does give details of Council procedures
and areas of activity:

> ... serves to increase communications between resi-
> dents and staff. ...   [A] vehicle which promotes the
> opportunity for a free flow of ideas and problems,
> providing an opportunity for understanding of the con-
> cerns of both. ...   [A]llows residents to take an
> active role in problem solving and exposes them to
> the varied expectations which are part of organiza-
> tional activities found in the community. ...   [A]llows
> residents to demonstrate responsible behavior and
> utilize various skills in planning, organizing, and
> implementing constructive projects.

Any resident in the Men's Reformatory who in the
previous three months has had no disciplinary report resulting in loss of good-time credits, may be elected by his fellow workers to represent a designated work area.   A president and a services secretary are elected by the Council
membership.

Administrative and Correctional-Treatment Services
personnel alternate as the staff group meeting each week
with the seventeen Council members.   Other staff may be
invited to discuss special problems or may attend on their
own initiative.   A typed summary of discussions is distributed to all residents and staff and written decisions are
provided later by staff on all matters not resolved in the
meeting.   In order to provide for idea input by residents
and to make them aware of departmental problems, procedure provides for Council appointment of subcommittees to
meet with department heads.   The Council derives income
from three sources, a movie screened twice a week, profits
from visiting room vending machines, and donations from
the community.

Expenditures of this income are determined by the

Council for the benefit of all residents. Interestingly, Council members assist housing-unit staff in resolving interpersonal relationship problems, either resident-staff or resident-resident. Council members are assembled as a first move in coping with a possible disturbance. The overall effectiveness of the Council at a given period is regarded as a reflection of its leadership. [75]

Information obtained in 1966 from the Women's Reformatory, Rockwell City, as presented herein was reviewed recently and returned with no change other than to note the name of the present superintendent, Ted Wallman. In order to provide the women an opportunity to express their concerns to the administration as well as to foster their involvement with the staff in program development, a Women's Council was organized in August 1966 at the Women's Reformatory. Three representatives from each cottage are elected by secret ballot to six-month terms. The superintendent is the chairman and secretary. The philosophy of the administration toward the council concept and an evaluation of council usefulness was made by Acting Superintendent James E. Allen:

> I think the most pressing need in adult institutions today is simply to be aware that women living in a group have concerns about the way they would like to live, and that the majority of their suggestions are fairly valid. The way in which the Women's Council is currently organized gives the top administrator the full advantage of purposefully involving the women in program planning, receiving an ongoing feeling of the tone of the institution, and an effective tool in group control since the members of the council are leaders in their units. The Women's Council is a semi-administration-inmate group that can serve many purposes. The group has been fairly effective both for the total population and for the staff. [76]

Bureau of Family and Children's Services

The Bureau of Family and Children's Services administers the two state facilities for juvenile delinquents. At the Iowa Training School for Girls, Mitchellville, the Superintendent's Advisory Council was organized shortly after the incumbent superintendent was appointed in September 1972. Each cottage elects a representative by secret ballot.

An at-large representative is elected by all girls in the
school.   Meetings are held each Monday with the superintendent to discuss administrative policies only.   A Council
also selects the weekly movies.   Other program modifications are planned to insure participation by girls in operations planning.   A team-approach is now being implemented
which will provide twice weekly meetings of team personnel
and cottage residents. [77]

        At the Iowa Training School for Boys, Eldora, a
Student Council was organized among the boys in the discipline unit which had undergone a physical, psychological, and
philosophical facelifting.   Renamed Health Center, the philosophy was changed from punishment and suppression to
medically oriented treatment of both physical and emotional
disorders.   The Council operated from 1961 to 1965 as an
integral part of the program.   A president, vice-president
and one representative from each wing of the building were
elected by secret ballot.   Weekly meetings were held with
the staff, at which time the boys presented matters related
to the unit program.   The meetings were described in a recent article:

        Inmates are expected to bring up in the meeting fac-
        tors disturbing to the general progress of the pro-
        gram; oftentimes considerable responsibility is shown
        in this area.   Suggestions made in writing by in-
        mates are read to the population by the council offi-
        cers and they frequently lead to important discussions
        about one another's behavior.   That the plotting of
        escapes has been reported on several occasions
        seems indicative of the strength of the council and of
        staff-council rapport.   Comments about the personal
        shortcomings or successes of inmates are often in-
        troduced by their fellows for discussion, for example:
        'Why does Sam keep wiping his nose on the dish
        towel?'; 'Joe has been slugging me and I want him
        to stop it'; 'Jack did a nice job of planning the party
        last night. '   Staff members, too, must be strong
        enough to accept critical comments directed toward
        them.
            The activities of the student council are closely
        supervised and care is taken that it not degenerate
        into a kangaroo court.   It serves a valuable function
        in providing a forum for the expression of inmate
        feelings.   It teaches some measure of community
        responsibility and it has been especially helpful in

the ego development of boys elected to official positions. 78

Since 1965, daily community meetings have been held which have eliminated the Student Council. These meetings, attended by both staff and boys, are seen as more desirable than council meetings to meet the six objectives of: catharsis, problem solving, development of communication skills, development of self-awareness, development of ego strength, and staff development. In mid-1966 these community meetings were made a part of the program in all living units of the school. 79

KANSAS

Department of Penal Institutions

The Department of Penal Institutions administers five institutions and four honor camps for adult and youthful felony offenders. Inmate councils as such are not authorized. 80 At one time there were inmate councils in two honor camps, both being disbanded as they were used by inmates as nothing more than a bartering agency which offered little toward resolving problems. 81

Division of Institutional Management

The two facilities for juvenile delinquents are under the jurisdiction of the Division of Institutional Management, State Board of Social Welfare. Shortly after he took office in September 1969, the present superintendet of Boys' Industrial School, Topeka, established a Student Advisory Council. The weekly meetings of sixty to ninety minutes provided a direct line of communication between the superintendent and the boys, facilitating his understanding of their program experiences and learning of their frustrations. Program changes have resulted from this interchange, giving the boys a sense of participation. 82 Prior to 1969, small committees were utilized to plan cottage activities and recreation events, with the staff chairman having full veto powers. 83

A Student Government Program was initiated in August 1966 at the Girls' Industrial School, Beloit, to provide opportunities for the girls to both plan and participate in

extra-curricular activities and institutional policies. [84] Initially members were encouraged to assume responsibility
in dealing with problems of inappropriate behavior and were
given disciplinary authority.   This was discontinued when
the girls demonstrated a tendency toward unreasonable harshness and a frequent misuse of authority by aggressive acting-
out and venting of anger on weaker students.

Each of the four cottages elects three officers, a
president, vice-president, and secretary, to serve as a
Cottage Council for four months.   These officers provide
leadership in the one-hour weekly cottage meetings.   The
meetings are a medium by which all students may participate in decisions regarding group programs and activities,
express dissent with cottage programs, and suggest changes.
There is also a Campus Council, under the leadership of
the director of Child Care Services, comprised of the presidents and vice-presidents of the four cottage councils.
Staff utilize the meetings at each level to interpret the rationale for decisions and suggestions.

Although the original rather loose structure of the
Student Government Program has been retained, operational
experience has brought about the establishment of certain
parameters of function.   More frequent behavioral difficulties and an increased rate of unresolvable conflicts were attributed to heightened anxiety levels engendered by the increased responsibilities placed on the students by the program.   The administration believes that although the process may not be as democratic as initially conceived, the
restructuring has resulted in a more therapeutic, beneficial,
and generally constructive Student Government Program.

KENTUCKY

Department of Corrections

The Department of Corrections administers five institutions for adult and youthful felony offenders.   Inmate
advisory councils have been organized in each with the exception of the Kentucky State Penitentiary, Eddyville.   At
that institution a pilot project is underway in which two staff
members and two inmates have been appointed to represent
any inmate cited to the Adjustment Committee for an infraction of the rules.   Inclusion of this approach in the programs of the other institutions is a future possibility. [85]

The Inmate Advisory Council at the Kentucky State Reformatory, LaGrange, is composed of thirty-six members elected by secret ballot to serve a six-month term of office to which an incumbent may once succeed himself. There are nine dormitories, each with four wings from which one representative is elected by secret ballot. Inmates residing in a dormitory wing nominate candidates who are screened by the casework staff to insure that the criteria are met of no major disciplinary reports during the immediate prior three months, four-months' residency in the population, and a like period remaining to serve until tentative or actual release date. The Council elects from the membership a chairman, co-chairman, secretary, co-secretary, and five committeemen. These persons constitute an Executive Committee. A Racial Relations Committee, with four white and four black members, is mandated by the constitution which became effective in September 1972. The Council meets monthly with the superintendent or his designee, to discuss a previously prepared agenda to which topics have been submitted by both the Council and the administration.

Under a constitution and by-laws signed on March 5, 1973, a Resident Affairs Council of five members was established at the Frenchburg Correctional Facility, Frenchburg. The institution was opened in 1969 to provide residential treatment primarily for younger men undergoing a first confinement experience. Members are elected by secret ballot to serve a three-month term of office and may succeed themselves once. Elections are held each February, May, August, and November. Only residents who have a clear conduct record for the two months immediately preceding the election, and who have been at the facility for six weeks with at least two months remaining prior to a scheduled appearance before the Parole Board, may run for office. The Council presides at a monthly meeting of the population, and meets each month with the superintendent to discuss an agenda whose topics have been contributed by both Council members and the administration. Council representation is present at weekly Treatment Committee meetings of the staff. The president of the Council may be present in an advocate/advisory capacity at meetings of the Adjustment Committee.

At both the Kentucky State Reformatory and the Frenchburg Correctional Facility, the stipulation is made that the Council will have no policy making powers. At the latter institution, however, the constitution states that the

Resident Affairs Council will have a distinct voice in some
areas of the policy making process.   At each installation it
is stressed that the superintendent is vested by law with
both the authority and responsibility for institutional operations, and reserves the right to veto actions of the Council.
However, the reasons for exercise of the veto power will
always be explained in writing.   No information was received
on the advisory councils at the Kentucky Correctional Institution for Women, Peewee Valley, and the Blackburn Correctional Complex, Lexington.

Department of Child Welfare

     The Kentucky Department of Child Welfare adminis-
ters fourteen facilities for juvenile delinquents.   The Youth
Council concept has been a program element for an unknown
number of years.   The operating manual of the Department
describes a process in use in residential programs:

> Youth Council--In order for a youth to have a voice
> in the treatment program, there is set up on a bi-
> monthly basis a council that meets with the superin-
> tendent for the purpose of making recommendations
> about the program.   A representative from each
> group brings suggestions and recommendations for
> discussion and consideration.   Notes from these
> council meetings are typed up and posted on the bul-
> letin board and also posted in the log for the entire
> staff to read.   The youth also make suggestions for
> camp agreements during these meetings and also in
> a camp meeting relating to problems that affect the
> entire camp population in their living together as a
> group.   These agreements are posted on the youth's
> bulletin board. 86

LOUISIANA

Department of Corrections

     The Department of Corrections administers eight
facilities for adult and youthful felony offenders and delinquent, neglected, and dependent juveniles.   An Inmate Council was organized on December 10, 1955, at the Louisiana
State Penitentiary, Angola.   Written rules and procedures

stated: "The Inmate Council is a privilege granted to the inmate population by the Warden. The Council and its members are given the privilege to negotiate with the Warden or any member of his staff and to discuss in a proper manner any problem or situation affecting or of interest to the inmate body as a whole. "

A councilman was elected by majority vote in each dormitory and camp, as were two in each of the two cellblocks. The term of office was one year. An appointee of a councilman assisted him in his area of representation. This appointed representative was permitted to attend the regular monthly meetings with the warden at which was discussed items included on an agenda prepared at an unsupervised previous meeting. The written rules stated that councilmen should not attempt to discuss personal matters at Council meetings.

The administration of the State Penitentiary at that time regarded the Inmate Council as being helpful by bringing to the Warden's attention reasonable requests and problems. Additionally, the Council sponsored holiday inmate talent shows annually, initiated an eyebank, assisted with the yearly March of Dimes campaign, and began a fund to provide postage for indigent inmates. Successful operation of the Council was attributed to an understanding by all concerned of its purpose and function. 87

Information received in 1966 indicated that (a) inmate politics, which lessened the caliber of candidates, (b) administration apathy, and (c) loss of confidence in the Inmate Council by the inmate population were major factors contributing to a decreasing effectiveness of the Council. These together with a work stoppage brought about the discontinuance of the group in August 1965. 88

In 1967 four other facilities reported no present or past advisory councils. 89 Current information states there is no representative inmate organization at the Louisiana Correctional Institute for Women, St. Gabriel. It is assumed that no councils exist other than at the Louisiana State Penitentiary inasmuch as mention is made of the possibility that as a result of efforts commenced there in 1972 inmates and students will be allowed to elect representatives to advisory councils. 90

In October 1972 the first scheduled mediation team

meeting was held as a part of a plan to reactivate inmate representation at the Louisiana State Penitentiary. Team membership includes inmates, ex-offenders, representatives of the Department of Corrections, the penitentiary, the United States Department of Justice Mediation, and a legal aid attorney appointed by the Federal District Court. Inmates are being given a voice in the formulation of rules and regulations and in making the problems of the prison population known to the administration. Results have been promising and it is hoped that meaningful representation from inmates can be established and maintained on a permanent basis.

MAINE

Bureau of Corrections

All facilities for adult and youthful offenders and juvenile delinquents are administered by the Bureau of Corrections of the Department of Mental Health and Corrections. No current data have been received regarding advisory councils. Information was obtained in 1966 that no self-government program existed at either the Maine State Prison, Thomaston, or the Men's Correctional Center, South Windham, but that there was a great deal of self-government among the inmates of the Women's Correctional Center, Skowhegan. [91]   No details on the latter were received.

Reportedly, about forty to forty-five years ago an inmate council at the Maine State Prison used its privilege to meet in the evening within a cellblock to plan and execute an escape attempt. One of the guards was severely beaten. That episode ended the council.

In 1967, the then superintendent of the Stevens School, Hallowell, who had been in the position a relatively short time, reported there was no student advisory council. A study, made prior to the superintendent's arrival, mentioned a student "Gripe" Council, the discontinuance of which was recommended because of the negative implications. [92]

According to information received in 1967, there had been no inmate advisory council for at least two decades at the Boys' Training Center, South Portland. However, there

were then informal student groups participating and express-
ing their ideas, under staff direction, in athletic and extra-
curricular cottage life activities. [93]

MARYLAND

All facilities for adult and youthful felony and misdemeanor offenders, juvenile delinquents and children in need
of supervision are under the jurisdiction of the Department
of Public Safety and Correctional Services.

Division of Correction

The Division of Correction administers six institutions
for adult offenders, one of which is a Reception Center for
males, and five camps comprising the Maryland Correctional
Camp System.   Information obtained in 1960 indicated the
existence of an Umpires and Referees Association at the
Maryland Penitentiary, Baltimore, described as having many
of the principles inherent in self-government.   Under the
direction of the supervisor of recreation, the Association
inmate staff conducted instructional classes and gave exam-
inations to aspiring arbiters.   Suggestions made at weekly
meetings were often accepted and adopted by the administration as recreation program policy.   An Alcoholics Anonymous
Program, also reported as being active, was sponsored by a
member of a community Alcoholics Anonymous Chapter.
There was also an Inmate Adoption Fund Plan sponsored by
the Director of Education.   Administered by a Board of Directors, the group met monthly, or at the call of the Chairman, to discuss gifts, receive a financial report, and to
discuss means of continuing the fund.   No other information
was provided concerning the specific function or activities
of the group except the unsupervised taping of a monthly
radio program. [94]

Another group, sponsored by the director of education, was the Colts Corral #954, described as a professional
football fan club which met monthly to view films of games,
hear sports-figure speakers, and meet with various visiting
professional teams and community sports reporters.   Additionally, the group initiated drives to assist underprivileged
children. [95]

In late 1966, a Presidential Organizational Council was formed at the Maryland Penitentiary. The assistant warden for correctional treatment was administrative advisor to the Council whose membership was composed of the presidents and vice-presidents of the thirteen inmate groups then active. Alcoholics Anonymous and the Maryland Penitentiary Umpires and Referees Association were cited as examples of the types of groups involved. The purpose of the Council was to develop better communication between the inmate groups and to discuss organizational and institutional problems. [96]

Current information regarding the institutions administered by the Division of Correction[97] reveals that the Maryland Penitentiary does not have an inmate advisory council. Only one of the nine self-help groups in existence prior to July 1972 is now active. Following a disturbance during that month, all groups with the exception of the Junior Chamber of Commerce rejected the conditions for their continued operation contained in a set of rules promulgated by the warden.

There was also a disturbance in July 1972, at the Maryland House of Correction, Jessup. As a consequence, all self-help groups and the Inmate Advisory Council were suspended. Recently, however, the Council was reactivated. An Inmate Advisory Council at the Maryland Correctional Institution, Hagerstown, meets monthly with pertinent institutional personnel. A report in February 1967 told of plans under contemplation to organize an inmate advisory council at the Maryland Correctional Training Center, Hagerstown, a thousand population institution then being opened. [98] Recently, the Council was placed on inactive status pending the report of the superintendent's task force appointed to evaluate the whole concept of the Council.

In 1940 the Maryland State Reformatory for Women, Jessup, was opened and admitted the eighty-three female prisoners who until then had been housed at the nearby Maryland House of Corrections. The facility was redesignated the Maryland Correctional Institution for Women on July 1, 1964. Current information states that an inmate advisory council meets frequently with the superintendent. A 1967 report mentioned four annual meetings of the group to plan extracurricular activities such as variety shows and athletic events. An attempt was made to have a different cottage representative at each meeting. [99] There are no

inmate advisory councils in the five facilities of the Maryland Correctional Camp System.

Department of Juvenile Services

Of the ten facilities administered by the Department
of Juvenile Services, only one has an advisory council.[100]
The Montrose School for Girls, Reisterstown, receives
twelve-to-eighteen-year-old females adjudged to be delinquent and/or "children in need of supervision. " The Advisory Council is composed of ten members, each elected
by her cottage residents.   The Council meets bi-weekly with
the superintendent, and such other staff as may wish to attend, to discuss topics regarding cottage and institutional
policies and procedures, with discussion of personal problems prohibited unless applicable to the cottage situation.
Council members have no vote in determining overall School
policy, functioning only as an advisory group with the objective of facilitating staff-student communication.   The superintendent reports that his relationship with inmates is facilitated by the meetings.   Additionally, the meetings have resulted in positive changes in both girls and staff, producing
significant program changes readily accepted by both
groups.[101]

MASSACHUSETTS

As we have seen, Massachusetts was the setting for
the first actual experimentation with inmate participation in
administration involving both youth and adult populations.
Although the experience at the New York House of Refuge
antedated that of the Boston House of Reformation by approximately three years, it was only at the latter that inmate participation was purposefully used for its experience
value to the individual.   At the Massachusetts State Prison,
the Society for Moral Improvement and Mutual Aid represented the first instance of adult inmates being placed in a
formal communication with administration.   Additionally, the
past and present at the Correctional Institutions, South Walpole, and Norfolk were related in Part I.

Department of Correction

The Department of Correction administers five institutions for adult offenders, and a Prison Camp division
comprised of three facilities.   No current data has been received.   The account herein is based on information obtained
in 1966.   The Commissioner of Correction, an office established following the report of the Wessell Committee in
1955, has issued no directives regarding inmate councils,
leaving their use to the discretion of each institution executive.

The Correctional Institution, at West Concord, was
built in 1878 to replace the State Prison at Charlestown.   It
served that purpose for six years until May 21, 1884, when
legislation ordered return of the adult prisoners to Charlestown and establishment of Concord as the Massachusetts Reformatory on December 20, 1884.   The present designation
was given by the Acts of 1955.   Concord is a maximum
security institution.   Prior to 1955 no one over the age of
30 could be committed there.   While today there is no age
limitation, the population is used mainly for the younger
group.

The administration at Concord reports that takeover
by aggressive individuals who controlled voting through in-
timidation and threat has been the cause of disbanding inmate councils organized in the past.   A Self-Development
Group which has been functioning for three years claims an
impressive record of rehabilitation among its members.
While believing this group has great potential, the administration voices concern that it may also be taken over by the
wrong element. [102]   The constitution of the Self-Development
Group cites its aim as being: "to extinguish our anti-social
habits by replacing them with new modes of behavior acceptable to ourselves and the community. "   The only requirements for membership are a wish to stay out of prison
and a willingness to help others do likewise.   Using methods
similar to those of Alcoholics Anonymous and Synanon, the
Group utilizes "Seven Points" toward self-betterment. [103]

The Correctional Institution at Framingham was the
second in the country to be built exclusively for women
prisoners.   Opened in 1877 as the Reformatory Prison for
Women, it lost the word prison in 1911 since it had become
essentially a reformatory in spirit and operation.   Attempts
to form student councils have been made at different times

but none have been significant in institution programming.
In 1929 a council was organized following an escape regarded by the members as a slur on their efforts to uphold
a high standard of citizenship throughout the institution.
Records made no further reference to a council until 1956
when the Two-Side Club was formed.   Approximately forty
girls were elected to represent the work departments, living areas and the institution clubs.   Subject to approval of
the superintendent, four officers were elected twice yearly
by secret ballot.   These four, president, vice-president,
secretary, and historian, held monthly meetings at which
arrangements were made for important functions, such as
assemblies, holidays, fairs, and plays. [104]

The Two-Side Club had no noticeable affect on policy
changes made at the time.   When the present superintendent
arrived in 1958 there were no remnants of any inmate organization.   The average period of confinement of nine or
ten months is cited as the potential source of many difficulties in organizing a council.

The Massachusetts Correctional Institution at Bridge-
water, housing over 2000 persons, contains in its four
separate units alcoholics and drug addicts, the criminally
insane, defective delinquents, and sexually dangerous persons.   No attempt has ever been made to discourage the
establishment of inmate councils.   The availability of top
echelon staff to any patient has possibly eliminated the need
for organizing such groups. [105]

Following the national trends toward the construction
of minimum security institutions, in 1951 the legislature authorized the construction of prison camps on land under the
control of the Department of Natural Resources.   The first
of the Massachusetts prison camps was opened in 1952.
Located near historic Plymouth in the Myles Standish Forest,
this 14,000 acre institution is the only camp to have had an
Inmate Council.   The Council functioned briefly in 1953, but
it was found to be unnecessary in a population averaging
only fifty.   The relaxed informal atmosphere of the camps,
conducive to a positive staff-inmate relationship, negates the
necessity for councils. [106]

Department of Youth Services

During the past year [1972-73] all juvenile institutions

in Massachusetts have been closed.[107]   When a survey was
made in 1966 and 1967, there were ten facilities in Massachusetts for the care of juvenile delinquents, all administered by a Youth Service Board.   Information was received
regarding two of these, the Industrial School for Boys,
Shirley, and the Lyman School for Boys, Westborough.
There was no inmate advisory council at the former and no
definite plans to organize one.[108]

At the Westborough facility, a Student Council had
been organized in late 1965.   Two representatives were
elected by the boys in each of the nine cottages.   Under
by-laws drawn by them, these representatives elected a
president, vice-president, and secretary, who directed
Council meetings under the supervision of the Clinical Department staff.   A chronic understaffing of that department
was given as the principal reason for the gradual dissolve-
ment of the Council.   The administration believed that the
Council was an effective advisory group and a beneficial experience to the boys by providing an opportunity to function
in a group situation where they had a voice in policies and
programs directly affecting them.[109]

MICHIGAN

Department of Corrections

The Department of Corrections administers five institutions and a system of corrections-conservation camps
for adult and youthful offenders.   A Reception-Diagnostic
Center at the State Prison of Southern Michigan processes
all committed male offenders.   Inmate participation in the
workings of the prison was recognized by the Department of
Corrections as being vital to both the welfare of the institution and increased efficiency in programs of treatment and
training.   After an examination of the systems of other
states, the formation of advisory councils was the method
selected to provide such participation.[110]

A directive issued March 28, 1972, entitled "Prisoner Representation," directs that each institution establish
procedures by which inmates may elect representatives to
meet with the staff for the purpose of increasing inmate-
administration communication.   Guidelines for forming these
advisory groups provide for secret ballot selection of

volunteer candidates to serve a maximum tenure of six
months as housing unit representatives. The number of
representatives to be elected is determined by each institution, and must reflect the overall racial composition of the
population. Representatives are to be encouraged to work
closely with the housing unit staff in solving issues arising
at that level. Other issues and problems may be discussed
at a monthly meeting of the representatives and the head of
the institution. Additionally, the representatives are to select two inmates to serve as voting members of the institution Benefit Fund Committee.

Screening of candidates is also directed. Disqualification may result if reasonable grounds exist to believe that
a candidate would prove irresponsible or disruptive to the
work of the group. An appropriate official will discuss the
reasons for such action with any affected individual. As of
mid-February 1973, there had been no disqualifications.

The State Prison of Southern Michigan, Jackson, formally instituted the council system in July 1971, about nine
months prior to the issuance of the "Directive on Prisoner
Representation, " after having experimented with the meeting
concept in late 1970. Procedures established there provide
for the secret ballot election of six representatives in each
cell housing unit, including the hospital, and four representatives in each barracks housing unit. These Unit Committees meet monthly, or more often if the need arises,
with two Housing Unit Team Members. Written minutes
of these minutes are posted on the housing unit bulletin
board.

Each Unit Committee selects one member to serve
on the Warden's Forum which meets bi-monthly to consider
institution-wide issues and problems. Recordings of these
meetings are broadcast over the closed circuit radio system.
Actions taken as a result of discussions at the Warden's
Forum include the advancing of the evening count time to
provide a longer recreation period, the option of keeping
cell lights on all night, a change in the hours of several
activities and programs to better accommodate the participants, the rewriting of the Resident Guide Book at a language level more generally understood by the intended read-
ers, and the installation of telephone booths in all cell units
for the placing of collect calls. On many occasions the successful resolution of the problems and concerns of an individual resident has resulted following presentation of his
situation by staff to the housing unit committee.

Staff has also introduced at the Warden's Forum problems involving groups of residents. For example, two groups appeared determined to display discourtesy during the performance of entertainers from the community. Retaliation was threatened by other residents who resented the behavior of the two groups. Discussion of the situation at the Warden's Forum was followed by discussion at Housing Unit Committee meetings. The latter groups then held discussions with the individuals concerned. This procedure resolved the problem.

By September 1972, the other four institutions and the camps had implemented the directive under procedures similar to those established at the State Prison of Southern Michigan. At each facility other staff members, as deemed appropriate by the warden, also attend the monthly meetings. Usually these are the deputy wardens, the director of treatment, a counselor, or a psychologist.

Office of Youth Services

The Office of Youth Services, Department of Social Services, administers all facilities for juvenile delinquents, which include a reception-diagnostic center, three training schools, and two youth camps. In the training schools basic youth treatment groups are reported as being very much involved in administering the programs. Youth groups of nine or ten students each are expected to cope with management type problems in cooperation with a staff team. The latter routinely seek student recommendations on operational matters. [111]

Both of the youth rehabilitation camps have a camp council in operation as a part of the administration. These are Camp Victoire, Grayling, and Camp Nokomis, Prudenville, each with a capacity of forty-eight. Information was received in 1967 that upon their opening in 1963 and 1964, respectively, each facility immediately organized a camp council composed of six boys nominated and elected by secret ballot to a two months' term of office, to which they could succeed themselves. The purpose of the councils was to provide an official, direct, and uninhibited channel of communication from boys to staff. Although it was noted that council membership often altered a student's position with his peers who perceived him as in effect being a part of the administration, this apparently did not inhibit the

effectiveness of the councils in resolving problems.   Racial
conflict and scapegoatism were cited as illustrative of the
type of problems resolved through council intervention. 112

        To accomplish the goals of (a) stimulating positive
leadership skills, (b) providing a quasi-official role in certain areas, (c) creating identification with program planning
and structuring, (d) fostering the objective analysis of policies and issues, and (e) providing a means for staff to obtain insight into the boys' viewpoint, certain guidelines have
been established which provide the boundaries of council
functions.

        (1) Planning decisions made by the group are to be
for the benefit of all and must take into consideration the
purpose, goals, and regulations of the camp.
        (2) While discussion topics may cover any area,
tone and approach must be constructive, realistic, and not
involve character assassination.
        (3) Council discussions are to be handled confident-
ially.

                         MINNESOTA

        All institutions for adult and youth offenders and ju-
venile delinquents are under the jurisdiction of the Minnesota
Department of Corrections.   The information given here was
forwarded to the present administration in December 1972
and returned with no comment other than modifications as
mentioned.

Division of Adult Corrections

        The Division of Adult Corrections administers three
institutions for adult and youthful felony offenders.   At the
Minnesota State Prison, Stillwater, there was an inmate advisory council for about one year in 1960-61.   Initially,
elected committeemen were quite stable persons.   However,
demands made upon councilmen by their constituents lessened
the desirability of the office.   Consequently, the caliber of
candidates deteriorated, leading to the election of irresponsible persons whose unreasonable demands and threats to
demonstrate and riot could not be tolerated.   After attempts
to create a sense of responsibility met with an unimproved

response, the council was discontinued. [113] It is reported
that currently a council is being organized.

There has never been an inmate council at the Minnesota State Reformatory for Men, St. Cloud, although occasionally inmate ad hoc committees have been appointed to
deal with specific problems. [114] A council has never been
formed at the Minnesota Correctional Institution for Women,
Shakopee. [115]

Division of Youth Conservation

The Division of Youth Conservation has administrative control over five facilities, two of which are youth
forestry camps. Although the central office has issued no
directives regarding student councils, all facilities have been
encouraged to establish good two-way communication between
students and staff. [116] Because of the short-term nature of
the program, the Minnesota Reception and Diagnostic Center, at Circle Pines, has never organized a student council. [117]

A Student Council was operative at the State Training
School, Red Wing, for about six months, being discontinued
in June 1966. The group promoted several innovations described as worthwhile, including a student government day;
student assistance in the selection of a new style of clothing; the liberalization of policies involving visiting and the
wearing of jewelry; and a change in smoking policies. The
council was discontinued upon the inception of a Guided
Group Interaction program, featuring individual cottage committees providing the students a voice in parole readiness,
home visits, cottage programs, administrative decisions, and
presenting and discussing new ideas. The present administration firmly believes in student representation and would
have continued the Student Council had the Guided Group
program not evolved. [118]

Two elected students from each of the eight cottages
form a Student Advisory Council which meets periodically
with the group living supervisor at the Minnesota Home
School, Sauk Center. Although the Council is not a policy
making group, policy may result from the information it
provides. Rated by the administration as a successful endeavor, the purpose of the Council is to serve primarily as
a feedback device to advise staff of students' feelings

regarding all aspects of the program. [119]

In the Fall of 1965 a Student Council was formed at
the Youth Vocational Center, Rochester, A constitution and
by-laws was drafted providing for the election of representatives from the student body.   However, the introduction of
a Guided Group Interaction program in March 1966, and
shortly thereafter the activation of weekly Community Meetings, supplanted the need for the Council. [120]   This Center
is now closed.

The St. Croix Camp, Sandstone, had a Student Council from 1962 until 1965, when it was discontinued because
of dominance by a few boys who used it to further their own
interests.   In September 1966 a limited form of self-government was introduced through Camp meetings held every two
weeks at which the superintendent presided.   Problems related to Camp operations could be introduced either by staff
or students.   Should the discussion topic require it, only
students could vote. [121]   This Camp is now closed.

Although the Thistledew Lake Forestry Camp, at To-
go, has no student council at present, there has been experimentation with such groups in the past; these produced only
limited success.   Apparently a departure from the original
democratic purposes occurred in each instance and the
group meetings became gripe sessions.   One of the factors
in the staff decision to discontinue councils was that participation did not result in any visible treatment value for the
student. [122]   A Student Council was in operation for a short
time but was discontinued in 1965 at Willow River Camp,
Minnesota.   Staff-inmate communication is at a fairly high
level due to the one-to-four ratio. [123]

MISSISSIPPI

Mississippi State Penitentiary

The Mississippi State Penitentiary, Parchman, is the
only institution in the state for adult and youthful felony offenders.   No current information has been received regarding inmate advisory councils, but in 1966 it was reported
there was then no form of inmate self-government nor any
knowledge of such a group ever having existed. [124]

Mississippi Training Schools

        The two facilities for juvenile delinquents are admin-
istered by the Central Office, Mississippi Training Schools.
No current data regarding advisory councils has been received. Information obtained in 1966 indicated that there
had never been an inmate council at the Columbia Training
School, Columbia. The report of the Board of Trustees
and Superintendent, Oakley Training School, Raymond, for
the biennium 1963-65, received in February 1967, contained
no reference to a council. [125]

                            MISSOURI

Department of Corrections

        There are no formally structured inmate councils in
the seven facilities for adult and youth felony offenders administered by the Missouri Department of Corrections. Ad
hoc committees are appointed for special activities. However, there is a full honor dormitory and two semi-honor
housing units at the Intermediate Reformatory which may be
regarded as self-governing in certain respects. The one
hundred fifty young men who live in units sign themselves
in and out and establish their own rules for conduct and
community living. This is also true to a large degree at
the Fordland Honor Camp located near Springfield. [126]

State Board of Training Schools

        The State Board of Training Schools administers three
facilities for juvenile delinquents. In the Training School
for Boys, Boonville, the Training School for Girls, Chillicothe, and the Youth Center, Poplar Bluff, the group counseling program often stimulates the individual and the group
toward an improved government of self. Each group member is responsible for recommending the release of each
other group member as well as recommending other appropriate institutional changes. However, there are no advisory council groups in operation. [127]

MONTANA

Department of Institutions

The four facilities in Montana for adult and youthful felony and misdemeanor offenders and juvenile delinquents are administered by the Department of Institutions. The Montana State Prison, Deer Lodge, had an Inmate Council from 1956 through 1959. Officers and representatives were elected by the general population. Cliques gained control and insured that only candidates acceptable to them were elected. This led to intrigue, special privilege, and eventually to violence in the form of a riot in 1959. The opinion that a Council would be detrimental to internal organization was expressed by a previous administration. However, no indictment was made of groups per se. Encouragement of organizations such as Jaycees and Alcoholics Anonymous was expressed. [128]

At the Pine Hills School, Miles City (formerly the State Industrial School), a Student Council was organized in 1968. Two representatives are selected by the ten to twenty-five boys residing in each of the six lodges. Suggestions made at lodge meetings and presented by the representatives at weekly meetings with the superintendent and assistant superintendent have resulted in constructive changes in program. Council members conduct tours of the School, and sponsor activities both on and off the campus. Recently, the superintendent initiated discussions with Council members, on rehabilitation concepts, lodge and student problems, and other topics they might wish to introduce, as a means of providing opportunities for both self-expression and learning about the philosophy and planning on which School operations are based. [129]

The Mountain View School, formerly designated as the Vocational School for Girls, was established at its present site, seven miles north of Helena, in 1919 after operating from 1893 as a part of the Boys' and Girls' Industrial School, Miles City. A student government was in operation several years ago but there is no information available regarding its procedures or reasons for discontinuance. Shortly after he was appointed in 1966, the present superintendent initiated a Student Government program in which a president and council members are elected by the students. [130]

Since its opening in July 1968, the Swan River Youth

Forest Camp, Swan Lake, has had a Camp Council whose
five members, elected by secret ballot, hold office until released or removed for certain disciplinary measures, or
who present reasons for resignation acceptable to a majority
of all boys in the population which averaged twenty-two in
1971 within an age range of sixteen to eighteen years. In
addition to a president, vice-president, and secretary who
records notes of all meetings for posting on bulletin boards
after transmittal to the staff, there is an Orientation Committee whose two members provide full orientation for all
newly arrived boys. [131]

The goals of the Swan River facility Camp Council
are to provide a means of boy-staff communication, develop
an esprit de corps, and help boys learn to handle their responsibilities. The duration of weekly meetings is determined by the topics introduced for discussion and may range
from a few minutes to several hours. Simplicity of operation, staff input, and a staff attitude of respect for the
group are factors cited as having made the Council effective
and useful.

NEBRASKA

Division of Corrections

The five facilities for adult and youthful offenders
and juvenile delinquents are administered by the Division of
Corrections of the Department of Public Institutions. Information obtained in 1967 regarding the youth development
centers at Geneva and Kearney, and the Nebraska Penal and
Correctional Complex, Lincoln, was sent to the Division of
Corrections for review. It was returned with no comment
other than a marginal notation that the Student Council at the
Kearney facility is no longer active. According to 1967 information, there has never been an inmate advisory council
in the Girls' Training School, Geneva, now the Youth Development Center. [132]

In 1967, a Student Council was reported as having
been functioning since 1961 in the Youth Development Center,
Kearney, then known as the Boys' Training School. The
purposes of the group were to promote the students' general
welfare and insure better student-faculty understanding. A
constitution provided for the election of senators and con-

gressmen from each cottage to serve a three months' term
of office.   Nominees must have been at the School for four
months and in good standing.   The council was regarded as
an opportunity for pupil participation in government and not
for so-called self-government.   A feature was a Council
Court which might hear a defendant's case and pass its decision to the superintendent.   The president and vice-president of the Council acted as judges, the senator from the
defendant's cottage was the prosecuting attorney, with the
defense being assumed by the congressman.   The remaining
councilmen formed the jury.   The superintendent at that
time met once a week with the Council.   Having been at the
School only a brief time he made no evaluation of the effectiveness of the group. [133]

The Penitentiary and the Reformatory were combined
in 1963 to comprise the Nebraska Penal and Correctional
Complex, Lincoln.   In 1967, an Athletics and Recreation
Committee was reported as functioning under a constitution
and by-laws providing for the ballot election of five members
who met monthly with the warden to consider topics on an
approved agenda.   The favorable attitude of the warden in
office at that time toward the organizing of advisory councils
was well known to the inmates.   (While warden at another
institution he had had an advisory council that was able to
accomplish a number of things.)   The lack of sufficient interest among the inmates to warrant the development of an
Inmate Advisory Council was cited as being due possibly to
activities of the Athletic and Recreation Committee and a
Junior Chamber of Commerce.   The latter was involved in
functions normally regarded as those of an Advisory Council.
Other groups active at the time were Alcoholics Anonymous,
Checks Anonymous, and a Gavel Club. [134]

At the State Reformatory for Women, York, each living area is administered in part by an Inmate Council.
Representatives start as errand runners in the maximum
security unit, progressing in responsibility in each living
area.   The three members elected in the Trusty Dormitory
have almost all decision making responsibility for that unit.
In all instances final decision and actual authority rest with
the staff and administration. [135]

NEVADA

Adult and youthful felony offenders are committed to the Nevada State Prison, Carson City, comprising three facilities: a Maximum Security Prison, a Medium Security Prison, and the Women's Prison. All are under the administration of the warden.

Information obtained in 1966 indicated that inmate advisory councils were first organized at the Nevada State Prison in 1955 and were originally called Inmate Committees. [136] Three-member and six-member councils were reported as being operative, respectively, in a Reception-Guidance Center and a Minimum Security Facility. Candidates for election to the six-month term of office in each group were screened by the administration to insure their capability of best serving the interests of other inmates. At the Minimum Security Facility, it was additionally specified that candidates must have a minimum of six months remaining to serve on their sentences, and a six months' period of clear conduct.

These councils had an active part in presenting to the administration suggestions and grievances (the latter accepted from individuals only when it was felt to be indicative of popular opinion); presenting to the inmates of those suggestions which the administration felt were in order; scheduling television and radio programs; coordinating holiday programs; and compiling information regarding potential purchases authorized under Inmate Welfare Fund provisions. No participation in custodial methods or procedures was permitted nor were personal criticisms of staff.

Currently, there is an inmate advisory council in each of the three facilities of the Nevada State Prison. The members are nominated and elected by the population, with the warden reserving the right to deny the nomination of any person. Otherwise, the Councils function in accordance with guidelines contained in the American Correctional Association Manual of Correctional Standards. Regarding as good his experience in having always worked with an inmate advisory council, the warden believes such a group is of primary importance as a vehicle of information exchange between inmates and administration. He stresses that a council should function only in an advisory capacity and not be permitted to assume administrative responsibility or authority. [137]

Department of Health, Welfare and Rehabilitation

The two facilities for juvenile delinquents are under
the jurisdiction of the Department of Health, Welfare, and
Rehabilitation.   Information was obtained in 1967 that neither
had an advisory council. [138]   No current data has been received.

NEW HAMPSHIRE

There is no Department of Corrections in New Hampshire.   The facility for juvenile delinquents and the institution for adult and youthful felony offenders are autonomously
administered.   No current information has been received
regarding advisory councils at the New Hampshire State
Prison, Concord.   A survey in 1960 indicated there had
never been any form of inmate council because of the small
population census, then about two hundred. [139]

In February 1971, a new program of differential
treatment was instituted at the New Hampshire Industrial
School, Manchester.   Town meetings involving both staff and
students are held weekly in each of five residential cottages,
to discuss policies and procedures.   Suggestions emanating
from these meetings may be implemented after administrative
clearance, the latter being regarded more as a means of
communication rather than an administrative rein on the decision making process.   The overruling of a Town Meeting
decision by the superintendent is reported as occurring
rarely.   Input into cottage operational procedures and programs has increased student supportiveness.   The School,
opened in 1858, is co-educational. [140]

NEW JERSEY

Division of Correction and Parole

All of the ten facilities for adult, youth, and juvenile
offenders are administered by the Division of Correction and
Parole, Department of Institutions and Agencies.   Although
the Division has not issued directives regarding the development of inmate advisory councils, it is evident that the

favorable attitude of Director Albert C. Wagner has influ-
enced the inclusion of such groups in facility programs.
The accounts of the advisory councils as follows are based
on information from the institutions, supplied through Director Wagner's office. 141

Training Schools

The Training School for Boys, Jamesburg, opened in
1866 to care for juvenile delinquents aged eight to sixteen,
with maximum termination of care at age twenty-one. A
new institution has been built in the state to care for those
aged eight to twelve. Jamesburg continues to care for the
thirteen- to sixteen-year-olds upon commitment. Most units
now have some form of self-government, such as the Ex-
plorer type programs in most cottages, and the Youth Council. The latter involves election by the resident body in
each of the cottages. The Council meets monthly with the
administration. Problems that arise from the residents
themselves are brought up for discussion, solutions found,
and subsequent administrative changes effected. The Youth
Council has been found to be a most positive program and
has led the way to many changes helpful to the population
and to the administration.

The Training School for Boys, Skillman, opened in
1968 to care for juvenile delinquents aged eight to twelve,
does not have an inmate council. The Training School for
Girls, Trenton, was established in 1871 and serves court
referrals of girls from eight to seventeen years of age. A
Campus Council consisting of one elected representative from
each cottage meets weekly with the superintendent. An alternate representative is also selected so that each cottage may
always have a council member present at the meeting.

Representatives are selected by secret ballot. The
only criterion is that a girl have the ability to speak for the
cottage group. As a result, the indigenous leader is usually
selected as the cottage representative. Council members
have no authority over other students in the institution, but
merely serve as a means of communication between the inmate group and the superintendent. The meetings are usually positive and of mutual benefit to both the administration
and to the students. The underlying theme in each of the
discussions is related to positive goals and ideas which may
improve the program.

Youth Correctional Institution Complex

Legislation effective January 1, 1964, created a complex of correctional institutions which had previously been designated as reformatories. Following classification at the reception center, an inmate is transferred to the facility within the complex best suited to serve his needs.

An Inmate Congress was established at the Youth Reception and Correction Center, Yardville, New Jersey, shortly after the institution opened in 1968, to maintain a constant means of communication between the inmate population and the administrative staff. The Congress, composed of a president, vice-president, secretary and one elected representative and alternate from each of the twenty-four housing units, holds one weekly meeting and meets once a month with the superintendent, the business manager, the correction captain, and eight housing unit officers to discuss an agenda submitted a week previously to the superintendent. The twenty-four representatives and alternates, elected by secret ballot, in turn elect the Congress officers. Elections are supervised by members of the custodial and treatment staffs. Officers of the Congress usually serve three months, with housing representatives elected as vacancies occur through parole. A written constitution guides the actions of the Congress, containing provisions for the removal from office of any member found guilty of a serious disciplinary infraction. A good disciplinary record for a period of ninety days then becomes a requisite to eligibility for reelection. Additionally, Congress representatives and their officers are responsible for communicating all proceedings to the inmate population and administration.

The Youth Correctional Institution, Annandale, was opened on April 16, 1929, as a minimum security institution for male first offenders between the ages of fifteen and twenty-six who had not been incarcerated in a correctional or penal institution before. The trend of the era that followed, and the enactment of legislation, changed the age range from fifteen to twenty-one, resulting in a predominantly youthful population. Until 1970, the institution was designated as the New Jersey Reformatory.

Under the supervision of the Education Department in cooperation with the custodial and administrative staff, a Cottage Committee program provides a means of direct communication between the inmate population and administrative

staff in matters concerning the general welfare of all. Each
of the eight cottages has a committee of three elected by
hand vote from staff approved nominees who have resided in
the cottage for at least one month, have good disciplinary
records and good or better marks. The kitchen and several
work details also have representation. Additionally, a nominee must have the best interest of the cottage in mind.
Committeemen must attend all scheduled or special meetings,
and one member from each cottage must act as recorder so
that topics discussed may be conveyed to the cottage populations. Minutes are later printed and distributed to each
cottage. No committeeman may have authority over other
inmates under any circumstances, derive any special privileges from his position, nor succeed himself after serving a
two months' term of office.

Weekly in each cottage a meeting of all residents is
held to discuss questions pertaining to the general welfare.
Twice a month the Cottage Committees meet with the superintendent and department heads at which time answers to
specific questions are given, policies and procedures explained, and current problems discussed. The Attorney
General's Survey of Release Procedures mentions a formal
program of inmate participation at the Annandale institution:

> ... [T]he organization is much the same as at Nor-
> folk, Massachusetts. The inmates of each of the
> eight cottages hold a weekly meeting, elect their own
> officers, and select a cottage committee. The cot-
> tage committee meets weekly with the cottage officer
> to discuss and help solve cottage problems. All cot-
> tage committees meet weekly with the superintendent,
> the director of recreation and the officer of the day
> to consider serious problems affecting the entire in-
> stitution. [142]

A report received in 1966 described a Cottage Committee program implemented on May 5, 1960. It was stated
that a program of the same name existed prior to that date
but its purpose and functions were entirely different. It is
not clear as to whether or not the latter program was the same
one mentioned in the Attorney General's Survey of Release Procedures. Essentially the description of the organization, purpose, and function of the Program as contained
in the 1966 report is the same as that currently in operation. [143]

The Youth Correctional Institution, Bordentown, was
opened in 1937 as a prison farm and designated as the New
Jersey Reformatory from 1948 to 1972.   An Inmate Congress was organized in 1949 and operates under a constitution and by-laws.   Secret ballot elections are held semi-
annually to elect housing unit representatives.   Nominees
must work inside the institution, live in the housing unit
represented, and have sufficient time left to serve their
three-month terms.   The Bordentown Inmate Congress currently operates in much the same manner as described in a
1951 account, except that meetings are now held weekly with
a supervisory officer available to answer questions:

> Meetings of the representatives are held periodically
> without officer participation or supervision.   Some
> matters brought before it are settled immediately
> and discussed with the superintendent.   These dis-
> cussions range from 'There are too many specks left
> in the potatoes when they are peeled' to a suggestion
> that the Congress assume partial responsibility for
> the cooperation of the men in taking counts.
>   It is necessary, if the institution is to have an ef-
> fective inmate council, that the men be allowed free
> discussion of their problems, both among themselves
> and later when presented to staff.   We must give
> their problems prompt and sympathetic handling.   It
> is often necessary to take men into our confidence,
> explaining such items as budget limitations, public
> attitudes toward institutions, and the administration's
> need for insistence on security.   It is, parenthetical-
> ly, a constant surprise to find how easy it is to deal
> with the men at this level.   A good many problems
> are turned back to the men for their own determina-
> tion with perhaps a word or suggestion on procedure.
> Actually, some of the best ideas for improvement of
> the institution have come from the Inmate Congress.
>   The objectives of the organization were framed by
> the men themselves with only gentle hints from the
> staff.   We feel that in some measure, at least, the
> objectives are being accomplished.   They are: 1.
> To give official recognition to inmate expression, via
> the Congress, thus attempting to reduce the wide gap
> existing between the inmate population and the admin-
> istration personnel; 2.   To bring to the attention of
> the administration such problems as arise spontaneous-
> ly from the population; and 3.   To permit the men to
> govern to some extent their own affairs and, by

discussing problems pertinent to the group, to aid
them in eventually developing a sense of social responsibility.

In essence, inmate participation means free and
easy access of inmate to staff and staff to inmate,
the work staff including officers as well as professional people; an easy relaxed communication in the
shops, the dining room, the housing units, even perhaps during mass movements. Such easy access of
inmate to officer becomes a practical necessity where
there is a good treatment program. [144]

Prison Complex

In a 1919 article, [145] Winthrop D. Lane stated that a
moderate degree of inmate control had been suggested as a
remedy for publicly exposed administrative difficulties in the
New Jersey State Prison, Trenton, but there is no evidence
that any action was taken on the suggestion. However, following a disturbance in the State Prison, an Inmate Council
was established on May 9, 1952. The first election resulted in the formation of a group not believed to be truly
representative of the population. Another election was held.
During a May 28 meeting the members announced they would
not leave the room until they received definite information
on Parole Board policy regarding the indeterminate sentences
of some inmates. Additionally, they demanded that two
committeemen be authorized to inspect the operation of the
Inmate Council at the Rahway Prison Farm, some forty
miles distant. The attitude of the members was one of ar-
rogance and defiance and their actions more akin to rebels
making demands rather than a representative group seeking
redress of grievances. The sit-down strike continued until
June 3, 1952, after the Commissioner of Institutions and
Agencies and the Prison Board of Managers stated they would
not meet with the group while in a state of rebellion. A
meeting was held on June 10, 1952, at which rules were
adopted to govern the relationship between the Inmate/ Council
and state and institution officials. While there is no further
official reference to the Council, a staff member who was
active as a staff-council liaison officer recalls that some of
the councilmen became intoxicated, acted in a somewhat
obstreperous manner, and brought about the demise of the
group. [146]

In December 1971, an inmate congress type

organization, the Inmate Representative Committee, was formed for the purpose of establishing representation to consult with the administration and as an attempt to improve conditions in the prison for all concerned. Currently, nineteen housing unit representatives are elected for terms of office of one year, secret elections being held at six-month intervals. The Inmate Representative Committee selects from the membership eight representatives to comprise the Inmate Council. Formal meetings are held between the administration and the Inmate Council twice a month to discuss items on an agenda submitted to the administration at least one week prior to the meeting.

Emergency meetings can and have been called by the superintendent. Housing Unit representatives attend in an observer capacity, with only the Inmate Council members having a voice. Still functioning actively, the Inmate Representative Committee is regarded as having played a vital role in improving the administration-inmate relationship at the Trenton institution.

Following a lack of success in implementing an inmate council in 1952 at the parent (Trenton) State Prison, no like effort was made at either the Leesburg or Rahway State Prison Farms. In early spring 1964 Rahway State Prison ceased its farm operation and by legislative action in 1969 became known as New Jersey State Prison, Rahway.

On the eve of Thanksgiving, 1971, a major disturbance took place with inmates seizing control of two large housing wings and the auditorium. They took the superintendent and five correction officers hostage, all of whom received injury. Two officers were released early during the disturbance. The superintendent and the remaining three correction officers were rescued by a faction of inmates who protected them throughout a major portion of the twenty-four hour seige. Negotiations were attempted by the administration with several of the inmate groups. Governor William T. Cahill, standing near by the scene, agreed to select a committee to meet with elected inmate representatives to review the fourteen grievances presented at the close of the disturbance Thanksgiving night, 1971.

A nineteen-member committee was elected by the population, representing the eighteen housing units and the Spanish-speaking inmates. The group met periodically throughout 1972 with a committee appointed by the governor representative of the administration and the community. After response to the grievances was issued by the governor's office both the inmate and governor's committees were dissolved since their mission was considered accomplished.

During the first week of January 1973, an institution-wide election was conducted and a fifteen-member committee was elected by the population. The function of this committee is to be of much broader scope than the group just dissolved. They are to meet each month with institution administration to discuss any and all matters as they relate to the general welfare of the residents. Every effort is being made by inmates and administration to firmly establish this means of communication.

The New Jersey State Prison, Leesburg, with a population of approximately eight hundred, is divided into two units. A medium security unit and a minimum security unit each has an inmate committee, established January 8, 1971, and March 4, 1971, respectively, to provide greater communication between the inmates and the administration in matters affecting groups of inmates or the general inmate body. Individual complaints or grievances must be resolved through personal interviews with individual staff members. The medium facility has six housing units each of which has three representatives on the Committee. The minimum facility has five housing units with two committee members each. No man may serve as a committee member who has had a serious disciplinary charge within the previous three months. A serious violation of the rules will be sufficient cause for removal from the committee. All committee members are selected by secret ballot and each serves for six months, not to be re-elected until off the committee for six months. Individual inmates may bring problems concerning groups or suggestions for improvement of the institution to the attention of any committee member in his unit. Each committee meets with the superintendent, assistant superintendent, deputy keeper, business manager and other pertinent personnel once a month. Printed minutes of the meetings are distributed to committee members and posted on each housing unit bulletin board.

The past and present situation regarding Student Government at the Correctional Institution for Women, Clinton, is contained in Part I.

NEW MEXICO

Department of Corrections

The Department of Corrections administers three facilities for adult and youthful felony offenders and juvenile delinquents. The author was the warden of the Penitentiary
of New Mexico, Santa Fe, from August 1967 through February 1970, and during the last eight months of that period
also directed the newly created Department of Corrections,
serving as the first Secretary of Corrections.

By 1967, an Inmate Council had been in operation for
several years, according to staff statements, but there were
no records available to determine its date of origin, procedures, or accomplishments. Reportedly, members were
elected by secret ballot and the group met occasionally with
the associate warden for treatment to discuss a variety of
topics.

There were no advisory councils at the three satellite
installations, the New Mexico Honor Farm located approximately eighty-five miles south, a Forestry camp some one
hundred miles north, and the Women's Institution, a separate building adjacent to the penitentiary. The low census,
usually under twenty, and the small number of employees,
there being only three until latter 1967, had no doubt been
factors inhibiting the development of an advisory council at
the Women's Institution. The idea of vitalizing the Advisory
Council was discussed with both staff and residents at periodic meetings. The consensus was that an attempt should
be made to implement a group which could play a meaningful
role in an advisory capacity to management. Accordingly,
a Resident Advisory Council was established under a constitution whose provisions were similar to those of the 1963
Council reorganization at the U. S. Penitentiary, Terre
Haute, Indiana.

Elections were held and several meetings took place,
but the attention of both residents and staff became diverted and
the council never completely fulfilled its intended role. During
this time the institution was undergoing a metamorphosis from
a custody institution to one of treatment-orientation, with a
focus on the needs of both residents and staff. It was a dynamic
period for all concerned. For some, it was a stressful time as
they faced the challenge of perspectives new to their experience.
However, most of the residents became involved in the many

academic-vocational-social programs being implemented at many levels, and the majority of the staff plunged thoroughly into the newly established intensive in-service training and academic programs designed to aid them in redefining their individual roles from agents of custody to agents of care and treatment.

The Resident Advisory Council managed to retain its identity and from time to time it provided helpful feedback to the deputy warden and the associate wardens regarding the reaction of the resident population to the efforts to create a positive climate and a staff attitude of professionalism. A constitution dated March 3, 1972, was signed by the present warden of the Penitentiary of New Mexico, establishing a Resident Advisory Council for which the first elections were scheduled to occur on June 19, 1972.[147]   The provisions of the constitution are similar to those previously referred to.   No information was received as to the actual operations of the organization.

A six-member Student Advisory Council was recently organized at the New Mexico Girls' School, Albuquerque. The girls of each of the three cottages elect two representatives.   Presiding leadership is rotated in order that each member may gain experience in that role.   One of the first tasks of the Council was to make suggestions on the structuring of cottage government.   The plan submitted by the group was rapidly implemented by the administration.   At cottage meetings, Student Council members obtain topics for discussion at their weekly meetings.   A three-member staff committee provides direction and acts as resource personnel.[148]

There was some development of a cottage government structure between 1966 and 1969 at the New Mexico Boys' School, Springer.   No information was received as to the present situation.

NEW YORK

Department of Correctional Services

All facilities for adult and youthful felony and misdemeanor offenders are administered by the Department of Correctional Services.   Additionally, the Department

administers the Division of Correctional Camps, composed
of four facilities for young offenders aged sixteen to twenty-
five.   A report in 1966 indicated that the Department of
Correction did not permit inmate self-government groups. [149]
Contacts made in 1966-67 with thirteen major institutions in
the state confirmed that neither self-government nor inmate
advisory councils existed in twelve of them.

The Bedford Hills Correctional Facility, Bedford
Hills, opened in 1901 as the Westfield State Farm.   In 1933
the female population of Auburn Prison was transferred to
Westfield.   In 1967 the institution was reported as having
three divisions under one superintendent: a Reformatory
Division, a Prison Division, and the New York City House
of Detention Annex.   The women lived in cottages in the
Reformatory Division and in wards at the Prison Division.
Subject to staff approval, each living unit elected a representative called a chairman.   A candidate was required to
be a cooperative person, capable of leadership with the interests of others at heart, familiar with campus procedure,
and have approximately six months yet to serve when
elected.   Disciplinary action for a serious incident during
the six months preceding an election was disqualifying.
Chairmen held weekly meetings in their units with the director of education and the recreation supervisor of each division, and periodic meetings with the superintendent.

Minutes of these meetings were circulated to staff and
residents.   In most instances the woman selected as chairman was favorably regarded and her counsel sought by the
other women.   This was regarded as usually being conducive
to the personal growth and development of the chairman.
On some occasions, staff had major reservations about
the election of certain individuals, only to see her develop
into a dependable leader.   This was reported as applicable
to both the aggressive personality and the shy, introverted
woman.   The program was reported as having been in operation since about 1929. [150]

On January 18, 1972, the Department of Correctional
Services issued an administrative bulletin entitled "Establishment and Operation of Facility Inmate Liaison Committee."
Guidelines attached to the bulletin directed the establishment
of inmate liaison committees and contained a suggested format for constitution and by-laws to be submitted to the commissioner not later than March 1, 1972, with operational
evaluation reports to be made quarterly, the first such being

due during June 1972. Additionally, it was directed that all personnel and inmates be informed of the objective, organization, and function of the inmate liaison committees, the former through in-service training and the latter via appropriate means. [151] The objectives of the program were stated as:

    1.   Effective communications with the inmates for accurate dissemination of information.
    2.   Consideration by management of worthwhile suggestions covering facility operations.

    The guidelines specified that no grievances or gripes of individiuals may be presented; the personality of individuals, either employee or inmate, shall not be discussed; the committees are to serve in a liaison capacity only with no disciplinary or administrative functions; and no committeeman be granted special privileges because of his membership.

    Each facility may define its membership qualifications, its voting districts or precincts, such as housing units and various work assignments, and its nomination system. Supervised elections provide for secret balloting on mimeographed lists of candidates to serve in any capacity for not more than six months during any twelve. At his option, a superintendent is empowered to restrict from membership those inmates who have been recent or chronic disciplinary problems.

    The superintendents feel that the inmate liaison committees are assets in that they provide channels through which grievances and problems are conveyed to the various administrations. Opportunistic use by individuals of a committee as a forum to advance personal causes or demands is mentioned as a major problem which has thus far emerged. Committees now function at almost all of the facilities and have been assisted by a Department of Correctional Services Lawyer in establishing their constitutions.

Division for Youth

    Information obtained in 1967 regarding student councils in the facilities for juvenile delinquents was sent to the Division for Youth for review and updating. The accounts which follow were provided by the Bureau of Children's Institution Services of the Division. [152]

The training schools in New York State are presently
administered by the New York State Division for Youth, State
Executive Department, Albany. There are twelve such
schools and centers of varying sizes and program focus,
geared either to a specific type or age grouping of youngsters. They accept juvenile delinquents and persons in need
of supervision up to the age of seventeen who have been
placed by the Family Courts of the state for acts committed
or for ungovernable behavior prior to their sixteenth birth-
day. Placements are made for a period of eighteen months
with possible successive extensions for additional periods of
one year each. No directives on student councils have been
issued by the Division. Each facility is free to establish a
council in the form best suited to its population and program.

The School for Boys at Industry, formerly designated
as the State Agriculture and Industrial School, had a Boys'
Council for many years, but currently operates without one.
The recent development of the unit system with its built-in
daily meetings has rendered it unnecessary at this point. A
Boy's Council started in January 1957 provided a forum for
the discussion of a wide variety of subjects including release, education, cottage adjustments, recreation, staff
roles, and interpretation of administrative rules and directives. Initially, council members were prone to subjective
discussions but as time went on they became more conscious
of their role and personal problems gave way to group considerations.

Experience with the council indicated apprehension by
staff at the outset. To offset this a close line of communication was established to inform staff of the content of council discussions. In addition, cottage staff members and
community representatives were also invited to participate in
the meetings. Community representatives sometimes included Youth Bureau personnel, legislative representatives,
and Job Corps staff.

In March 1956 the first Student Congress was established at the Otisville School for Boys, Otisville, under a
constitution and by-laws. Constant turnover of students, the
average length of stay being about eight months, was a major
contributing factor to discontinuance of the group shortly after. Reorganized again in October 1959, the Congress is
regarded by the administration as an important feature in
communication within the school and has made a substantial

contribution to improving programs and maintaining an atmosphere of shared responsibility of boys and staff for the life of the institution community.

All residents of each cottage are members of a cottage congress, each group electing its own officers, a president, vice-president, and secretary. The president and secretary of each cottage attends the monthly meeting of the Institution Congress. The assistant superintendent serves as chairman of this group, the functions of which are to promote program participation, suggest new programs, and solve problems together. In addition to the general cooperation of all staff, specific assistance is required from particular areas for a successful Student Congress. No staff member is expected to be at cottage congress meetings for the purpose of supplying direct answers to problems which are brought up for discussion, but staff are there to help the students find their own answers. No staff member is expected to force a cottage to prolong a meeting which it decides it does not want or need; the philosophy is that each Cottage Congress should be an opportunity for the students, not a burden. The School was formerly named the State Training School for Boys.

The Goshen Center for Boys, Goshen, which opened on January 6, 1947, occupying two buildings in the former New York City Reformatory at New Hampton, was originally designated as the Annex of Boy's Training Schools. Its present facilities, completed in the fall of 1962, have a maximum capacity of one hundred boys. A boy government in council has always been a part of the program, continued by succeeding directors. Called Center Council, each of its five members is president of his wing council, sponsored by the head child care worker and the recreation director. Wing council meetings are held monthly, with the Center Council meeting held every four to six weeks to consider an agenda derived from the wing meetings. Examples of programs either initiated or expanded through the Center Council include a weekly honor roll system, a seasonal recreation program, off-campus sports and other activities, personal clothing, home visits, a personal hygiene and health program, and canteen services. The administration plans to continue the councils stating that programs operate more successfully when boys have had a hand in their implementation.

The Director's Council at the Brookwood Center for

Girls, Claverack (formerly the Brookwood Annex of the
Training School for Girls, Hudson), originally formed in
January 1967, is no longer in operation. During the time
it was, two representatives from each of the four wings
were elected by secret ballot to serve until released. Nominees had to meet several qualification criteria which included desirable personal traits, good deportment, and average or above academic grades. Weekly meetings with the
director were followed by informal wing meetings.

The Warwick School for Boys, Warwick, has no current student advisory council but has had such groups in the
past. However, students are involved in policy-making decisions through frequent consultations. Although there has
never been an advisory council at the South Kortright Center for Boys, South Kortright, in the past known as the
Branch of the Boys' Training Schools, there has always been
a weekly town hall forum since the facility opened in 1963.
These meetings involve the total population of fifty juveniles
and serve as a combined group interaction program as well
as a forum for student expression.

At the Hudson School for Girls, Hudson, originally
the Training School for Girls, each of the cottage units elect
by secret ballot a representative to serve a two-month term
of office on the Superintendent's Council. Weekly meetings
are used to disseminate information to the students who also
present questions and problems from their cottages. Minutes are distributed for review by staff and students.

The Student Council at the Tryon School for Boys,
Johnstown, was formed on October 27, 1971. The purpose
of the Council is to have boy representatives meet with department heads and administrative staff to review all phases
of the program. Student Council representatives are selected
by the boys of each cottage. Originally, the Council met on
a weekly basis; however, it was found that more time was
needed between meetings to follow up on suggestions and
questions raised. At the present time, meetings are held
on a bi-monthly basis. Since its inception, the Student
Council has met with various administrative and program
staff including the assistant superintendent, business officer,
recreation supervisor, food services manager, clinic director, and principal child care worker. A sampling of matters discussed in Student Council includes: daily activity
schedule, church requirements, phone calls, group incentive,
family visits, off-grounds activities, and hair policy. An

administrative review of the function of Student Council recently suggested that boys attending Student Council were not
truly representative of the rest of the boys in their cottage,
but more often presented their personal opinions, although
tempered somewhat by the known views of other boys in the
cottage.   It was agreed that in reality Student Council is a
sampling of opinion but is considered worthwhile even in this
form.   Plans include reviewing the organization of Student
Council early in 1973 in order to update procedures and make
the Council more meaningful.

Although the Highland School for Children, Highland,
formerly known as the State Training School for Boys, which
serves children under age thirteen, did have a Student Council in its early years, it was discontinued because of the
age of the youngsters.   The Overbrook Center for Children,
Red Hook, established in 1966 and serving younsters age
seven to eleven, has no student council.   The Wynantskill
Training School for Girls, which closed in 1971, held weekly
meetings in each cottage to discuss matters of common concern, but did not have an organized Student Council.[153]

NORTH CAROLINA

The Department of Social Rehabilitation and Control
has jurisdiction over all facilities for adult and youthful felony and misdemeanor offenders and juvenile delinquents.

Department of Correction

The Department of Correction administers seventy-
five facilities for felony and misdemeanor offenders.   Although various planning, steering, and guidance committees
have been formed, the only inmate advisory council is at
one of the original youth centers.[154]

The Umstead Youth Center, Butner, opened in 1949.
In October of that year an advisory council was formed,
which is still in existence, known as the Mayor and His
Council.   By secret ballot election the boys at Umstead
Youth Center elect from a slate of four nominees, one to
hold the office of mayor for a six-month term.   Any boy is
eligible for nomination provided he is not on restriction or
extra duty.   Provision is made for his removal should he

violate a major rule or the staff deem such action necessary.
Regulations prescribe that the mayor should be a boy of high
moral character, definitely interested in helping others.   In
addition to presiding at twice monthly meetings of his Council, the mayor is expected to set a good example for others,
encourage them to obey orders, work willingly and to make
good use of their time.

Additionally, seven group leaders are elected to four-
month terms to serve as members of the Mayor's Council.
Any boy not on restriction or extra duty may stand for election.   Those elected are expected to work closely with the
staff counselor to insure observance of rules and regulations
by his constituents, offer informal counsel to other boys,
supervise recreational activities, and work as a leader on
clean-up details or other work assignments.

Office of Youth Development

A student council has been developed over the past
two years in seven of the eight facilities for juvenile delinquents administered by the Office of Youth Development.   At
the Dobbs School for Girls, Kinston, a Campus Council has
been in existence since the School opened in 1944.[155]

The organizing of student councils was perceived by
the administration as a means of providing students a voice
in day-to-day activities.   Since there had been no such prior
involvement of students except at the Dobbs School for Girls,
the process of planning and implementation, including the
orientation of both students and staff, required much time.
The rate of progress varied among the facilities, with one
completing development only recently.

Student council members are elected to represent cottages.   Officers, which include a president, vice-president,
secretary, and parliamentarian, are elected by the entire
student body.   Committees are appointed to be concerned
with matters such as cottage planning, dress code, philosophy, orientation, food services, recreation, and social activities.   Council members are assigned as chairmen of the
committees with the membership composed of both council
members and appointees.   Each school has an administrator's advisory council whose members include both staff and
students.

Additionally, in 1972 there was developed what appears to be an innovative plan to obtain meaningful participation in program planning by those most directly affected. Three "recipient of services committees" were organized in three schools. The dozen members of each group represent six former students who have received discharges and over whom the Office of Youth Development has no authority, three students in the community under conditional release status, and three students currently enrolled at a school. One day meetings are held semi-annually at each School or in the vicinity. A representative of the commissioner of Youth Development, and five officials of the school meet with that school's committee. The latter include the School director or assistant director, director of social services, director of cottage life, principal of the academic and vocational programs, and the chief vocational counselor. Evaluations of current or proposed programs are made to determine the degree to which there has been, or is a potential for, meaningful assistance to students in both residential and community programs. The administration feels that maximum services delivery depends on knowing what has been, or can be, of optimal value to those who receive the services. Suggestions made by those still in the various stages of recipiency and those who have successfully been reintegrated into the community is regarded as a valuable resource.

"Recipient of services committees" at the other five schools are scheduled for activation by mid-1973.

NORTH DAKOTA

Office of Director of Institutions

The state facilities, one for adult and youthful felony offenders and one for misdemeanor offenders and juvenile delinquents, are administered by the Director of Institutions. Because of a relatively low census of usually less than one hundred and fifty, good inmate-staff rapport, and the existence of inmate organizations which represent various segments of the inmate population, there is no need felt to establish any kind of inmate council or self-governing group at the North Dakota Penitentiary, Bismarck.156

The North Dakota Industrial School, Mandan, had a

Student Council prior to 1965 which functioned similarly to a
high school student group. Demand on staff time was a
factor in its discontinuance. During the 1965-1966 school
year a Campus Council was formed with representation on
the basis of classes as well as living units. Meetings with
a staff supervisor provided an opportunity for the expression
of negative feelings about institutional programs, and served
as a sounding board for the staff. [157]

In recent years the Campus Council has been renamed
the Policy Making Committee, with student representation
from each of the living units and staff representation from
the work areas. The group, usually numbering twelve, has
had authority to review and modify all policies. Active during 1971 and 1972, the Committee has been inactive in 1973
largely because of administration planning for procedural
changes designed to provide increased student interaction.
The administration believes that this type of involvement is
important and meaningful to students. [158]

OHIO

Department of Rehabilitation and Correction

The eight Ohio institutions for adult and youthful offenders are administered by the Department of Rehabilitation
and Correction. In April 1972, the Department of Rehabilitation and Correction issued regulations stating that inmate
advisory councils are to be established at each correctional
institution. Constitution and by-laws, approved by the director of the Department, must specify an electoral process
of nominations, free elections, and a secret ballot voting
system. Representation may be by either work assignment
or housing unit, as approved by the superintendent of the institution concerned. The superintendent has the right to remove from office any member he considers unsuitable to
represent the population in a constructive and adaptive manner. Instances have occurred where removal has been necessitated, e. g. , violation of institution regulations and conduct of such type as to render the individual unsuitable to
properly represent those who had elected him. Those elected
to a six months', non-successive term of office shall meet
at least monthly with the superintendent or his designee to
discuss an agenda submitted a week in advance. Each institution is to provide a convenient place, furnished with

equipment and related supplies, where its council shall have
the right to meet weekly.   Honor dormitories and honor
camp units located outside a main institution may also establish councils.   Under procedures established in another
regulation, the council may represent individual inmates in
grievances through an institution liaison officer.   Otherwise,
councils shall function in a liaison advisory capacity only
with no authority to establish or administer institution policy.

        All of the institutions within the Department of Re-
habilitation and Correction have implemented the regulation
regarding the establishment of inmate advisory councils with
varying degrees of success.   As a result of certain activities and involvement, some councils are not currently functioning.   There has been a mixed reaction at various staff
levels to the establishment of councils, ranging from complete cooperation to some resistance. [159]

Ohio Youth Commission

        Various forms of student councils exist in three of
the ten facilities administered by the Ohio Youth Commission.   Information was obtained regarding past experiences,
projected plans, and current thinking toward such groups. [160]
Although the Zanesville Youth Camp, Zanesville, has no student council, the superintendent does occasionally receive
indication of the need for some policy changes through discussions arising in group therapy sessions conducted with
students by social workers.   Since the number of students
is small, usually about thirty-five, the superintendent is
accessible to both students and staff to hear problems.

        Currently, there is no student council at the Training
Center for Youth, Columbus, a special treatment unit for
boys ages ten to seventeen.   Here again, open communication and ready access to the superintendent and staff is enhanced by a student body whose census averages ninety to
one hundred.   The establishment of a student council will be
considered at the Juvenile Diagnostic Center, Columbus,
upon completion of the planned conversion to a treatment
facility where the students will remain for a much longer
period of time.   It is assumed that the brief time students
spent at the Center has heretofore made organization of a
student council impractical.

At the present time the Fairfield School for Boys, Lancaster, does not have a student council. However, the administration hopes that one will be developed with the expansion of a program, now in its initial stages, referred to as a Zone System. The administration of the Maumee Youth Camp, Liberty Center, recognizes the value of student opinion input in the preparation of its program, but in early 1973 had no crystallized plans as to the optimum method of utilizing this resource in the operational structure.

The discontinuance of a Student Council program at the Mohican Youth Camp, Loudonville, approximately two years ago is attributed to problems such as the low motivation of students, the difficulty of maintaining active involvement by the assigned teacher representative, and scheduling conflicts with other activities. Two students are currently involved in the planning of menus, one from the educational program, the other from the work training program. Evaluation is being made of the feasibility of establishing an advisory board composed of students in the Orientation-Prerelease Cottage to insure the opportunity of participation by school and work training students under staff direction and supervision.

All students at the Riverview School for Girls, Powell, are involved in groups which are given considerable responsibility in the formation of policies concerning group routines and in planning and organizing group functions and programs. The ultimate goal of this group program approach is to have girls involved in truly meaningful and critical decisions--for instance, the readiness of a girl to return to the community.

A Campus Council was initiated recently at Scioto Village, Powell, to encourage students to participate in activities and to better familiarize themselves with all aspects of living at the facility. A representative is elected by each cottage and membership on the Council is reported as being a prestigious position. A girl, who has been at the facility for at least eight weeks, has a minimum time of three months remaining until release, and who is doing reasonably well in the academic, vocational, or on-job training, may be nominated to stand for election provided she can obtain (1) the endorsements of: one youth leader in her cottage, her guidance counselor, and one other staff member from any department; and (2) the endorsements of at least five students from her cottage. The Council is the official body

which provides communication between students and staff.
The group meets monthly under the direction of the recreation leader to discuss the ways in which the operations of
various departments affect the life of the students.

The Training Institution for Central Ohio, Columbus,
at one time had a Boy's Committee, described below. The
present administration has invited students to meet with staff
to provide their viewpoints, such as at budget meetings.
Currently two to four student representatives visit all cottages and invite inquiries and opinions, later meeting with a
Volunteer Council to discuss matters so obtained. This
procedure provides feedback to both the Volunteer Council
and the student body.

The Boy's Committee, organized in the latter part of
1965, was discontinued in early 1967, after members began
to be negative and anti-authority. Information obtained in
1966 regarding the Boy's Committee indicated that each of
the eight cottages selected a representative to meet weekly
with the superintendent. The agenda to be discussed could
include almost any topic the members chose. There were
two strictures: no individual names were to be mentioned
when discussing a complaint, and no use of offensive language was allowed in reference to any staff member. Discussions at the meetings were occasionally instrumental in
formulating or modifying facility policy. An example was
cited of changing the bedtime from ten to ten-thirty p. m.
The original precipitating reason for organizing the Boy's
Committee centered around a rumor that the deputy superintendent insisted that every boy remain at the institution a
minimum of eighteen months before being considered for release. Through the Committee, the superintendent hoped to
forestall such rumors, and to clarify whatever misunder-
standings regarding institutional policies existed among the
boys. The net evaluation was that the meetings had proven
to be useful in at least a limited way, especially in the area
of communication. [161]

OKLAHOMA

Department of Corrections

The Department of Corrections administers six institutions for adult and youthful felony offenders. No advisory

councils exist and none are planned. However, an ombudsman position is being established as a means of effecting inmate-staff communications. [162] In 1966 information was received that the Oklahoma State Penitentiary, McAlester, did
not have an advisory council. However, two inmates were
members of the Inmate Welfare and Recreation Board, a
statutory organization of seven members: the warden, two
state employees and two inmates selected by the warden,
and an appointee each of the State Board of Public Affairs
and the Commissioner of Charities and Corrections. [163]

Bureau of State Homes and Schools

There are no student councils in the three facilities
for juvenile delinquents administered by the Bureau of State
Homes and Schools, Department of Institutions, Social and
Rehabilitative Services. Various group-process techniques
are utilized in the treatment programs at the facilities but
these are not regarded as systems of self-government. [164]
According to information obtained in 1966 development was
then underway of a Student Advisory Council for recreational
services and programs at Girls' Town, Tecumseh, and a
cottage committee plan at the other facilities for juveniles. [165]

OREGON

All facilities for adult and youthful felony offenders
and for juvenile delinquents are under the jurisdiction of the
Department of Human Resources.

Corrections Division

The Corrections Division administers three institutions
for adult and youthful felony offenders. Material obtained in
a previous survey was reviewed by the present administration and updated with information on developments at the
Oregon State Penitentiary and the Oregon Women's Correctional Center. [166]

The first Inmate Council of record at the Oregon State
Penitentiary, Salem, was formed in June 1951 following several weeks of tension in the institution. Two general inmate
assemblies were called to permit open nomination of

candidates and discussion of procedural methods. By secret
ballot six councilmen and two alternates were elected to
serve six-month, non-successive terms of office. The group
met with the warden a week later, electing a chairman and
vice-chairman. Sixteen topics were presented for discussion, most being acted upon favorably by the warden. A
council on recreation was scheduled to be formed in November 1951, although there is no evidence to indicate that
either the Inmate Council or the Recreational Council ever
became a voice in the institution. Two groups periodically
held meetings in the recreation yard, but minutes are not
available nor is it known if they were ever made. Staff
members recall that successive administrators ignored the
existence of any council. The groups met, talked over their
grievances, and then adjourned. Apparently the councils
were neither listened to nor instructed to disband. It is indicated that both groups were abolished the night of July 10,
1953, when a riot began. [167]

Following a riot in March 1968, a demand for the
development of an inmate council was met by the administration. During the ensuing months the Council thus formed
became increasingly militant and demanding, moving from a
representative to a leadership role. A series of assaults on
staff, two strikes, and the death of a correctional officer
appeared attributable to Council activities and the organization was disbanded by the superintendent in April 1969. [168]

The Oregon State Correctional Institution, Salem, was
opened in May 1959. A new unit was completed and occupied
in October 1966, raising the capacity to five hundred, most
of whom are first felony offenders. An Inmate Relations
Council was organized in October 1960 and continued in
operation until about 1964. Inmates whose conduct record
had been clear for six months and who had demonstrated a
constructive attitude toward institutional goals, if proposed
by at least five fellow housing unit residents, could stand
for election by secret ballot to a six months' term of office.
The four-man council chose a secretary and chairman from
its membership. The minutes of monthly meetings were
reviewed by the superintendent who then met with the Council officers to give his decisions on suggestions or questions.
While the Inmate Relations Council was a means of advising
the superintendent of matters inmates were interested in,
for the most part the latter's suggestions were predominantly
oriented to creature comforts. Lack of interest on the part
of individuals whose leadership could have been positive in

nature, pressure tactics on weaker men by candidates at election time, and the shallowness of council referrals combined to weaken the image of the group in the eyes of both inmates and staff. Resistance on the part of a few self-styled operators to the manner in which an election was held precipitated discontinuance of the council. [169]

At the Oregon Women's Correctional Center, Salem, the superintendent meets on request with the members of the various activities groups to discuss matters of concern. This accessibility, together with unrestricted and uncensored correspondence with the Director of the Corrections Division, the Penitentiary and the state ombudsmen, the governor, and the courts, appears to result in prompt and satisfactory resolution of most major concerns of the inmates. [170]

Children's Services Division

The Children Services Division, created in 1970, administers the two facilities for juvenile delinquents. Several years ago at the Hillcrest School of Oregon, Salem, in an effort to gear policy and program to the expressed needs of the girls, bi-weekly luncheons were held to stimulate communication between staff and representatives of each housing unit. The program was discontinued in 1966 at which time it was planned to establish a student council to be composed of two representatives from each cottage, one to be elected by the girls, the other to be selected by cottage staff. As of early 1967, the council had not been organized. [171]

Currently it is reported that through a long and difficult participatory process involving both staff and students, a constitution and a bill of rights have been recently written at the Hillcrest School, with a similar process going on for the past year at the MacLaren School for Boys, Woodburn. [172] The constitution establishes the Robert S. Farrell High School Student Body Council, declares membership open to any student enrolled in the Farrell High School, and provides for three elected representatives, and alternates, from treatment team groups who elect from the membership a president, vice-president, secretary-treasurer, and sergeant-at-arms, all to serve until released from the facility or removed from office for absence without permission, violence, or non-attendance at meetings. The school counselor is designated as advisor, together with a teacher and a

cottage staff member each selected by the group to serve for
a period of six months.   Twice weekly meetings are scheduled and special meetings may be called by the Council
president, the school principal, or one of the advisors.
These three may also call a student assembly to be conducted by the Council.

A Black Student Union has been organized and functions under a constitution which limits membership to Black
students, but allows non-voting participation by others.   The
membership elects a chairman, secretary, and treasurer
who serve until released.   A teacher is elected as sponsor.
Both the Student Body Council and the Black Student Union
have adopted the "Student Bill of Rights" signed on October
20, 1972, reproduced here in its entirety:

STUDENT BILL OF RIGHTS

The Constitution of the United States of America explicitly guarantees the freedoms of speech,
press, assembly, self-identity, personal appearance, and religion.   Along with these, we have the
right to be secure in personal effects and against
unreasonable search and seizures without probable
cause, and also to have fair representation and
due process in matters involving discipline or
suspension from school.   The enumeration in the
constitution of certain rights does not mean one
can deny others the rights retained by the people.

1.   Students have the freedom of verbal expression.   This freedom cannot be restricted
unless its exercise interferes with orderly conduct and work.
Students and staff or students and students
should not violate the first right which is the
freedom of speech.   If a person harasses another
person, they have violated their freedom of
speech.   An example of this would be calling
another person a name with malicious intent
which causes the other person to lose their tem-
per and become disorderly.   This example would
be a violation of the freedom of speech because
it is designed for the harassment of an individual
instead of the expression of an idea.

2.   Students are entitled to a free press.

This does not give the license to slander or abuse individuals. Students must be able to defend what they write with logic and evidence. Students have the freedom of the press as long as they do not violate the guidelines established by the journalism class.

3. Students have the right to self-identity. This identity may be sought and expressed in any of the following arenas: political, cultural, racial, individual, or religious. This expression can be perpetuated in appearance (grooming, dress) and should not be limited unless these present a clear and present danger to health and interfere with work or order.

4. Students have the right to assemble with or without supervision according to choice. The assembly is to be conducted in an orderly manner. It is understood that to assemble for the purpose of overthrow of the institution or conducting a riot will not be condoned.

5. Students have the freedom to participate or not participate in religion or religious activities of their choice.

6. Students have the right to possess personal property. This does not pertain to articles which have been proven harmful. These problems should be decided upon by a group of staff and students.

7. It seems necessary that in order to maintain due process and fair representation in relation to the school program that a judicial review board would be created and implemented. This review board would be composed of staff and students.

8. To be searched as a matter of routine (being stripped upon return from a home visit) is an example of disrespectful treatment of students. The time and reason for searching or seizing, if it is necessary, should be a mutually agreed upon process between student and staff.

9.   Students have the right to be treated with
respect at all times.

In 1967, information was received regarding the Mac-
Laren School for Boys, Woodburn. [173] Boys were reported
playing a significant role in the development and evaluation
of policy and procedures through their representation and
participation in the Youth Council which was organized May
8, 1962.   Two boys who had lost no privileges were chosen
from each living cottage, one by secret ballot and one by the
cottage manager, to participate in weekly Council meetings
with the superintendent or a staff advisor.   By majority
secret ballot the members elected among themselves a president, vice president, secretary, and two board directors.
Members could be removed by the superintendent or by a
two-thirds vote of Council members in attendance, by reason
of parole or other permanent assignment off-campus, or the
loss of full privileges.   The Council was popularly known
as the JC-YC since it was sponsored by the Woodburn, Oregon, Junior Chamber of Commerce.   Boys were able, via
the Council, to present suggestions and recommendations to
the staff and make significant contributions to the Woodburn
community by assisting in various civic projects.

The then superintendent, under whose administration
the Youth Council was organized, reported experience with
such groups for many years.   He expressed his belief that
it is essential that all humans have an opportunity to feel
that they have some voice in decisions that affect them, and
that persons involved in decision-making become more re-
sponsive to rules, regulations, policies, and procedures.
He was also firmly convinced that inmate councils should
not become governing bodies nor should they have responsibility for treatment plans or discipline.

In its then less than five years of operation, the
Youth Council was credited with several important accomplishments.   For example, boys were formerly permitted
to have only one home visit a month; as a result of YC action, boys with sixty consecutive days of full privileges are
entitled to two home visits each month.   Other changes provided for unsupervised movement from cottages to school
and return; unlimited mailing privileges to parents and girl-
friends; the wearing of personally owned clothing; and the
consultation with Youth Council m. nbers by the administration prior to the purchase of new institutional clothing.

PENNSYLVANIA

Bureau of Correction

The Bureau of Correction, Department of Justice, administers eight institutions--six for adult and youthful felony offenders, one for youthful felony and misdemeanor offenders and juvenile delinquents, and one for adult and youthful felony offenders and juvenile delinquents. Although all of the institutions have many resident organizations, e. g., Jaycees, only the latter mentioned has an advisory council. [174]

At the State Correctional Institution, Muncy, an institution for female felony and misdemeanor offenders, and juvenile delinquents, three representatives are elected from each of the five cottages to a Resident Advisory Council which was organized in the summer of 1971. [175] For the first several months the superintendent attended the bi-weekly meetings during which time the purpose and scope of the Council's responsibility were determined. The principal obligation of Council members is to provide a liaison between population and administration; they have no responsibilities for institutional programming and security. In February 1972, the deputy superintendent for treatment was designated as staff representative and now attends all bi-weekly and emergency meetings. Through Council representation all residents are provided an opportunity for input into the formulation of rules and regulations.

Revamping of cottage security rules and leisure time programming are examples of Council-administration activities. The Council has had an active part in dealing with unacceptable behavior of other residents in the Behavior Clinic. Factors cited as determining Council continuation are the responsibility demonstrated by the population in the quality of representation elected, the evident high calibre performance of those representatives, and the insight into resident concerns provided to the administration.

Bureau of Youth Services

The Bureau of Youth Services, Office of Children and Youth, administers nine facilities for juvenile delinquents. No current information regarding student councils has been received. In 1966 a survey made of the nine facilities then under the Office of Children and Youth, Department of Public

172   The Right to Participate

Welfare, revealed that five had councils, two had discontinued them recently, and two utilized ad hoc committees for
specific events. Although the superintendent of one of the
last mentioned had never had experience with a council he
was convinced of the validity of the criticisms of such
groups and preferred not to organize one. 176

     At the Youth Development Center, Canonsburg, with
a population of two hundred and thirty-nine (of which one
hundred and two were girls), a Student Council operated from
1958 until 1966, when it was discontinued because of a reorganization of the staff. Several methods of membership
selection were tried, the principal two being popular vote
and selection by staff as an earned privilege. Despite various problems, including a tendency of some Council members to misuse their office, the staff felt the group was a
desirable activity and planned to reactivate it.

     The Youth Development Center, Loysville, with an
October 1966 population of a hundred and five, established a
Student Council in May 1966 that operated under a constitution stipulating that the organization has no policy making
powers and citing among its purposes cooperation with the
administration, the promotion of programs fostering the welfare of the students, the recommendation of conduct and behavior norms, and the opportunity to obtain experience in
democratic practices. Two representatives of each living
unit were elected for six-month terms of office. These
members elected their own president, vice-president, and
secretary who conducted the monthly meetings. A staff advisor was appointed by the superintendent.

     In the North Philadelphia Youth Development Center,
with a population then of two hundred and twenty-three, a
student council was organized October 13, 1965, to provide
a modified experience in democratic living and the opportunity to discover the close relationship between privilege and
responsibility, and to serve as a means of developing leadership qualities. As of October 1966 it was reported that
expectations had been realized.

     In October 1966 there had been no student council
among the hundred and forty-seven boys at the Youth Development Center, Warrendale, for more than a year. Individual cottages intermittently had attempted to organize a
student council or a staff approved "junior counselor" role.
Although the staff was not in favor of the council idea, it did

utilize the emerging leadership abilities of the boys through the use of ad hoc committees to plan special events.

A Girls' Council of six members had been in continuous operation since December 1961 at the Waynesburg Youth Development Center.   In June 1966 a Junior Council of four girls was formed as a source from which to fill vacancies occurring on the Girls' Council.   The fact that many girls sought Council status for the prestige and privileges involved was the main reason for creation of the junior group. The Girls' Council met regularly with the superintendent and was directly responsible to her.   In addition to planning special activities, discussions were held on the behavior of particular girls which might be detrimental to the others.

Council members were chosen on the basis of good adjustment, sense of responsibility, and a demonstrated ability to work toward realistic goals.   Each was expected to set a good example.   A Council girl decided for herself whether or not to share her observations of the behavior of others for the protection of all.   The staff believed the Girls' Council had a definite and significant place in the program of the Center, and cited two reasons for its successful operation: members receive added privileges which serves as an incentive to good behavior in order to attain membership; and members are not required to report on the behavior of others, which enables them to retain their peer group status.

The aid of the Girls' Council might be sought in situations where the administration was concerned about a potential absconder, in which instance the Council girls may volunteer to talk with the girl or keep her under surveillance, and in the case of a girl's illness, in which two members might be asked to sit with her until medical help becomes available.

Youth Forestry Camps Numbers 1, 2, and 3 are located respectively at Hookstown, Hickory Run State Park and Aitch, Pennsylvania.   At Hookstown a Campers Activities Council was formed in May 1966 to plan and coordinate social and recreation activities for the fifty-one students. Members of the Council met with similar groups from other institutions regarding such joint activities as dancing, dinners, and outings.   The superintendent believed that the Council provided a positive experience which could be the basis for inculcating feelings of trust and responsibility.   It

was planned to utilize the Council concept in other areas of
the camp life program as staff became more skillful in its
administration.

Hickory Run State Park Camp organized a Camper's
Committee in March 1958 when a poor climate of staff-
camper relationships made the need for a participating group
apparent.   This group was reported as being successful in
promoting the achievement of common goals.   As with most
organizations it fluctuated in its effectiveness among the fifty
boys.   Its value was summed up in the superintendent's observation that the most turbulent moments of the camp occurred during the times the Camper's Committee was at its
weakest.   Ad hoc committees concerned with craft and special recreational programs for the twenty boys were utilized
at the Aitch Camp.   A rapid turnover of population was given
as the principal reason for preferring that arrangement
rather than a permanent council.

RHODE ISLAND

The Department of Corrections administers all institutions for adult, youth, and juvenile offenders.   A complex
of three adult institutions and two training schools are located at Howard.   In 1971 the Juvenile Diagnostic Center
was opened at Cranston.

Adult Correctional Institutions

No current information has been received, but a 1966
report stated there were no inmate advisory councils in the
Adult Correctional Institutions. [177]

Juvenile Correctional Institutions

In 1967 it was reported there had never been an inmate advisory council at the Rhode Island Training School
for Girls since its opening in 1882. [178]   No current information has been received.   Reportedly, no inmate councils have
ever existed at the Rhode Island Training School for Boys. [179]

SOUTH CAROLINA

Department of Corrections

The Department of Corrections administers seventeen institutions for adult and youthful felony offenders and misdemeanor offenders. There are no advisory councils at the Reception and Evaluation Center, and the Thomas P. Stoney Psychiatric Center, both at Columbia, and six community pre-release centers. The other nine facilities have active councils. [180]

An Inmate Council was organized in March 1968, at the Central Correctional Institution, Columbia. Constructive suggestions, as well as complaints, are brought to staff attention through the Council, whose authority is limited to the making of recommendations. Sections established within the institution may each elect one representative and one alternate who, after final approval by the warden, serve a one-year term of office. Representatives may succeed themselves once. No prerequisites for membership have been established. The Council, meeting twice a month with the warden or his representative, has proven to be a useful method of communication and has provided the staff with constructive criticism. An example is the modification of the twice-daily count process. As a result of the interchange of views within the Council meeting framework, more efficient and mutually agreeable procedures were devised.

The Givens Youth Correction Center, Simpsonville, Inmate Council was organized in 1970. Its activities declined, however, and it was reorganized in February 1972 with a membership of five elected to represent the dormitories. In July 1971, an Inmate Council was organized at the Goodman Correctional Institution, Columbia. The warden, chief correctional supervisor, and all inmates attend the meetings.

Two members are elected from each of three housing areas as representatives to the Inmate Council formed in December 1972 at the Maximum Detention Retraining Center, Columbia. The Wateree River Correctional Institution, Boykin, Inmate Council was begun in August 1970. Two representatives, one white and one black, are elected from each of the seven wards. Each ward elects its own representatives to the six-member Inmate Council in existence since August 1971, at the Manning Correctional Institution, Columbia.

The Inmate Council at the Harbison Correctional Institution for Women, Irmo, dates back to November 27,
1964. The membership of six is composed of three elected
representatives from each of the residential buildings. A
six-member Inmate Council selected from the wards was
formed in January 1971 at the Walden Correctional Institution, Columbia. An elected representative from each of the
five dormitories is a member of the Inmate Council organized in July 1971 at the MacDougall Youth Correction Center,
Ridgeville.

Department of Youth Services

The Department of Youth Services administers six
facilities for juvenile delinquents, including a Reception and
Evaluation Center, Columbia. There is a Student Advisory
Committee at the John G. Richards School for Boys, Columbia, about which no information has been received. [181]

SOUTH DAKOTA

State Board of Charities and Corrections

Three facilities, one for adult and youthful felony offenders, one for juvenile misdemeanants, and a forestry
camp for selected youthful offenders, are administered by
the State Board of Charities and Corrections. The South
Dakota Penitentiary at Sioux Falls has no advisory council.
Approximately five or six years ago a Jaycees chapter was
organized which is regarded as a good medium of communication supplementing almost daily contacts with population by
the administration. [182]

The South Dakota Training School, Plankinton, previously had a Student Council which functioned principally in
the areas of planning recreational activities and the conducting of tours. Currently, Guided Group Interaction is the
treatment technique in use. It is believed that this method
of involving students in their own treatment provides them
with more possibilities to participate in the formulation of
rules and procedures. [183] The Youth Forestry Camp, Custer, established in 1967, has no advisory council but does
require participation in peer groups of four to seven campers
from which recommendations may be made through a counselor regarding camp procedures. [184]

TENNESSEE

The Department of Correction has jurisdiction over all facilities for adult and youthful felony offenders, misdemeanor offenders, and juvenile delinquents.

Adult Services

The Adult Services administers four institutions for adult and youthful felony offenders. A Self-Government Program is operative at the Tennessee Penitentiary, Nashville, and the Tennessee Prison for Women, Nashville.

A program designed to provide residents with a large measure of responsibility for their personal behavior has been established in a housing unit at the Tennessee State Penitentiary, Nashville.[185] A resident who has maintained a clear conduct record in the general population for twelve months, been employed in his present position for a minimum of six months and earning incentive time credits in the immediate past three grading periods, and whose work supervisor is of the opinion that he can function in a minimum supervision situation, may be referred to a three-member staff selection board representing treatment, security, and industry. If approved by that group, the resident may then be assigned to the special unit where he may continue to reside as long as he continues to earn incentive time credits. Other than a requirement to be present in his cell at the nine p.m. daily count, a resident has the freedom of the unit. While present in the unit he has possession of the key to his cell. He is responsible for the cleaning of his cell, and may be selected by the staff in charge for other clean-up assignments. A Rules Committee, selected by the residents, may submit suggestions on governing the unit for consideration by the administration.

A Self-Government Group, organized about three years ago at the Tennessee Prison for Women, Nashville, is composed of residents who have been rated as above average in work or training in the dormitory. The Group reviews all applications for membership, referring acceptances to a staff committee for final approval. Members are given additional privileges. They are allowed to have their own food, keep later hours, and visit in each other's rooms. The Group also disciplines its members if rules are broken. Additionally, members operate a snack bar on weekends, assist in the orientation of new admissions to the institution, and engage in community projects such as visiting nursing homes and sending Christmas baskets to needy families. [186]

For an unspecified period of time between February and September, 1960, there was an elected inmate committee at the now closed Brushy Mountain Penitentiary, Petros. However, the members used their position for personal gain and some members became agitators. The organization was permitted to expire of its own accord. [187]

Youth Services

The Youth Services administers five facilities for youth felony and misdemeanor offenders and juvenile delinquents. Each facility has or is organizing a student council to serve as an advisory group. Generally the councils are composed of one or more representatives from each dormitory and a president elected at large and they hold weekly meetings. [188]

Information was received in 1966 and 1967, that a Student Council was in operation at the Tennessee Youth Center, Joelton. Organized in 1965, just three years after the Center opened, the Council was composed of one representative from each vocational course. Members were selected by the students and held weekly meetings with a staff advisor at which criticisms of program and suggestions for modifications were made. The president of the Council, a student elected by the membership with no staff involvement, was a member of the staff discipline committee which also included two vocational instructors and the academic school principal. This student member had freedom of expression regarding the situation of any disciplinary case and usually entered into all discussions. He could offer any suggestion for disposition and staff often acceded. [189]

TEXAS

Department of Corrections

The Department of Corrections administers fourteen institutions for adult and youthful felony offenders, including a Diagnostic Unit, Huntsville. Inmate councils are not utilized in any institution. [190]

Texas Youth Council

     None of the fourteen facilities for juvenile delinquents administered by the Texas Youth Council has an advisory council. 191

UTAH

Division of Corrections

     The Division of Corrections administers the Utah State Prison, Draper, which is the single facility for adult and youthful felony offenders. In 1966 information was received that the first Inmate Advisory Council was organized in the main institution in October 1957, and another later in the Minimum Security Facility which was regarded as being more effective. The opinion was expressed that a more pressurized situation existed among the type inmate housed in the main institution, enabling the more aggressive and assaultive person to gain election to office. 192

     Under the provisions of a Constitution and By-Laws, each representative to the Inmate Advisory Council upon taking office was required to sign a pledge to "represent my constituents, and the inmate body as a whole, honorably and to the best of my ability ..., observe all requirements of the Constitution and By-Laws, and ... refrain from engaging in personalities at the meetings. I will do nothing to embarrass the Council ... [and] will not abuse the privileges that go with membership...." Two members from each housing unit were elected by secret ballot to six-month terms of office. The Council selected a chairman and vice-chairman from the membership. The Secretary was chosen by the warden from a slate of three persons nominated by the Council. "Robert's Rules of Order" governed the conduct of the weekly unsupervised meetings and the monthly meeting with the warden. No current information has been received.

Division of Family Services

     The Utah State Industrial School, Ogden, is the state facility for juvenile delinquents. The program is co-educational, with girls comprising approximately one-third of the population. The facility was established in 1888 as the

Territorial Reform School, adopting its present designation in 1896.

For the past eighteen to twenty years there has been a Student Council program. In the early years, the Council was operative only during the school year. Membership included a president, vice-president and secretary elected by the students, and representatives of each homeroom. In March 1965, a Group Living Student Council was organized in addition to the school group. Since 1970, there has been a single Student Council program to accomplish the purposes of developing treatment programs appropriate to student needs through student-staff communication, and to provide Council members and the student body with a series of developmental educational and social experiences. The program is under the supervision of the assistant superintendent and the director of education. No criteria for Council membership have been established. Each cottage selects representatives by popular vote, and the leadership--president, vice-president, and secretary--is chosen by vote of the Council members.

Student Council members meet on occasion with the executive staff and the superintendent, and attend other meetings concerned with the management and the life style of the students in residence. Currently, there is under consideration a plan to establish for Student Council members a daily social science laboratory-type program designed to develop an understanding of the relationship between the regulations involved in the management of a Student Council and regulations at all levels of government. The administration strongly advocates the student council system in facilities for juvenile offenders, commenting that perhaps growth in social responsibility is one of the greatest gains to students as they participate in the management of others. [193]

VERMONT

Department of Corrections

The Department of Corrections administers seven facilities for adult and youthful felony and misdemeanor offenders and juvenile delinquents. The small population, thirty to fifty, in five of the facilities makes possible regular

meetings involving all residents and staff. The maximum
security Correctional Facility at Windsor has a Liaison
Committee composed of five residents elected by the population and the supervising officer of the Facility. Other staff
members meet with this group when the discussion topic is
pertinent to their functions. No council has been organized
at the Weeks School, Vergennes. [194]

Several years ago an Inmate Council was in operation
for about one year at the Windsor facility which was then
designated as the Vermont State Prison and House of Correction for Men. In addition to becoming a "gimme" group,
the Council began analyzing the situations of various inmates
and demanding the right to correspond with social agencies
to express views on the handling of social problems of certain individuals. [195] The Women's Reformatory, Rutland,
opened in 1921 and closed a few years ago, reportedly had
no advisory council. [196]

VIRGINIA

The Department of Welfare and Institutions has jurisdiction over all institutions for adult and youthful felony and
misdemeanor offenders, and juvenile delinquents.

Division of Corrections

At the present there are no inmate advisory councils
in the five institutions administered by the Department of
Corrections. [197]

At the Southampton Correctional Farm, Capron, a
facility for youthful first offenders, a council was organized
in February 1965 under a constitution and by-laws providing
for the secret ballot election of two representatives from
each housing unit with terms of office varying from two to
six months. After endorsement by at least ten others in his
housing unit, an inmate who had been in the institution not
less than two months with a clear conduct record and with
a minimum of six months left to serve could stand for election if approved by a Staff Committee which included the
superintendent, assistant superintendent, and department
heads. Twice monthly meetings during working hours were
authorized to discuss matters relative to the general welfare

of the population. No problems of individuals were to be
discussed except when it was apparent they could affect other persons generally. A like situation was provided for
relative to matters covered by state statutes, discussion being allowed if it was believed the statutes were being ignored
to the detriment of inmate welfare. Despite these rather
liberal and permissive conditions, lack of inmate interest
brought about the demise of the council late in the same
year. 198

Division of Youth Services

The Division of Youth Services administers seven
facilities for juvenile delinquents. A Reception and Diagnostic Center for Children, Bon Air, is operated as a separate unit in conjunction with the Bon Air School for Girls.
In 1966 none of the five facilities then in operation had a
student council. At the present time each facility has a
student council or a similar organization. 199 Information
was obtained regarding four facilities.

Student government in its present form has been in
existence since 1968 at the Hanover School for Boys, Hanover. Prior attempts to organize such a program were
made but no details are available. Two representatives are
elected by the boys in each of the eight cottages. Weekly
cottage meetings are held under the direction of counselors.
Later a campus Student Government meeting is held to which
representatives bring complaints and suggestions made in the
cottage meetings. Staff sponsors are a counselor and an
academic teacher who act as liaison with the administration.
During the past eighteen months the success and effectiveness of the Student Government has been generally poor.
Since there have been few actions taken by the administration on suggestions channelled through the group, a belief
has grown among many of the boys that the making of suggestions is a waste of time. This reaction is also manifested
by representatives choosing to participate in other activities
rather than to attend the Student Government meeting. The
scheduling of Student Government meetings concurrently with
other group meetings has been recognized as a factor contributing to the lack of attendance. Reorganization of the
Student Government in the near future is hoped for. 200

A Student Council was organized in 1968 at the Beaumont School for Boys, Beaumont, and functioned for several

years with some success. It was found that the compara-
tively short stay of a student at the School, at that time it
was six months, resulted in more time being spent in election of representatives and officers than in constructive activity. Since discontinuance of the Council, several other
methods have been found to involve the students in school
function and administration, of which two are cited. A
Positive Peer Culture program requires groups of students
to assume responsibilities for improving their daily living
situation, and to play a major role in deciding when individual group members are ready for release. Also, an atmosphere of accessibility has been developed in which students
may freely approach staff of any level with the realization
that their complaints, suggestions, and recommendations,
involving only self or the entire facility will be listened
to. [201]

Several attempts to organize a student council since
the opening of the Juvenile Vocational Institute, Honaker, in
October 1967, have been unsuccessful. The major difficulty
cited, in addition to lack of staff experience with such
groups, was an organizational structure which permitted the
gaining of control by the negative element among the student
body. Using the experience of past errors, development is
underway by the administration of a new organizational structure for a student council. [202]

The lack of success in attempts to establish a student
government at Pinecrest Center, Richmond, is attributed
basically to the age of the boys, none being over twelve,
and their concern with personal and immediate goals rather
than with a group program. [203]

WASHINGTON

Facilities for felony offenders and juvenile delinquents
are under the jurisdiction of the Washington Department of
Social and Health Services, Social Services Division.

Services Delivery Division-Adults

In the aftermath of the riots and disturbances that
swept over the United States in the early fifties, the State
of Washington made a general reorganization of its adult

correctional institutions. Inmate advisory councils were authorized by the then Department of Institutions in a 1954
directive for the purpose of promoting good will and to provide free and efficient inmate-staff communication. Through
council activities it was believed that inmates might become
more sympathetically aware of the problems of prison administration and, conversely, staff might become more
acutely aware of the psychological stresses and strains of
prison life. Although council members were to be granted
considerable leeway in the selection of topics for discussion,
it was stipulated that none were to be given authority to
implement administration-approved suggestions or to involve
others, either inmates or staff, except as directed by the
Superintendent. [204]

Despite the mandatory provisions of the first paragraph in the directive--"There shall be established at each
correctional institution an Inmate Advisory Council consisting of seven to fifteen members"--a survey made in 1966
found only one advisory council in existence. Another institution had discontinued a council, and the small population
at each of the honor camps allowed such a high degree of
staff-inmate interaction that councils were felt to be un-
needed. Ad hoc committees were in use at the Reformatory
and the Corrections Center to deal with the blood bank,
movie selection, inmate talent shows, and athletic events,
being disbanded upon completion of the activity. [205]

A directive was issued in 1970 to supersede that of
1954. Under its provisions each of the six institutions, including two honor camps, has a resident governmental council composed of members representing housing units or program areas, elected by secret ballot and limited to a six-
months' term of office. Procedures are governed under a
constitution prepared by the residents and approved by the
superintendent and the central office. It is regarded as essential that all residents understand how and by whom they
are represented on the councils and have the opportunity to
participate in the open elections. Community representatives
may attend meetings of the councils. [206]

At the Washington State Penitentiary, Walla Walla,
the Inmate Advisory Council was organized in 1956, composed of eleven members limited upon election by secret
ballot to a single six-month term of office. Although elected
by the residents of his housing unit, the scope of each councilman's responsibility was institution wide. To be eligible

for office, a candidate must have had his minimum sentence
set by the Parole Board, a suitable conduct record, and at
least six months to serve if elected. A chairman and a
secretary were chosen from the membership to conduct and
record the semi-monthly meetings, one of which was attended by the superintendent or his representative. [207]

As a result of the 1970 directive, the name of the
Walla Walla institution council was changed to Resident Governmental Council and a new constitution was drawn up.
The eleven member composition was retained. However,
the franchise of each voter was enlarged so that he could
cast eleven votes to be distributed as he chose. Council
members elect from their ranks a president, vice-president,
and executive secretary. Each of the other members is assigned to head project ad-hoc committees as needed. Interesting features are the publication of a newspaper by the
Council under a five-member resident-staff Editorial Review
Board, the Council privilege to contact the news media provided the superintendent has been given a courtesy copy of
the communication, and a Citizens' Advisory Committee.
This latter group has six members selected by the superintendent and the council president from civic, fraternal, and
service organizations, and individuals who are permitted access to all institution residents and areas at any time. The
Committee advises the Resident Governmental Council and
the administration on matters of mutual concern, and may
invite officials from all levels of government and private
citizens to observe, participate in discussions, and offer advice at Council meetings. The constitution is currently under revision. [208]

Resident Governmental Council representatives participate in staff meetings, adjustment committee hearings, and
classification committee meetings as well as staff-resident
committees. Results of this participation are evaluated as
being productive of both positives and negatives. Hopefully,
experience will increase the former and eliminate the latter. [209]

An Inmate Advisory Council was established in 1954
at the Washington State Reformatory, Monroe. Operating
under the directive of the Department of Public Institutions,
the organization was never fully accepted by line employees
who from time to time expressed considerable hostility
towards its philosophy and function. This presented the
Council with a dilemma--the expectations of their

constituents pressed them squarely into the face of the disapproval of the keepers.   In February 1965 it was determined that an inmate boycott of the dining room was carried out by Council, which was disbanded following the transfer of its members to the penitentiary.   Investigation suggested that the boycott was a retaliation against the superintendent for not approving as many proposals as the Council
wanted. [210]

Service Delivery Division-Juvenile

All Washington juveniles who are adjudged delinquent
are committed to the Department of Social and Health Services.   Residential care is provided in fourteen facilities
which include a reception-diagnostic center, a children's
center, five group homes, five youth forest camps, and two
treatment centers (schools).   Information obtained in 1967
was referred to the Social Services Division, Department of
Social and Health Services, to determine its current validity.   No changes were made by the Social Services Division
other than to note that one facility reported on in 1967 is
now closed. [211]   No information was received on the five
facilities opened since that time.

At the Maple Lane School, Centralia, a council program organized in 1950 operates under a constitution and by-
laws amendable by a two-thirds majority vote and staff advisor approval, which provides for the election of a council
in each cottage, the presidents of each comprising the Campus Council.   When a girl is regarded as ready to handle
responsibility her name is placed on a Cottage Council membership eligibility list.   Chosen by a simple majority on a
secret ballot, a member is elected to an indefinite term of
office from which she may be removed for failing to assume
necessary responsibility.   Each Cottage Council elects a
president, vice-president, and secretary.   These groups
meet weekly with a staff member present.   Suggestions, requests, or complaints may be referred to the Campus Council which meets every other week with a staff advisor from
the Cottage Life Department to consider suggestions for re-
ferral to the staff.   Suggestions may be only on facilities,
programs, or special projects.   Recommendations of a disciplinary nature or pertaining to the physical or mental
health needs of an individual are excluded.   Chairmanship
and secretary functions are rotated weekly.

The Camp Council of the Youth Camp, Naselle, was organized November 1, 1966, just two weeks after the first students were received at the facility. The four living units are called lodges. Each lodge council chooses three of six staff-selected boys to run for a two-month term of office. Voting is by secret ballot and the nominee receiving a majority vote is declared lodge chief. Two other councilmen are elected to one-month terms. Two bay chiefs are appointed by the staff to two months terms. Qualifications for council membership include two months' camp residence for bay chiefs and councilmen, three months for lodge chief, and a willingness and ability to handle the job in a manner beneficial to the Camp, with a further consideration of what benefits the particular council member might gain by being in office. Lodge councils meet weekly with a staff leader. At all Camp Council meetings, held on an irregular basis, the lodge chiefs and their staff leaders may plan athletic, recreation, and social activities as well as community projects, discuss relationships between Lodges, and consider suggestions on Camp policies and procedures.

The Cedar Creek Youth Camp, Littlerock, has student councils in operation in both its Timberline and Alpine programs, the latter being a subsidiary facility. Each council is representative of the student population and meets with a member of the counseling staff to discuss policy and procedure, make recommendations for modifications of procedures, assist in planning and evaluating recreational activities, participate in the integration of new students and, under staff supervision, work with students who are experiencing difficulty.

In the original Cedar Creek program, Timberline, a Student Council was organized in 1954 with a membership of ten. Six of these were work program crewleader or foreman positions designated as "Colored Hats." To be eligible for a colored hat, a boy must be in the program a minimum of three months. He is appointed by staff on the basis of his work ability and leadership qualities. One member of the Council is the "Camp Kick," a representative of the student population elected by secret ballot to a one-month term. A candidate for this office must have been in the program a minimum of four months and in good standing. The remaining members, representing the three dormitories, must have been in the program two months. Election is by secret ballot and tenure of office continues until paroled. The Council has no officers or constitution and by-laws.

In the Alpine program, a Student Council was developed in December 1959, but discontinued in 1961 because of a drop in the age level of the boys to fourteen/fifteen years.   In the latter part of 1963, when the Camp again began to receive older boys, the Council was reinstated and has functioned well since that time.   Its membership is composed of two staff-appointed crewleaders, a Camp Kick, and two elected crew representatives.   Qualifications, tenure, and organization are similar to the Timberline program.

The Student Council at the Spruce Canyon Youth Forest Camp, Colville, also known as "Colored Hats," was established in 1961 and has continued effectively since.   The positions of colored hats are: one camp kick (red), two crew leaders (green), and five squad leaders (yellow).   The first position is filled by secret balloting on a nominee slate selected by the staff from boys who have demonstrated outstanding work ability and above average peer and authority relationships to serve a term of one month.   The other positions are filled by staff appointment.   Potential for positive leadership and personal improvement are primary selection criteria.   The Council meets bi-monthly with the supervisor of student life to consider suggestions for betterment of camp living.

When the Woodinville Group Home opened in 1965, a Student Council was organized to give the boys an opportunity to express their feelings toward operations and the development of programs.   The capacity of the facility is sixteen boys, with all taking part in the twice monthly meetings with staff.   A president, vice-president, secretary, and master-of-arms are elected by majority vote to serve until released or asked by staff to step down because of poor behavior. Disbursements from a student fund financed by a ten percent contribution of each boy's earnings are determined at Council meetings.

The Pioneer Group Home at Tacoma has had group participation since shortly after the facility opened in 1962, the purpose for which is to establish rapport between students and staff regarding program and goals.   Additionally, the group makes decisions on expenditures of student funds and group recreational activities.   Due to the small population, membership in the group is automatic.

The Fort Worden Treatment Center, Port Townsend, was opened in 1958 and closed recently.   In 1967

information was received that a group of boys and girls,
elected from the cottages, met with the recreation staff to
plan co-educational activities.   The group was not regarded
as being a student council, however.

WEST VIRGINIA

Department of Correction

The Department of Correction administers three institutions for adult and youthful felony offenders and five
facilities for delinquents.   One of the latter also receives
youthful felony offenders.   According to information obtained
in 1966, there were no advisory councils.   However, the
Department of Correction was seriously considering experimenting with such groups. 212   No current data has been received.

WISCONSIN

Division of Corrections

All facilities for adult and youthful offenders and juvenile delinquents are administered by the Division of Corrections, Department of Health and Social Services.   Ad hoc
advisory councils have been in existence from time to time
for special activities.   Some are functioning at present
[1973].

In March 1973 inmate participation advisory committees, elected by the inmates, were organized at the Wisconsin State Prison, Waupun; the Wisconsin State Reformatory,
Green Bay; the Wisconsin Correctional Institution, Fox Lake;
and the Wisconsin Home for Women, Taycheedah.   Each
committee has an equal number of inmate and staff members
and is headed by the clinical director assigned to the institution by the Bureau of Clinical Services.   The members are
to meet regularly and make recommendations to the Council
on Criminal Justice, a state planning agency funded by the
Law Enforcement Assistance Administration, on grant requests in the field of correction.   Although limited experience at this time precludes a definitive statement, it does
appear that several valuable goals will be achieved through
this approach. 213

In the early 1940's an inmate council was in operation at the Wisconsin State Prison, Waupun. Reportedly individual complaints were given undue weight when handled by the council rather than through ordinary procedures, resulting in unwarranted attention to many minor and ridiculous matters. The elections of representatives of the major departments soon resulted in the formation of committees whose membership was drawn from aggressive nonconformists. It was felt that the council was a factor in a major disturbance in 1944; this led to its abandonment.[214]

No current information has been received regarding advisory councils in the Wisconsin Correctional Camp System. In 1967 it was reported there were no councils in the seven camps then in operation.[215] No current information has been received regarding advisory councils at the four facilities for juvenile delinquents.

In 1967 the Kettle Moraine Boys School, Plymouth, had no advisory council, nor did the Wisconsin School for Boys, Wales. At the latter facility, however, representative groups from the various cottages could confer with the superintendent regarding problems not solved in the group counseling programs conducted in all living units by a psychiatrist, psychologist, or social worker. At the Black River Camp, Black River Falls, a facility for juveniles, the relatively short service period of five months was reported as having inhibited the development of an inmate advisory council.[216]

In 1967 it was reported that the therapeutic community program at the Wisconsin School for Girls, Oregon, featured Community Meetings and Cottage Representatives. In the former, all girls of a cottage met together for one hour daily with a counselor and a social worker. The content of the meeting varied as did the function: the focus might be on the problems of one girl; the determination of appropriate disciplinary action for an individual or a group; or the solution of everyday cottage living problems. The social worker might ask for recommendations or decisions, reserving the right to overrule either. Any conclusions reached were subject to staff approval. The Cottage Representatives program provided for an informal weekly meeting of the superintendent and the elected representatives of the ten cottages. Representatives reported on the progress of programs, and could give their views on contemplated modifications or innovations.[217]

WYOMING

State Board of Charities and Reform

The three facilities for felony and misdemeanor offenders and juvenile delinquents are administered by the State Board of Charities and Reform. Recently, information previously obtained was sent to the Board. It was returned with no notations other than current information concerning the Wyoming Girls School, Sheridan.

The Wyoming State Penitentiary, Rawlins, had an Inmate Advisory Council for a brief period in 1955. It was abolished because of unreasonable demands by the members. In July 1966, a three-member popularly elected Inmate Council was formed which now meets twice a month with the warden to discuss topics relating to the health and welfare of the population. There are no written rules or regulations governing its function. [218]

Student government was tried during the early years of the present decade at the Wyoming Girls School, Sheridan. Variations in structure and changes in rules and regulations did not produce results warranting documentation of methodology. [219] Currently, student participation in School affairs is an integral part of organization dynamics. This was brought about through group meetings regarded as both therapeutic and functional. All group meetings are subject to staff approval or veto.

In 1967 it was reported that although the administration was favorably disposed toward the idea of an inmate advisory council and during the prior two years had given consideration to organizing one, no council then existed at the Wyoming Industrial Institute, Worland. [220]

SOURCES TO PART II

1. Letter from then Commissioner A. F. Lee, Board of Corrections, Montgomery; October 3, 1966.
2. Letter from Lawrence D. Cottle, U. of Alabama Graduate Student in Social Work (for Supt. John H. Carr), Alabama Boys' Industrial School, Birmingham; March 21, 1973.
3. Letter from Director of Program Development Kenneth H. O'Dea, Alabama Industrial School, Mt. Meigs, Alabama; March 21, 1973.
4. Letter from Director of Social Services Margaret E. Lilly, State Training School for Girls, Birmingham; December 14, 1972.
5. Letters from Director Charles G. Adams, Jr., Division of Corrections, Juneau, December 26, 1972, and February 5, 1973.
6. Letter from Chief of Correctional Institutions P. L. Severson, Anchorage, March 20, 1967.
7. Policy Memorandum No. 23, "Inmate Council Procedure," Office of the Director, Youth and Adult Authority, December 12, 1966.
8. Op. cit.
9. Letter from Community Services Administrator E. J. Aitken, Dept. of Corrections, Phoenix, November 29, 1972.
10. Letter from Commissioner Terrell Don Hutto, Dept. of Correction, Little Rock, April 5, 1973; "Inmate Council Constitution and By-Laws," Arkansas State Penitentiary, November 1972; "Inmate Handbook," Dept. of Correction, November 1972.
11. Letters dated June 1967 from Supt. Anthony A. Shock, Arkansas Training School for Boys, Pine Bluff; Supt. R. E. Hemphill, Arkansas Training School for Boys, Wrightsville; then Supt. Clifton W. Shepard, Arkansas Training School for Girls, Alexander; Supt. R. M. Foster, Arkansas Training School for Girls, Fargo.

12. Letters from then Director Walter Dunbar, Dept. of
    Corrections, Sacramento, August 5, 1966; Chief,
    Community Relations and Information Philip D.
    Guthrie, Dept. of Corrections, December 12, 1972.
13. Letter from Associate Warden James W. L. Park,
    Calif. State Prison, San Quentin; September 20,
    1966.
14. Letters from Associate Warden S. P. Faustman,
    California State Prison at Folsom, Represa, Sep-
    tember 23, 1966; Associate Warden R. C. Thomas,
    December 18, 1972.
15. Letters from then Supt. G. P. Lloyd, California Cor-
    rectional Institution, Tehachapi, November 17,
    1966; Admin. Asst. F. L. Johnson, January 9,
    1973.
16. Scudder, Kenyon J. Prisoners Are People. Garden
    City, N. Y. : Doubleday, 1952; p. 71.
17. Correspondence from Kenyon J. Scudder, consultant,
    the Osborne Assn. Inc.; July 27, 1966.
18. Letter from then Supt. E. J. Oberhauser, California
    Institution for Men, Chino, August 5, 1966.
19. Letter from Admin. Asst. Earl Muff, California Insti-
    tution for Men, Chino, January 16, 1973.
20. Letters from Admin. Asst. F. W. Forden, Correc-
    tional Training Facility, Soledad, September 29,
    1966; Supt. W. T. Stone, January 3, 1973.
21. Constitution and By-Laws, Inmate Advisory Council,
    North Facility, Soledad, February 28, 1966.
22. Letter from Supt. L. N. Patterson, Deuel Vocational
    Institution, Tracy, December 14, 1972.
23. "Constitution," Inmate Advisory Council, Deuel, Voca-
    tional Institution, Tracy, March 1958.
24. Letter from Supt. T. L. Clanon, M. D. , California
    Medical Facility, Vacaville, December 15, 1972;
    "Constitution and By-Laws," Inmate Advisory Coun-
    cil, September 9, 1963.
25. Letter from Admin. Asst. Dean T. Greene, California
    Men's Colony, Los Padres, California, September
    9, 1966; "General Order No. 20, Inmate Organiza-
    tions. "
26. Letter from then Assoc. Supt. W. J. Estelle, Jr.,
    California Conservation Center, Susanville, Septem-
    ber 1, 1966; "Constitution and By-Laws," Council,
    Susanville, July 1, 1966.
27. Letter from Supt. W. D. Achuff, Southern Conserva-
    tion Center, Chino, September 20, 1966; "Adminis-
    trative Order No. 27," August 1, 1964; "Constitu-
    tion and By-Laws," Inmate Advisory Council.

28. Letter from Admin. Asst. Kenneth H. Tate, Sierra
    Conservation Center, Jamestown, September 20,
    1966; "Constitution and By-Laws," Inmate Advisory
    Council, Calaveras--Minimum Section.
29. Letters from Supt. Roland W. Wood, California Re-
    habilitation Center, Corona, September 20, 1966 and
    December 18, 1972; "Constitution and By-Laws,"
    Male Resident Central Committee, Rev. 1966.
30. Letter from then Supt. Iverne R. Carter, California
    Institution for Women, Frontera, October 11, 1966;
    "Brochure," CIW, 1966.
31. Letter and Reports from Director Allen F. Breed,
    Department of the Youth Authority, Sacramento;
    January 25, 1973.
32. Report from Unit Administrator William E. Dickerson,
    Southern Reception Center-Clinic, Norwalk; Novem-
    ber 16, 1966.
33. Report from then Supt. Beatrice D. Dolan, Ventura
    School for Girls, Camarillo; November 3, 1966.
34. Letter from then Supt. F. H. Butterfield, Fred C.
    Nelles School for Boys, Whittier; October 27, 1966.
35. Letter from then Supt. Sylvia F. Wolf, Los Guilucos
    School for Girls, Santa Rosa; October 20, 1966.
36. Letter from Supt. Frank R. White, Ben Lomond Youth
    Conservation Camp, Santa Cruz; October 18, 1966.
37. Letter from then Supt. C. A. Terhune, O. H. Close
    School for Boys, (Northern Youth Center), Stockton;
    November 16, 1966.
38. Letter from then Supt. Victor A. Kirk, Paso Robles
    School for Boys, Pasa Robles; October 20, 1966.
39. Letter from Chief Robert D. Trujillo, Division of Cor-
    rections, Denver; November 24, 1972.
40. Letter from then Chief Harry C. Tinsley, Division of
    Corrections, Denver, November 30, 1966.
41. Letter from Public Relations Officer Claire E. Nagle,
    Division of Youth Services, Denver, January 30,
    1973.
42. Letter from then Chief Mylton F. Kennedy, Division of
    Youth Services, Fort Logan, February 8, 1967.
43. Letter from then Warden Frederick G. Reincke, Con-
    necticut State Prison, Somers, September 6, 1966.
44. Letter from Asst. Director Mark S. Richmond, Federal
    Bureau of Prisons, March 2, 1967.
45. Letter from Supt. Janet S. York, Connecticut State
    Farm for Women, Niantic, October 18, 1966.
46. Letters from: Acting Director of Institutions Charles
    W. Dean, Dept. of Children and Youth Services,

Hartford, April 2, 1973; Asst. Supt. for Program
Gloria J. Busch, Long Lane School, Middletown,
July 17, 1973; "Constitution of the Long Lane
School, " July 1973.

47. Letter from Director John J. Moran, Division of Adult
Corrections, Smyrna, November 28, 1972.

48. Letters from Administrator of Preventive Services H.
Kirby Krams, Youth Services Commission, Wilming-
ton, September 16, 1966; Supt. Dorothy Banton,
Woods Haven-Kruse School for Girls, Claymont,
April 13, 1967.

49. Letter from Assistant Director Quanah F. Parker,
Division of Juvenile Corrections, Wilmington, April
5, 1973; "Procedure: The Student Council, " Ferris
School for Boys, September 22, 1969.

50. Letters from Admin. Asst. Gene E. Jenkins, Division
of Corrections, Tallahassee, January 16, 1973;
Supt. L. W. Griffith, Division of Corrections Road
Prisons, Tallahassee, February 17, 1967; then
Asst. Supt. A. F. Cook, Glades Correctional Insti-
tution, Belle Glade, February 2, 1967.

51. Letter from Asst. Bureau Chief Frank A. Zych, Bureau of Training Schools, Tallahassee; December 5,
1972.

52. Letter from Supt. Lenox E. Williams, Arthur G.
Dozier School for Boys, Marianna; February 28,
1967.

53. Letter from Commissioner Ellis C. MacDougall, Dept.
of Offender Rehabilitation, Atlanta, January 2,
1973.

54. Letter from Asst. Director Charles C. Ray, Social
Services Section, Dept. of Human Resources, Atlanta, January 19, 1973.

55. "Administrator's Directive No. 71, " Corrections Division, Honolulu, October 18, 1966.

56. Letter from Acting Administrator Moses Ome, Corrections Division, Honolulu, November 29, 1966.

57. Harper, Joe C. "Community Participation in the Prison Program. " 1956 Proceedings, American Correctional Association, pp. 33-36.

58. Letters from Director Raymond W. May, State Board
of Correction, Boise, November 30, 1972, and
December 20, 1972.

59. Letter from Director Ike A. Tolley, Social Services
Dept. , and Director Arvon J. Arave, Cottage Life
Dept. , State Youth Training Center, Saint Anthony,
March 23, 1973.

60.   Letter from Director Ross V. Randolph, Dept. of Pub-
        lic Safety, Springfield, October 31, 1966.
61.   Letter from Admin. Asst. Herbert T. Schaefer, Office
        of Institution Services, Juvenile Division, St.
        Charles, February 9, 1973.
62.   Letter from Supt. Olin W. Stead, Division of Correc-
        tional Services, Illinois Youth Commission, Spring-
        field, May 1967.
63.   Letter from Director of Classification and Treatment
        John W. Buck, Dept. of Corrections, Indianapolis,
        November 21, 1966.
64.   Letter from Warden Russell E. Lash, Indiana State
        Prison, Michigan City, January 30, 1973.
65.   Letters from Director John W. Buck, November 21,
        1966; Asst. Supt. Richard V. Schroeder, Indiana
        Reformatory, Pendleton, December 18, 1972.
66.   Letter from Supt. Donald L. Hudkins, Indiana State
        Farm, Greencastle, January 23, 1973.
67.   Letter from Supt. Dolores E. Schroeder, Indiana Wom-
        en's Prison, Indianapolis, January 24, 1973.
68.   Letter from Director James E. McCart, Reception-
        Diagnostic Center, Plainfield, February 7, 1973.
69.   Letter from Academic Counselor Frank Wallace, Indiana
        Boys' School, Plainfield, February 2, 1973.
70.   Letter from Coordinator Volunteer Services Mary E.
        Hanna, Indiana Girls' School, Indianapolis, February
        2, 1973.
71.   Letter from Asst. Supt. Richard Davis, Indiana Youth
        Center, Plainfield, January 22, 1973.
72.   Letter from Assoc. Warden for Treatment Lowell D.
        Hewitt, Iowa State Penitentiary, Fort Madison,
        October 25, 1966; "Brochure," Iowa State Penitenti-
        ary, November 30, 1972.
73.   Attorney General's Survey of Release Procedures, Vol.
        5, "Prisons," 1940, p. 133.
74.   Letter from Inmate Council Advisor A. B. Corne,
        Men's Reformatory, Anamosa, September 28, 1966.
75.   Letter from Warden C. H. Haugh, Men's Reformatory,
        Anamosa, December 28, 1972.
76.   Letter from then Acting Supt. James E. Allen, Women's
        Reformatory, Rockwell City, February 27, 1966.
77.   Letter from Supt. Dean Luxford, Iowa Training School
        for Girls, Mitchellville, December 21, 1972.
78.   O'Neil, Carl F. and Gregory, David. "The Metamor-
        phosis of a Training School," Federal Probation,
        June 1964, pp. 34-40.
79.   Letters from Supt. Carle F. O'Neil, Iowa Training

School for Boys, Eldora, February 20, 1967; December 22, 1972.

80. Letter from Asst. Director John C. Hazelet, Dept. of
Penal Institutions, Topeka, December 7, 1972.

81. Letter from then Supervisor of Honor Camps Wayne
D. Woolverton, Topeka, April 18, 1967.

82. Letter from Supt. Lawrence D. Penny, Boys' Industrial
School, Topeka, December 8, 1972.

83. Letter from then Supt. Jack C. Pulliam, Boys' Industrial School, Topeka, June 1, 1967.

84. Letters from Supt. Denis J. Shumate, Girls' Industrial
School, Beloit, June 6, 1967; December 8, 1972.

85. Letter from Exec. Asst. John D. Rees, Dept. of Cor-
rections, Frankfort, April 2, 1973; "Constitution
and By-Laws, " Inmate Advisory Council, Kentucky
State Reformatory; "Constitution and By-Laws, "
Frenchburg Correctional Facility Resident Affairs
Council.

86. Letter from Commissioner Evans D. Tracy, Dept. of
Child Welfare, Frankfort, December 18, 1972.

87. Letter from then Assoc. Warden J. Wayne Allgood,
Louisiana State Penitentiary, Angola, September 13,
1960; "Rules and Procedures, " Inmate Council,
Louisiana State Penitentiary.

88. Letter from then Assoc. Warden B. L. Harris, Louisiana State Penitentiary, Angola, November 28, 1966.

89. Letters from then Supt. J. D. Middlebrooks, Louisiana
Correctional and Industrial School, DeQuincy, March
6, 1967; Supt. Fred Lindsay (then Asst. Supt.),
Louisiana Training Institute, Monroe, March 6,
1967; Supt. Jack M. Pearce, Louisiana Training In-
stitute, Pineville, March 9, 1967; then Supt. Dallas
B. Mathews, Louisiana Training Institute, Baton
Rouge, March 8, 1967.

90. Letter from Director Elayn Hunt, Dept. of Corrections,
Baton Rouge, December 1, 1972.

91. Letter from then Commissioner Walter F. Ulmer,
Dept. of Mental Health and Corrections, Augusta;
November 29, 1966.

92. Letter from Supt. Pauline I. McCready, Stevens Training Center, Hallowell; February 1, 1967.

93. Letter from Supt. William H. Hughes, Boys Training
Center, South Portland; February 1, 1967.

94. Letters from then Warden Vernon L. Pepersack,
September 20, 1960, and Supervisor of Recreation
Edward V. Taylor, September 27, 1960, Maryland
Penitentiary, Baltimore.

95.   Letter from Warden Pepersack, Maryland Penitentiary,
       Baltimore, September 20, 1960.
96.   Letter from then Asst. Warden for Correctional Treat-
       ment James Jordan, Maryland Penitentiary, Janu-
       ary 30, 1967.
97.   Letter from Director of Classification Frederick E.
       Terrinoni, Division of Correction, Baltimore,
       April 4, 1973.
98.   Letter from Classification Supervisor Paul A. Wage-
       ley, Maryland Correctional Institution, Hagers-
       town, February 7, 1967.
99.   Letter from then Supt. Alice M. Blum, Maryland
       Correctional Institution for Women, Jessup, Janu-
       ary 30, 1967.
100.   Letter from James D. Mizelle, Program Consultant,
       Dept. of Juvenile Services, Baltimore, December
       6, 1972.
101.   Letter from Supt. Leonard F. Gmeiner, Montrose
       School for Girls, Reisterstown, December 19,
       1972.
102.   Letter from Supt. Samuel L. Freeman, MCI, West
       Concord, November 21, 1966.
103.   "Constitution, " Self-Development Group, MCI, West
       Concord.
104.   Letter from Supt. Betty C. Smith, MCI, Framing-
       ham, November 23, 1966.
105.   Letter from Supt. Charles W. Gaughan, MCI, Bridge-
       water, September 12, 1966.
106.   Letter from Director of Prison Camps Edward J.
       Dunn, Jr. , Dept. of Correction, Boston, Septem-
       ber 9, 1966.
107.   Letter from Commissioner Joseph M. Leavey, Dept.
       of Youth Services, Boston, March 15, 1973.
108.   Letter from Supt. John W. Hastings, Industrial School
       for Boys, Shirley, May 14, 1967.
109.   Letter from Supt. Francis A. Ordway, Lyman School
       for Boys, Westboro, May 15, 1967.
110.   Letters from Public Information Officer Joanna Fire-
       stone, Dept. of Corrections, Lansing, December
       11, 1972; February 12, 1973; "BCF Regulation
       D-18, Prisoner Representation, " March 28, 1972;
       "Resident Representative Procedure, " State Prison
       of Southern Michigan, Rev. May 1, 1972.
111.   Letter from Director Vergil M. Pinckney, Institutional
       Services, Office of Youth Services, Lansing,
       March 20, 1973.
112.   Letter from then Director of Youth Rehabilitation
       Camps, Prudenville, June 19, 1967.

113. Letter from then Warden R. H. Tahash, Minnesota
     State Prison, Stillwater, September 14, 1966.
114. Letter from then Supt. Jack G. Young, Minnesota
     State Reformatory, St. Cloud, February 20, 1967.
115. Letter from then Supt. Ruby C. Benson, State Re-
     formatory for Women, Shakopee, February 1967.
116. Letter from Director Delbert C. Leaf, Juvenile Insti-
     tutions, Department of Corrections, Saint Paul,
     March 1, 1967.
117. Letter from then Director Frederick J. Gelbman,
     Ph. D. , Minnesota Reception and Diagnostic Center,
     Circle Pines, March 20, 1967.
118. Letter from then Supt. Milton S. Olson, State Train-
     ing School, Red Wing, March 20, 1967.
119. Letter from then Supt. Kenneth F. Schoen, Minnesota
     Home School, Sauk Center, March 21, 1967.
120. Letter from Supt. Casimir Zantek, Youth Vocational
     Center, Rochester, March 31, 1967.
121. Letter from Supt. Robert I. Spills, St. Croix Camp,
     Sandstone, April 10, 1967.
122. Letter from then Supt. W. G. Najjar, Thistledew
     Lake Forestry Camp, Togo, March 23, 1967.
123. Letter from Supt. Ralph L. Nelson, Willow River
     Camp, Willow River, April 11, 1967.
124. Letter from then Supt. C. E. Breazeale, Mississippi
     State Penitentiary, Parchman; November 18, 1966.
125. Letter from then Supt. Lloyd McGehee, Columbia
     Training School, Columbia, November 18, 1966;
     "Twelfth Biennial Report, " Oakley Training School,
     Raymond.
126. Letters from then Director Fred T. Wilkinson, De-
     partment of Corrections, Jefferson City, Missouri,
     November 16, 1966, and Deputy Director Edward
     E. Haynes, December 6, 1972.
127. Letters from then Director W. E. Sears, State Board
     of Training Schools, Jefferson City, November 16,
     1966, and Acting Director Frederick O. McDaniel,
     January 16, 1973.
128. Letters from then Warden E. Ellsworth, Jr. , Mon-
     tana State Prison, Deer Lodge, September 9, 1966,
     and Warden Roger W. Crist, December 1, 1972.
129. Letter from Supt. Don T. Holladay, Pine Hills
     School, Miles City, November 28, 1972.
130. Letters from Supt. Don P. Robel, Mountain View
     School, Helena, September 28, 1966 and November
     27, 1972.
131. Letter from Supt. Mel Mohler, Swan River Forest

Camp, Swan Lake, December 1, 1972; "Camp
Council Constitution. "

132.   Letter from Supt. Donald E. Best, Girls' Training
School, Geneva, February 21, 1967.

133.   Letter from then Supt. E. Kent Hayes, Boys' Training School, Kearney, January 4, 1967.

134.   Letter from then Warden Maurice H. Sigler, Nebraska
Penal and Correctional Complex, Lincoln, January
4, 1967.

135.   Letter and Information Brochure from Supt. Jacqueline
Crawford, Reformatory for Women, York, Decem-
ber 21, 1972.

136.   Letter from Associate Warden for Classification and
Treatment Delbert E. Frost, Nevada State Pris-
on, Carson City, September 9, 1966; "Procedure
#16.00, Inmate Advisory Council Procedures, "
Minimum Security Facility, July 16, 1966.

137.   Letters from Warden Carl G. Hocker, Nevada State
Prison, Carson City, February 17, 1967 and
November 27, 1972.

138.   Letter from Administrative Secretary Jean H. Clark,
Dept. of Health and Welfare, Carson City, February 13, 1967.

139.   Letter from then Warden Parker L. Hancock, New
Hampshire State Prison, Concord; September 13,
1960.

140.   Letter from Director of Treatment and Clinical Services, New Hampshire State Industrial School,
Manchester; December 1, 1972.

141.   Letter and Reports from Director Albert C. Wagner,
Division Correction and Parole, Trenton, March
5, 1973.

142.   Attorney General's Survey of Release Procedures.
Vol. 5, "Prisons, " p. 134.

143.   Letter from then Supt. H. Samuel Vukcevich, New
Jersey Reformatory, Annandale, November 14,
1966; Booklet, "About Annandale and You, " 1965,
pp. 13-15.

144.   Wagner, Albert C.   "Inmate Participation in Correctional Institutions. " The Prison World, Septem-
ber-October 1951, Vol. 13 No. 5, pp. 9-11.

145.   Lane, Winthrop D.   "Democracy for Law Breakers. "
The New Republic, March 8, 1919; pp. 172-174.

146.   Letter from then Principal Keeper H. Yeager, New
Jersey State Prison, Trenton, February 24, 1967.

147.   "Constitution, " Resident Advisory Council, Penitentiary of New Mexico, Santa Fe, March 3, 1972.

148. The Highlights, publication of New Mexico Dept. of
     Corrections, February-March 1973, p. 3.
149. Letter from then Deputy Commissioner John R. Cain,
     Dept. of Correction, Albany, August 30, 1966.
150. Letter from then Supt. Lillian V. Fish, Westfield
     State Farm, Bedford Hills, March 13, 1967.
151. Letter from Executive Deputy Commissioner Walter
     Dunbar, Dept. of Correctional Services, Albany,
     April 12, 1973; Administrative Bulletin #19,
     "Establishment and Operation of Facility Inmate
     Liaison Committee," January 18, 1972.
152. Letter from Director Lawrence Wolfson, Bureau of
     Children's Institution Services, Division for Youth,
     Albany, January 4, 1973.
153. Letter from Director Harold R. Bissett, Training
     School for Girls, Wynantskill, April 10, 1967.
154. Letters from Programs Director Holly R. Britt, Dept.
     of Correction, Raleigh, December 22, 1972; Pris-
     oner Rehabilitation Director Martin M. Peterson,
     Prison Dept., September 19, 1966.
155. Letters from Deputy Commissioner R. Vance Robert-
     son, Office of Youth Development, Raleigh, Janu-
     ary 18, 1973 and February 6, 1973; then Commis-
     sioner Blaine M. Madison, Board of Juvenile Cor-
     rection, Raleigh, May 29, 1967.
156. Letter from Corrections Research Officer Edwin F.
     Zuern, Office of Director of Institutions, Bis-
     marck, March 19, 1973.
157. Letter from Supt. Cameron L. Clemens, North Dakota
     Industrial School, Mandan, September 12, 1966.
158. Letter from Supt. Clemens, July 16, 1973.
159. Letter from Director of Institutional Operations, Dept.
     of Rehabilitation and Correction, Columbus, Febru-
     ary 5, 1973; Administrative Regulation 846, "In-
     mate Advisory Councils," April 1972 (Rev. August
     1972).
160. Letter and Institution Reports from Asst. Director
     William M. Balson, Ohio Youth Commission,
     Columbus, February 28, 1973.
161. Letter from then Supt. Anthony Catalino, Training In-
     stitution, Central Ohio, Columbus, September 16,
     1966.
162. Letter from Director Leo E. McCracken, Dept. of
     Corrections, Oklahoma City, December 8, 1972.
163. Letter from then Warden Ray H. Page, Oklahoma
     State Penitentiary, McAlester, September 22, 1966.
164. Letter from Director of Institutions L. E. Rader,

Social and Rehabilitative Services, Oklahoma City, June 26, 1973.

165. Letter from Director L. E. Rader, Dept. of Public Welfare, Oklahoma City, September 20, 1966.

166. Letter from Executive Asst. O. R. Chambers, Corrections Division, Salem, April 10, 1973.

167. Letter from then Administrator George W. Randall, Corrections Division, Oregon State Board of Control, Salem, September 28, 1966.

168. Ibid.

169. Letter from then Supt. R. J. Williard, Oregon State Correctional Institution, Salem, February 1, 1967; "Constitution and By-Laws," Inmate Relations Council, October 1960.

170. Op. cit.

171. Letter from Asst. Supt. Dean B. Orton, Hillcrest School of Oregon, Salem, February 14, 1967.

172. Letter from Duane Shimpach, Youth Services Division, Salem, May 2, 1973.

173. Letter from then Supt. Amos E. Reed, MacLaren School for Boys, Woodburn, February 2, 1967; "School Brochure."

174. Letter from Commissioner Allyn R. Sielaff, Bureau of Correction, Camp Hill, December 7, 1972.

175. Letter from Supt. James P. Murphy, State Correctional Institution, Muncy, January 15, 1973.

176. Letter from Acting Commissioner Richard G. Farrow, Office for Children and Youth, Dept. of Public Welfare, Harrisburg, December 22, 1966; Survey made as of October 31, 1966.

177. Letter from then Warden Harold V. Langlois, Rhode Island Adult Correctional Institutions, Howard; September 5, 1966.

178. Letter from Supt. Donald D. MacDougald, Rhode Island Training School for Girls, Howard; February 9, 1967.

179. Letter from Asst. Director Anthony V. Orabone, Dept. of Corrections, Cranston; January 8, 1973.

180. Letters from Director William D. Leeke, Dept. of Corrections, Columbia, December 7, 1972; July 3, 1973.

181. Letter from Director Grady A. Decell, Dept. of Youth Services, Columbia; December 21, 1972.

182. Letters from Warden Don R. Erickson, South Dakota State Penitentiary, Sioux Falls, September 7, 1966; December 27, 1972.

183. Letters from Supt. Edward Green, South Dakota

Training School, Plankinton, November 18, 1966; December 14, 1972.

184. Letter from Director H. J. Venekamp, Youth Forestry Camp, Custer, December 7, 1972.

185. Letter from Director of Adult Counseling James W. Dickman, Dept. of Correction, Nashville, July 2, 1973; "Memoranda re Unit VI," Tennessee State Penitentiary, Nashville, February 1973.

186. Letter from Director of Treatment Susan B. McMillan, Tennessee Prison for Women, Nashville, August 2, 1973.

187. Letter from then Warden John D. Winsett, Brushy Mountain Penitentiary, Petros, September 6, 1960.

188. Letter from Director of Juvenile Counseling Services Frank G. Moseley, Dept. of Correction, Nashville, July 3, 1973.

189. Letters from then Supt. Seth Garrington, Tennessee Youth Center, Joelton, November 1966; March 7, 1967.

190. Letter from Director W. J. Estelle, Dept. of Corrections, Huntsville, January 11, 1973.

191. Letter from Director of Child Care, David E. Sandefur, Texas Youth Council, Austin, December 21, 1972.

192. Letter from Warden John W. Turner, Utah State Prison, Draper, September 16, 1966; "Constitution and By-Laws," Inmate Advisory Council, Rev. July 1961.

193. Letters from Asst. Supt. Donald F. Tatton, Utah State Industrial School, Ogden, December 9, 1966, and December 20, 1972.

194. Letter from Commissioner R. Kent Stoneman, Dept. of Corrections, Montpelier, December 14, 1972.

195. Letter from Warden Robert G. Smith, Vermont State Prison, Windsor, September 7, 1966.

196. Letter from Supt. Eleanor H. Holleran, Women's Reformatory, Rutland, January 31, 1967.

197. Letter from Director W. K. Cuningham, Jr., Division of Institutions, Richmond, January 26, 1973.

198. Letter from Director Cunningham, September 12, 1966.

199. Letters from Director C. R. Minor, Division of Youth Services, Richmond, August 30, 1966; December 14, 1972.

200. Letter from Asst. Supt. G. L. Stanley, Hanover School for Boys, Hanover, January 26, 1973.

201. Letter from Asst. Supt. J. T. Lawrence, Beaumont School for Boys, Beaumont, January 17, 1973.

202.   Letter from Asst. Supt. Geoffrey K. Byrd, Juvenile
       Vocational Institute, Honaker, March 28, 1973.
203.   Letter from Supt. R. H. Sutton, Pinecrest Center,
       Richmond, January 26, 1973.
204.   MO-Instruction 330.1, Establishment of the Inmate
       Advisory Council, Division of Correctional Institu-
       tions, Dept. of Public Institutions, Olympia, Sep-
       tember 27, 1954.
205.   Letter from Supervisor L. Delmore, Jr., Division of
       Adult Correction, Olympia, September 19, 1966.
206.   Memorandum #70-7, "Residents' Government, " Office
       of Adult Corrections, Division of Institutions,
       Olympia, November 6, 1970.
207.   Constitution, Inmate Advisory Council, Washington
       State Penitentiary, Walla Walla, 1956 (reprinted
       February 25, 1958).
208.   Constitution, Resident Governmental Council, Washing-
       ton State Penitentiary.
209.   Letter from Supt. B. J. Rhay, Washington State Peni-
       tentiary, Walla Walla, December 26, 1972.
210.   Letter from Supt. Roger F. Maxwell, Washington
       State Reformatory, Monroe, September 14, 1966.
211.   Letter and Survey from then Supervisor Thomas G.
       Pinnock, Division of Juvenile Rehabilitation, Olym-
       pia, June 15, 1967; Letter from Deputy Assistant
       Secretary Thomas G. Pinnock, Social Services
       Division, Dept. of Social and Health Services,
       Olympia, November 27, 1972.
212.   Letter from then Director C. Robert Sarver, Division
       of Correction, Charleston, September 19, 1966.
213.   Letter from Director Sanger B. Powers, Division of
       Corrections, Madison, April 19, 1973.
214.   Letter from Director Powers, September 15, 1966.
215.   Letter from Warden James W. Mathews, Wisconsin
       Correctional Camp System, Madison, May 1967.
216.   Letters from Supt. Paul D. Prast, Kettle Moraine
       Boys School, Plymouth, March 9, 1967: Supt.
       Roland C. Hershman, Wisconsin School for Boys,
       Wales, March 15, 1967; Supt. Larry A. Alberts,
       Black River Camp, Black River Falls, March 13,
       1967.
217.   Letter from Supt. Rex T. Duter, Wisconsin School
       for Girls, Oregon, March 7, 1967.
218.   Letters from Warden Leonard F. Meachum, Wyoming
       State Penitentiary, Rawlings, September 12, 1966,
       and November 14, 1966.
219.   Letter from then Supt. Phillip A. Whaley, Wyoming

Girls School, Sheridan, February 1967.
220.   Letter from then Supt. B. D. Kuchel, Wyoming In-
       dustrial Institute, Worland, February 1, 1967.

Part III

THE FEDERAL PRISON SYSTEM

The Federal Bureau of Prisons, Washington, D.C.,
administers forty-seven facilities for persons sentenced to
confinement for violations of federal laws. These facilities
range from close custody penitentiaries to minimum security
camps, including institutions for juvenile and youth offenders
and a medical center to care for the mentally ill and those
with serious medical disorders that cannot adequately be
treated in the other institutional hospitals.

Guidelines on the organization of inmate groups are
provided by a Policy Statement issued in May 1972 which
affirmed the previous policy of leaving the approval and
supervision of organized inmate groups to the discretion of
each institution's administrator.[1] Inmates wishing to form
an organization are required to obtain written approval of
the institution head prior to becoming active. A tentative
constitution and by-laws defining the organization's purpose
and operation must accompany the request for organization.
All organizations approved must be coordinated by a designated employee. Meetings may be held at such times not
competitive with regularly scheduled work and treatment
programs. All activities and projects sponsored by an organization must be approved by the institution head. Fund
raising projects are limited to those not requiring staff time
beyond the capability of resources available to the institution
and those not in competition with the commissary or inter-
fering with the orderly operation of the institution.

While a membership dues and a method of collection
may be authorized provided guidelines are established for an
appropriate bookkeeping system including an annual fiscal
audit, no inmate may be excluded from membership in an
organization solely on the basis of lack of funds for dues.
Most of the institutions have established advisory councils
under procedures prescribed by this policy statement.

Federal Penitentiaries

There are six United States Penitentiaries, all having a satellite camp with the exception of the institution at Atlanta, Georgia. The Atlanta penitentiary utilizes ad hoc inmate committees in a variety of programs. Staff members have mentioned an inmate advisory council having existed at one time, but there is no official record of it. [2]

The Attorney General's Survey of Release Procedures, published in June 1940, mentions that shop committees had been organized at the Leavenworth, Kansas, penitentiary. [3] Present records reveal that an Inmates' Advisory Council was in operation in February 1944, but the actual date of its formation is unknown. A constitution, revised January 1, 1947, provided for the secret ballot election of one representative for each of twenty-two work details to serve a one-year term of office. Candidates, chosen in a primary election, must have been in the institution six months and have at least a year remaining to serve. Representatives selected a chairman and a secretary from their membership or from the population. If selected from the population neither were permitted to vote in council deliberations. The council met monthly in closed session to determine the agenda to be presented to the monthly meeting with the warden or his representative. The constitution stipulated the advisory nature of the group, expressly prohibiting concern with individual problems. The election of all representatives and all proposals by the council were subject to approval by the warden. Operation of the council was discontinued on July 2, 1951, after it had apparently become only a sounding board for petty gripes and grievances. The Sports Committee of the Inmate Advisory Council at Leavenworth continued to function after disbandment of the parent group and was reorganized under its own constitution on February 2, 1953, as the Recreation Advisory Committee. This group was dissolved in July 1954, at the request of the members as they believed it no longer had a part to play in the organization. [4]

There has never been an inmate advisory council at the Lewisburg, Pennsylvania, penitentiary. For a few years there was an Inmate General Welfare Committee whose purpose was to provide financial aid to inmates, their families, former inmates, and worthy community welfare programs. This group was discontinued in January 1965, primarily because of the demands on staff time. In recent years ad hoc committees have been utilized extensively to deal with specific matters. [5]

The McNeil Island, Washington, penitentiary had an Inter-Relations Committee, organized about thirty-seven years ago but there is no information available regarding its structure or procedure. [6] A Men's Advisory Council was formed in 1960, to promote the general welfare of the inmates by providing a liaison with the staff. A constitution and by-laws, revised effective January 1, 1965, stated that any inmate of average intelligence and with an educational level not less than sixth grade could be a candidate to represent his housing unit for a six months' term of office provided he had been in the institution six months and had not incurred a record of major misconduct for the six months immediately prior to election. The twelve members were elected by secret ballot and selected from their membership a chairman, vice-chairman, secretary-reporter, and parliamentarian. The Council met twice a month to prepare an agenda of topics to be discussed by the Executive Committee, composed of the four officers, at its monthly meeting with the warden. The agenda was limited to five topics. Minutes of all meetings were disseminated via bulletin boards. Standing committees on blood bank, education-recreation, entertainment, publicity, rules and safety-sanitation were appointed by the Council, the chairman of each being selected by majority vote. Ad hoc committees were formed for specific purposes. [7]

R. W. Meier, warden at the McNeil Island Penitentiary, from October 1966 until mid-1970, continued the Men's Advisory Council essentially as described. Monthly meetings were utilized as forums of information exchange between staff and residents. Management input included, for example, discussions on the need for efficient operations by effecting economies in electrical power use, food, and clothing items. [8]

Currently, the administration reports being in an experimental stage in inmate communications. While no directives or policy statements have been issued, a number of inmate organizations and clubs are in existence with whom the administration meets regularly to discuss items on a previously drawn agenda. Consideration is being given to resuming the procedures followed by the Men's Advisory Council organization from 1960 to 1966. [9]

The Inmate Advisory Council was organized at the
Terre Haute, Indiana, penitentiary in 1941, less than one
year after the institution opened under the administration of
Warden E. B. Swope. The author observed the development
of the Council except for the periods of December 1943
through June 1946, and October 1953 through July 1959,
while respectively in the Army Air Force and assigned as
Chief, Classification-Parole at another institution. From
August 1959 until May 1964, the author was the associate
warden for treatment at the Terre Haute institution and provided the principal liaison between the staff and the Council.

While election by secret ballot was always a feature
of the Terre Haute procedure, in the beginning years the
elections were actually nominations subject to approval by
the administration. This resulted in a membership of more
mature and intelligent men. Meetings were held regularly
at monthly intervals. In accordance with a constitution, the
agenda for each meeting was approved in advance by the
warden and minutes were subsequently submitted to him.
In 1947, the associate warden for treatment was designated
as staff liaison officer with the group.

The Inmate Advisory Council was disbanded in the
early 1950's, largely because of staff disinterest. Attempts
to revive it met little success until 1956 when a new constitution was drawn which provided for a representative and
alternate to be elected in each housing unit by secret ballot
to a six months' term of office. Qualifications for candidacy
were ninety days residency in the institution and a minimum
of six months' time yet to be served.

The newly activated Advisory Council sought to function on what has been described as a forensic level--that is,
the administration conveyed plans and policies to the representatives as a means of enlisting inmate aid in realizing
institution goals. According to the then associate warden
for treatment, there was a respectful interchange between
the administration and inmates, with the latter accepting responsibilities earnestly with no secondary motives. Although
matters presented for discussion by Council members often
included those described by the staff as trivial, the administration avoided in any way minimizing the importance of any
topic. As an antidote to the practice of a member withhold-
ing action on a matter simply to provide himself with an item
for discussion at the next meeting, a plan was initiated to
have members report on improvements accomplished since
the last meeting. [10]

As with other such groups, the history of the Terre
Haute Council is a series of highs and lows. By the late
fifties the image of the Council was not favorable in the
eyes of many staff and inmates. In 1960, although no modifications were made in the constitution and by-laws, a
change did occur that overshadowed all other considerations.
The Inmate Advisory Council was accepted as being truly
representative of the institution population. Warden T.
Wade Markley, who had only recently assumed the position,
advised the inmates that they were to be regarded as members of the institution operating staff and that Council members, as their representatives, would be advised of financial
and other records relevant to management. The successful
results of that approach are evident in the excerpts of a
1961 report by Warden Markley:

> The Inmate Advisory Council has been in existence at
> this institution for several years. Organizationally
> it has remained about the same. However, in the
> past year we have drastically changed its orientation
> and functions.... We have communicated with the
> council extensively, tried to keep responsible inmates
> as members and have tried with considerable success
> to orient them toward providing leadership in estab-
> lishing and maintaining a decent place to live. They
> have assumed this responsibility to the best of their
> abilities and have contributed to the establishment of
> the good climate we have achieved....
>
> We are advising the entire inmate body of our al-
> lotments and how we allocate them. We have had
> some interesting sessions in which we allowed smaller
> groups such as the Inmate Council to study our allo-
> cations and try to find a source from which additional
> funds could be made available for food or clothing.
> They have been unable to find a better solution and
> usually give up in a short time when the effect of any
> transfers are pointed out. They have even developed in-
> sights into the needs for personnel and of the effect
> on them of personnel shortages. They also develop
> some understanding that the unfavorable publicity of
> their own acts has much to do with the lack of public
> acceptance which in turn is responsible for much of
> the limitations of appropriations.
>
> As a result of the understanding developed from
> these communications, the level of expectation was
> lowered considerably. Many even express surprise
> that the food can be so good. Thus we are able to

attain a position whereby to the inmate body the food
is as good as can reasonably be expected under the
circumstances and it has become acceptable.   There
is a second dividend that is even more important.
A toe hold for the development of an acceptance of
group responsibility is furnished.   They begin to see
that if they steal or waste food, or fail to take care
of clothing or maliciously damage bedding or equipment they are hurting only themselves.   They cannot
control the situation as individuals, but must act as
a group.   It has prompted spontaneous campaigns to
control waste and has actually reduced losses....
They are conducting sanitation campaigns and participate in the weekly inspections.   Also, they are conducting programs aimed at preventing waste and
malicious damage, controlling homosexuality and theft,
and against the use of vulgarity and inmate slang.

   In addition to setting an example and taking individual actions in the housing units, the council as a
whole has sponsored newscasts, issued leaflets and
posters, and prepared articles and a series of cartoons for the Terrescope (the inmate bi-weekly publication).   The cartoons are humorous but directed
toward improving behavior.   The two characters de-
picted are So Seedy, the typical inmate rationalizer
who contaminates himself and others, and Preston
Forward is the hero who always wins while So Seedy
is made to look ridiculous and the weakness of his
position is evident.   Another interesting innovation
in the council-administration relationship was the development of agenda for the monthly meetings held
with various staff members.   These agenda are issued prior to the meeting and allow the staff member
to consult with others if necessary and the council to
discuss and consider items before entering the meeting.

   The desirability of inmate councils has been de-
bated for years.   We feel that ours is a positive
force and that it increases program effectiveness.
Perhaps, desirability hinges upon approach and attitudes.

   Council operations continued on this level until late
1962.   A boycott of the dining room then occurred which investigation determined was encouraged by a small group, two
of whom were Council members.   The council then went into
a period of limbo during which time a complete review was

undertaken of the Inmate Advisory Council program.   One
thing was clearly evident: the program was not attracting
the men most qualified to represent others.   The question
was how to encourage such men to participate and at the
same time leave the selection of their representatives to the
men themselves.

Finally, in late March 1963, procedures were established based on the recommendations of a staff committee
chaired by the author.   A man wishing to be a candidate
would so inform his caseworker who would then forward his
application to the Adjustment Committee, provided that his
file reflected an adequate institutional adjustment, a minimum
of ninety days served at Terre Haute, and a minimum of
six months to be served beyond the next election.   The Adjustment Committee, in turn, would confirm the applicant as
a candidate if it was believed he had the potential for car-
rying out the duties of a councilman as indicated by his ability, adjustment, attitude and leadership.   Prior to an election the Adjustment Committee appointed a three-man nominating committee in each affected housing unit.   That committee selected a slate of four candidates from the list of
eligibles already certified as candidates.

The result of this innovation was to heighten the desirability of Council membership.   The process involved approval by significant staff members which gave prestige to
those qualifying.   In turn, it insured that thugs and clowns,
clearly incapable of meeting councilmanic responsiblities,
would not be elected.   The actual selection of those who
were to stand for election was left in the hands of the inmates through the nominating committee, and final selection
was still that of the general electorate via the secret ballot.

As it was desired to bring about a broad-based staff
interest, custodial supervisors were later designated to select the persons to serve on the nominating committees in
each housing unit.   Additionally, a staff-inmate coordinating
committee was appointed to provide the closest possible
liaison between the administration and the inmate population.
Chaired by the associate warden for treatment, the membership of this committee included the Council president, the
secretary and a third councilman appointed by the president,
plus five staff members who served for six-month periods.
Appointments were made by the associate warden from all
departments and included line personnel as well as supervisors.

The name of the council was changed to Resident Advisory Council and all men were thereafter referred to as residents rather than inmates. Emphasis was placed on the individual responsibility of each councilman in effecting an improved staff-resident communication. Each was given an opportunity to learn about institutional policies, procedures, and goals and encouraged to disseminate that knowledge to others. Councilmen became involved in the admission-orientation program for newly arrived men, being scheduled as speakers in what had been heretofore exclusively a staff function. Councilmen were appointed as members of staff committees on services, such as food and laundry. In addition, members attended staff planning committees on budget and vegetable gardens. A handbook on councilmanic duties and responsibilities was prepared.

This new approach was received enthusiastically by the residents and after some initial reservations the staff accepted it. The significant thing about it was that it accomplished its purpose of a more meaningful communication. The base of this communication was broadened by having inmate workers participate in departmental staff meetings. The views of residents were obtained in developing plans for the enrichment and strengthening of programs.

The Terre Haute Resident Advisory Council is no longer in existence, and reportedly has not been since 1964. Ad hoc committees are appointed for specific purposes under current procedures. [11] The Residents' Council of the Marion, Illinois, penitentiary operated for three years under a constitution similar to others already described.   In July 1972 it became necessary to disband the group. [12]

Federal Reformatories

There are three federal reformatories currently in operation. Information is also provided herein on the institution at Chillicothe, Ohio, which functioned as a federal reformatory from 1926 to 1966.

The Federal Reformatory for Women, Alderson, West Virginia, was opened in 1927. The first superintendent, Mary B. Harris, reportedly established a form of student government based on her experiences while superintendent in 1918 at the Clinton New Jersey Reformatory for Women. In 1940 there was a reference to inmate cooperative clubs functioning actively in the institution. [13]

Current records at Alderson indicate that a representative resident group has been in existence intermittently for many years. Reactivated in March 1965 as the Community Council, the group is predicated on the belief that residents and staff should share responsibility for the general welfare and management of the community (institution) and that improved communications provided through the organization will add to the insight of all in mutual expectations. Realizing that success of the program could be assured only by staff support, the reorganization was preceded by several meetings in which the nature and potential of an inmate council was discussed. Management expectations of staff role were incorporated into the operational procedures for each cottage housing unit. Although it is regarded as not without problems, the Council is believed by the administration to have more positive than negative aspects. Additionally, the administration believes that if the Council is to be really effective, the expenditure of considerable high-level staff time is necessary. [14]

The associate warden is staff advisor to the community council, which operates under a constitution revised on September 20, 1966, and again on August 26, 1970. A woman who has been in the institution for at least ninety days, and has a year remaining to serve from the date of election, may be nominated from the floor or by a three-member nominating committee to stand for election by secret ballot to be a representative of her cottage, provided she has resided there for sixty days. Two representatives of each cottage are elected to serve one-year terms of office. The Council elects a chairman, vice-chairman, and a secretary, who together with five other Council representatives selected by them, compose an Executive Committee. This group prepares background material on matters to be discussed so as to facilitate the monthly Council meetings. Items on the agenda are compiled by the secretary from reports of monthly cottage residents' meetings conducted by the two council representatives and the officer-in-charge. In addition, there is a Coordinating Committee of four members, appointed by the Council chairman, whose function is to inquire into any questions arising about Council representatives and to act as arbitrators in the event a problem cannot be resolved at the cottage level. [15]

The Federal Reformatory at Chillicothe, Ohio, was opened in 1926 and ceased to operate as a federal institution in December 1966, when it was ceded to the state of Ohio.

An Inmate Advisory Council was organized there on November 7, 1933, under a constitution whose preamble proclaimed its purpose to be to effect a closer cooperation among inmates and the administration, and to promote the general welfare of the inmate body.   The group attracted national attention a few months later when a leading periodical reported its formation.   "Inmates of the U.S. Industrial Reformatory at Chillicothe, Ohio, now have an advisory council of sixty-five members, one to every ten of the dormitory population, with an executive committee of fifteen, to bring matters of general welfare before the administrative officers. Early proposals concerned recreation facilities and suggested means for cutting down electric light bills. "16

From the long experience at the Chillicothe institution with advisory councils, in May 1966 the 101st Resident Advisory Council was elected, there developed several observations: good representation is of mutual benefit to the population and administration; an advisory group must be limited and controlled to avoid its ultimate downfall; domination by councilmen who place their own wishes ahead of the good of the group is detrimental to the viability of the council.   This last observation created guidelines for a listing of characteristics which should be applicable to all councilmen:

1.   Does his best to reflect the honest views he represents.
2.   Possess true leadership qualities and seeks ways to improve programs and rehabilitation efforts.
3.   Has the stature to stand up for the right things and assists his Quarters Officer and the administration in eliminating thievery, sex play, obscenity, and gambling.
4.   Is a tactful person who is effective through intelligent persuasion and example.
5.   Counters rumors and distortions with facts.
6.   Does his best to make his quarters as decent and wholesome a place to live as he knows how.
7.   Realistically and conscientiously tries to find ways and make suggestions for improvements in the institution.
8.   Is always polite, courteous, appreciative and considerate of others.
9.   Makes it a point to learn and know of the efforts and improvements being made in the institution and attempts to instill some degree of appreciation in

other inmates.

10.   Is considerate of the difficult job an officer has, and who does his best at all times to foster and improve good staff-inmate relationships.

11.   Is able to work out most of the problems in quarters with his Quarters Officer.

Dinner meetings were held after each election honoring the outgoing officers and welcoming the newly elected officers.   The guidelines for elections called for a ninety-day clear conduct record, a four-month term of office, and a willingness to remain in the same quarters (state-of-promotionlessness) during term of office.   Voting was by secret ballot with allowances for first, second, and third choices. All elections were subject to the final approval of the administration.   In addition to representation for quarters, there were members elected whose constituency and concern reflected the various industrial areas; such as chair factory, machine room, foundry.   The original constitution and by-laws was drawn up on November 7, 1933; the by-laws were amended on February 7, 1938, and a completely revised and amended constitution and by-laws was published on March 3, 1941.[17]   J. A. Mayden, who was warden at the Chillicothe institution from 1965 until 1966, classified advisory council activities as occurring at three levels;[18]

1.   Forensic Level--The advisory council is an organization utilized by the administration to convey information to inmates, and possibly to receive information from inmates.

2.   Administrative Aid Level--At this level, the advisory council is charged with responsibility in specific activities, such as the planning of radio, television and movie schedules, and arranging holiday events.   In the housing unit, the councilman's duties revolve primarily around helping to maintain a smooth operation.

3.   Policy Level--The advisory council at this level is included by the administration in discussions and decisions on policy.

Warden Mayden believed that the forensic level would be difficult to maintain, since there is little to sustain the interest of the participants.   He cited the administrative aid level as being the simplest in terms of management in that it obtained the aid of inmates with no danger of encroachment on the authority of the administration.

The third level was emphasized by Warden Mayden
as being the most productive to all concerned. One of the
gravest problems this level of advisory council operation
holds is the threat felt by personnel. Before council operations at this level can be successful and valuable several
ground rules must be established. These rules should include active participation by the warden or a representative
who can take action, sincerity of intent in participation by
the staff even when faced by challenges to cherished traditions, open and direct lines to high level staff for ready
consultation, and the inclusion in council membership eligibility of varied behavioral types in order that the administration may effectively approach the turbulent element in the
population. Warden Mayden stated that some of the most
productive councilmen had been of that element. He also
compared participation in council activities to group therapy.

The Chillicothe Councils functioned principally on the
administrative aid level as described by Warden Mayden.
The organization was used effectively by the supervisor of
education in recreational programming. On the housing unit
level the correctional officers and councilmen worked coop-
eratively. As the population of the institution was being reduced by the transfer of residents to other institutions in
anticipation of ceding the facility to the state, the council
was of considerable assistance to the administration.

At the El Reno, Oklahoma, reformatory an Advisory
Council was organized in July 1940, shortly after a serious
disturbance, and continued until sometime in 1960. The
development of new classification procedures, however, apparently opened up channels of staff-inmate communication
which supplanted those provided by the Council. [19] An Inmate Advisory Group was established at the El Reno institution on August 18, 1972, to function as a communicative
and advisory group between the residents and the administration. Two representatives are chosen by secret ballot from
each housing unit and one representative is selected from
each of the recognized cultural or civic groups such as
Jaycees, Black Heritage, and Indian Culture, to serve a
three-month term. Regularly scheduled meetings are held
twice monthly with a staff coordinator in attendance. [20]

For several years the Petersburg, Virginia, reformatory had two inmate advisory groups. One group, formed in
late 1966, whose membership was appointed by the administration, met with the warden quarterly. The other group,

whose members were appointed by the housing unit officers, met with the assistant supervisor of education to select television and radio programs.[21]

In April 1972, an institutional directive was issued which changed the structure and procedures of the program at the Petersburg institution, providing for one group to be known as the Inmate Representative Group. A representative from each housing unit is elected by secret ballot to a three-month term of office. Meetings are held monthly with the warden and various staff members to discuss an agenda composed of topics suggested by inmates or staff. The directive specifies that: "representatives will alternate between the Black and Caucasian races from quarter to quarter." Although the program is relatively new the administration believes that the Group serves as a valuable vehicle of inmate-staff communication.[22]

Federal Institutions for Juvenile and Youth Offenders

There are three federal youth centers for juvenile and youth offenders. An Advisory Council was in operation at the Federal Youth Center, Ashland, Kentucky, for approximately a year, beginning in early 1962. It was revived on two or three occasions for brief periods. Reportedly it was difficult to maintain a membership that was representative of the entire population rather than just of the more aggressive elements. The Council was regarded as negative with reference to staff-inmate relationships.[23] Currently it is planned to organize an inmate council within a few months. The activities of several inmate committees on programs, commissary, and food, to name a few, together with a treatment-team approach which encourages evaluation by inmates, are indicative of administrative concern with inmate-staff communication.[24]

In January 1967 a Student Advisory Committee was formed at the National Training School, Washington, D.C. The superintendent met every two weeks with the members who were selected by the housing unit officers for three months' terms. This communication was helpful to the administration, leading to some minor changes in several programs.[25] The School was closed in 1968.

The Robert F. Kennedy Youth Center, Morgantown, West Virginia, was opened in 1968, with facilities for juvenile

and youth offenders of both sexes.   Since June, 1970, there
has been a Student Advisory Committee consisting of elected
representatives from each cottage who meet each week with
the Program Management Committee, which consists of the
case management supervisor, education supervisor, chief
psychologist, and administrative officer. 26   Once a month
the director also attends the meeting.   The weekly meetings
with the Program Management Committee primarily serve
three purposes: (1) for students to seek review and clarification of existing policies and programs pertaining to them;
(2) for students to propose changes or additions to program;
and (3) for the administration to discuss with students programs and policies currently under development or review,
or matters needing student support.

Organizationally, each cottage has two elected representatives on the Student Advisory Committee with the exception of the Pre-Release Cottage which has one.   Presently no restrictions exist as to who may serve on the Advisory
Committee.   Representatives are expected to reflect the
views of the students in their cottage and to report back in
their cottage town meetings the results of their meetings
with the Program Management Committee.   The representatives select one of their members who serves as the chairman of the Advisory Committee and another who is vice
chairman.   There is also a staff member who assists them
in developing a weekly agenda in their preliminary meeting
and who prepares the minutes of the regular joint meetings
of the Student Advisory Committee and the Program Management Committee.   Agenda items can be submitted by either
staff or student with the only stipulation being that the item
pertain to a matter of general institutional concern and that
it not involve individual personalities.   In actual practice,
most agenda items are advanced by students.   Once a month
the meeting between the Committee and the Program Management staff is held in a large room and all interested
students are encouraged to attend.   The director periodically
attends, but keeps a low profile.   He regards the process
as workable and well worth the time involved.

Early in 1972, the administration commenced appoint-
ing students to serve with staff on special task forces.   The
initial step was to include students on the Task Force concerned with the revision of the Student Advisory Committee
By-Laws.   This was followed by student inclusion on the
Task Forces on Grooming and Student Behavior.   Reportedly,
the students involved performed fairly responsibly.

Additionally, each cottage has a weekly town meeting involving all students and staff on duty at that time. The meetings are primarily informational in nature with staff using the time to make administrative announcements and to discuss living unit problems and rumors. Students, in turn, are able to raise whatever questions or complaints they may have regarding the operation of the cottage or program. Town meetings are regarded as contributing to the successful operation of the institution.

A Resident Community Council was organized in October 1972 at the Federal Youth Center, Englewood, Colorado, creating a formal channel of communication between staff and residents. Among the goals established for the Council are the promotion of mutual action in problem solving, insuring the reception by appropriate staff of the existence of resident concerns, and the development of better resident-resident understanding. Nominees for Council membership are permitted to campaign by addressing their housing unit peers in regularly scheduled weekly sessions designated as Town Hall Meetings. Two representatives and one alternate are elected by secret ballot to serve an unspecified term. There is a limitation of two terms, consecutive or otherwise, during any three-year period. The twice-a-month meetings held with a staff ombudsman are so scheduled to insure minimal interference with other programs. The Council is encouraged to act as an advisory group with the realization that it has no power to dictate to staff. Additionally, there is an expectation that staff, through the ombudsman, will respond to the Council in an honest, expeditious manner. [27]

Federal Correctional Institutions

There are ten federal correctional institutions currently in operation. At the Danbury, Connecticut, institution an Advisory Council in existence for several years was discontinued in early 1963. [28] An Inmate Communications Committee was organized in March 1972, under an institution policy statement, for the purpose of improving inmate-administration communications on matters of general concern. It is specified that there is no intention of replacing individual inmate-staff communications. The two elected representatives of each housing unit serve until released or transferred to another unit. Minutes are prepared and posted on bulletin boards following each of the two ninety-minute meetings held monthly with the administration. [29]

A Resident Communication Committee was organized
in August 1972, under an institution policy statement, at the
Milan, Michigan, institution, as one effort to fulfill a policy
of facilitating communication. Results so far are rated as
successful. Members and alternates are elected by secret
ballot to represent their housing units for not more than
two terms of four months' duration. The Committee has
no decision-making power regarding the issues presented at
monthly meetings with staff members. The saliency of proposals by the Committee is regarded as the basis for its
effectiveness and influence. After six months of operation
the administration planned to evaluate the program and, in
cooperation with the Committee, make some modifications
that were believed to be necessary. [30]

During the period from 1948 to 1959, the Federal
Correctional Institution, Sandstone, Minnesota, was used by
the state of Minnesota as a medical facility. When it reverted to the jurisdiction of the Federal Bureau of Prisons
in 1959, Ray W. Meier was assigned there as warden.
During his administration (1959-1964), a Men's Advisory
Council was organized. A nominee approved by the administration could stand for election to a six-month term of office as a representative of his housing unit. Tenure was
limited to one term. An unsupervised meeting of the Council was held each month to prepare an agenda for the monthly meeting with the warden. The agenda was limited to five
topics and the duration of the latter meeting could not exceed one hour. Minutes of the meeting were posted on the
bulletin boards in all housing units. [31]

According to information received in 1967, an Inmate
Council was organized at the Sandstone, Minnesota, institution on November 19, 1964. Meetings held monthly with the
warden, associate warden, and other concerned personnel
were regarded as being productive. A constitution provided
for the secret ballot election of a representative from each
housing unit to serve a six-month term of office with one
succession possible. Only those persons who had been in
the institution for six months and who had a like period remaining to be served could stand for election. A disciplinary report during the six months prior to election disquali-
fied a nominee applicant. [32]

It is not known how long the Inmate Council organized
in November 1964 lasted. An institutional policy statement
established an Inmate Council in June 1972 to improve

inmate-administration communications on matters of mutual concern in order to facilitate improved institution operations for staff and inmates. It was specified that there was no intention that the Council supplant individual inmate-staff communications. [33]

A representative of each housing unit, chosen by secret ballot, together with representatives elected by minority groups, comprise the membership who hold two-hour meetings twice each month, one of which is attended by the warden or his representative. Minutes of the latter mentioned meeting, after approval by the warden, are posted on all bulletin boards.

Six months served and six months remaining to be served, no disciplinary reports for a like period, and three months' residency in the Sandstone institution are the qualifications for any man wishing to be elected to serve a six-month term of office, to which he may once succeed himself. Council members choose among themselves a chairman, vice-chairman, and a councilman-at-large, the latter acting in the dual capacity of sergeant-at-arms at Council meetings, and as a mediator among housing units. A secretary is appointed by the chairman from either the elected membership or the population.

The preamble to the constitution of the Inmate Council at the Sandstone institution cites the purposes of the organization as being the fostering of effective idea exchanges, the development of a harmonious atmosphere, and the enhancement of inmate morale. It is further stated that councilmen are both expected and required to so conduct themselves as to avoid criticism personally or of the Council. Members must never act to impair the Council or to negatively influence their peers.

On January 20, 1959, the Seagoville, Texas, institution organized an Inmate Advisory Council. Under procedures established in a constitution, a representative from each housing unit, and one alternate, could be elected to a six-month term of office by secret ballot. There was no limitation on succession. Any man who had attained an eighth-grade education, or its equivalent, and who had been in the institution for ninety days could run for office provided he had a six months' clear conduct record and more than ninety days remaining to serve. A meeting was held each month with the warden and associate wardens to discuss

various activities.   In some instances the Council was helpful to the administration in regard to management problems.
Line staff, in general, had few favorable comments on the
function of the Council. [34]

The Inmate Advisory Council at the Seagoville institution was discontinued around June 1969.   When a Unit
Management System was adopted in April 1972, various types
of town hall meetings were initiated in each of the five
eighty-man units.   On June 15, 1973, an institution policy
statement established a Staff-Resident Communications Committee, culminating discussions held during the prior year
on the need to reestablish such a group to facilitate interchange between the population and the administration. [35]

Membership of the Staff-Resident Communications
Committee consists of the warden, associate warden, chief
of correctional programs, executive assistant to the warden
(who is designated as the staff coordinator), supervisor of
education, and two representatives from each of the five living units.   Following secret ballot elections, each unit
manager lists the names of the three residents receiving the
highest number of votes.   From these lists the warden selects two persons to serve six-month terms as official committee members.   The third person is designated as an alternate member.   Tenure is limited to two consecutive
terms.   The Committee meets once a month to discuss the
items on an agenda prepared and published the previous
week at a meeting of the executive assistant and one representative from each Unit.   Matters involving institution security, orderly operation, and facility emergencies are
stated as being staff prerogatives.   Discussion topics must
be those clearly definable as program or general welfare
concerns, with no inclusion of a resident's personal problems.

An Inmate Advisory Council was organized in October
1951 at the Federal Correctional Institution, Tallahassee,
Florida.   The constitution provided for secret ballot election
to a six-month term of office as a representative of his
housing unit for any man with a clear conduct record who
had been at the institution at least ninety days and who was
regarded as acceptable for membership by the associate
warden.   At the twice-monthly meetings, councilmen considered suggestions tendered by their constituents.   These
suggestions, by/majority vote, could be forwarded to the administration.   Each councilman assisted the housing unit

officer in disseminating pertinent information and was responsible for television program scheduling. Additionally, the councilman played an important role in orienting new men to the unit. The then administration viewed the Council program as being mutually beneficial to staff and inmates by promoting better communication and by offering an opportunity for the latter to develop leadership qualities as well as civic pride. [36] When the present warden of the Tallahassee institution took office in June 1972, the Inmate Council was not functioning. A committee whose members are chosen by popular vote now selects movies and television and radio programs. [37]

Both the Men's Division and the Women's Division of the institution at Terminal Island, California, have advisory councils. The Men's Council was originally organized in 1958 and has functioned on a sporadic basis. The Women's Council, known originally as the Inter-Relations Council, was organized in March 1962. Both groups functioned under a constitution similar to others already mentioned. While the author was associate warden of the Men's Division from May 1964 through July 1967, the group was redesignated as the Terminal Island Council. Occasional enthusiasm by a few members would lead to short-lived periods of activity. In October 1965, staff attention and effort were directed to implementing the Work Release Program. The Council continued to function, meeting on an irregular basis.

During the period 1967 to 1969, Council activity was quiescent, reactivating only occasionally. Since that time it has been quite active, however. Representation is by housing unit, ethnic group, and social groups, all elected, and meeting at least once a month with various staff members. Communication between Council and staff is credited with limiting a November 1971 work stoppage to a one-day duration. [38]

At the Lompoc, California, institution, an Inmate Advisory Committee functions under a Policy Statement dated December 7, 1972. Each officially recognized inmate group may designate a member as its representative to the Committee. There were fourteen organizations at the time of the Policy Statement issuance, representing ethnic, racial, hobby, and self-help groupings. The Committee meets monthly for sixty to ninety minutes with an administrative group composed of the two associate wardens, chief correctional supervisor, chief of case management, and the group

activities coordinator.   Other staff members are invited
when the discussion topic falls in their area of responsibility.   Minutes of the discussions held on the items listed on
the previously prepared agenda are distributed to meeting
participants and posted on housing unit bulletin boards after
approval by the associate wardens.   The Committee is not
a decision-making group, but the Policy Statement reflects
the possibility of staff decisions based on discussions presented by the Committee. [39]

Believing that effective correction in an institutional
setting requires an adequate forum for expression of resident views to administration, and that if given appropriate
opportunities residents will make positive contributions to
the improvement of operations, especially in areas immediately involving them, the Fort Worth, Texas, institution
established several resident representative councils in April
1972.   Three groups mentioned in a policy statement are a
Consumer Council, a Programs and Operation Council, and
a Residents' Council on Corrections. [40]   In the first mentioned group, the membership is composed of one representative from each housing unit elected by secret ballot to
serve a three-months term.   The group meets monthly with
the warden's executive assistant and the chief of client management to discuss and recommend changes in procedures
on commissary, movie selection, release clothing, and community entertainment groups.

Each established program unit selects by secret ballot a representative to serve a three-month term of office
on the Programs and Operations Council.   This group meets
monthly with the associate wardens to present recommendations regarding institution programs and operations, other
than those areas reserved for the Consumer Council.

The Residents' Council on Corrections at the Fort
Worth institution is interesting, and although not novel it is
certainly not widely employed.   Council members are selected for ninety-day periods to meet with the warden to
discuss philosophies, and to contribute their views on the
status of contemporary corrections.   Selection of members
is based on an assessment of the individual's capacity for
serious discussion.   Consideration is also given to maintaining a proper representation based on ethnic origins, criminal sophistication, and sex.   The institution has facilities
for both males and females.

Neither the LaTuna, Texas, or Texarkana, Texas institutions have inmate advisory councils. [41]

Federal Prison Camps, Detention Centers, Community Treatment Centers, Medical Center

There are no resident advisory councils at the federal prison camps located in Montgomery, Albama, Safford, Arizona, and Eglin Air Force Base, Florida. Current plans call for the organization of a council in the near future at the latter institution. [42]

No information was sought from the detention centers located in New York City and Florence, Arizona. The rapid turnover of population prevents the organization of advisory councils at either of these two facilities.

For the past eleven years the Bureau of Prisons has operated a series of community treatment centers, half-way houses, in major metropolitan areas. Currently there are nine centers and five satellite facilities. The establishment of resident advisory councils in these centers is not feasible nor warranted in view of the community orientation of their programs.

There is no inmate advisory council at the Medical Center for Federal Prisoners, Springfield, Missouri. [43]

SOURCES

1.   Policy Statement 7300.115. "Inmate Organizations, " Federal Bureau of Prisons, May 4, 1972.
2.   Letters from then Warden O. G. Blackwell, U. S. Penitentiary, Atlanta, Georgia, March 28, 1967; Warden James D. Henderson, December 12, 1972.
3.   The Attorney General's Survey of Release Procedures. Vol. 5, "Prisons, " p. 335.
4.   Letters from then Warden J. T. Willingham, U. S. Penitentiary, Leavenworth, Kansas, December 30, 1966; Warden S. J. Britton, December 26, 1972.
5.   Letters from then Warden J. J. Parker, U. S. Penitentiary, Lewisburg, Pennsylvania, April 6, 1967; Warden M. R. Hogan, December 13, 1972.

6.   The Attorney General's Survey, op. cit.
7.   Letter from then Warden R. W. May, U. S. Penitenti-
      ary, McNeil Island, Washington, September 27,
      1966.
8.   Letter from R. W. Meier, President, Man-Ser, Inc.,
      Lake Havasu City, Arizona, February 7, 1973.
9.   Letter from Warden L. E. Daggett, U. S. Penitentiary
      McNeil Island, Washington, December 12, 1972.
10.   Letter from then Warden J. A. Mayden, Federal Re-
      formatory, Chillicothe, Ohio, August 23, 1966.
11.   Letter from Warden Noah L. Alldredge, U. S. Peniten-
      tiary, Terre Haute, Indiana, December 11, 1972.
12.   Letter from Warden G. W. Pickett, U. S. Penitentiary,
      Marion, Illinois, February 7, 1973; "Constitution,"
      the Resident's Council, August 25, 1972.
13.   The Attorney General's Survey, op. cit.
14.   Letters from Warden Virginia W. McLaughlin, Federal
      Reformatory for Women, Alderson, West Virginia,
      October 6, 1966 and February 7, 1973.
15.   Constitution, Federal Reformatory for Women Commu-
      nity Council, Rev. September 20, 1966; Rev. Au-
      gust 26, 1970.
16.   The Survey, February 15, 1934, p. 53.
17.   Report from then Associate Warden S. V. Westerberg,
      Federal Reformatory, Chillicothe, Ohio, August 23,
      1966.
18.   Letter from Warden Mayden, op. cit.
19.   Letter from then Warden A. E. Pontesso, Federal Re-
      formatory, El Reno, Oklahoma, April 12, 1967.
20.   Letter from Charles H. Young, Executive Asst. to the
      Warden, Federal Reformatory, El Reno, Oklahoma,
      December 18, 1972; "Policy Statement," July 28,
      1972, and "Constitution," Inmate Advisory Group,
      October 6, 1972.
21.   Letter from then Warden D. M. Heritage, Federal
      Reformatory, Petersburg, Virginia, April 26, 1967.
22.   Letter from Warden G. R. McCune, Federal Reforma-
      tory, Petersburg, Virginia, December 8, 1972.
23.   Letter from then Director C. E. Harris, Federal
      Youth Center, Ashland, Kentucky, April 3, 1967.
24.   Letter from Director Irl E. Day, Federal Youth Cen-
      ter, Ashland, Kentucky, December 14, 1972.
25.   Letter from then Supt. R. E. Gerard, National Train-
      ing School, Washington, D. C., March 28, 1967.
26.   Letter from Director Jay F. Flamm, Robert F. Ken-
      nedy Youth Center, Morgantown, West Virginia,
      February 13, 1973; "Operations Memorandum,"

Operation of the Student Advisory Committee, September 3, 1970.

27. Letter from Director Lee B. Jett, Federal Youth Center, Englewood, Colorado, December 11, 1972; "Policy Statement," Resident Community Council October 20, 1972.

28. Letter from then Warden Frank F. Kenton, Federal Correctional Institution, Danbury, Connecticut, April 5, 1967.

29. Letter from Warden J. J. Norton, Federal Correctional Institution, Danbury, Connecticut, January 5, 1973; "Policy Statement," Inmate Communications Committee, March 24, 1972.

30. Letter from Warden C. J. Hughes, Federal Correctional Institution, Milan, Michigan, December 13, 1972; "Policy Statement," Resident Communication Committee, June 27, 1972.

31. Letter from R. W. Meier, op. cit.

32. Letter from then Acting Warden J. J. Yates, Federal Correctional Institution, Sandstone, Minnesota, April 5, 1967.

33. Letter from Warden R. L. Aaron, Federal Correctional Institution, Sandstone, Minnesota, December 13, 1972; "Policy Statement," Inmate Communications Committee, June 12, 1972.

34. Letter from then Associate Warden C. J. Hughes, Federal Correctional Institution, Seagoville, Texas, March 29, 1967.

35. Letters from Warden Jack H. Wise, Federal Correctional Institution, Seagoville, Texas, February 6, 1973, and July 6, 1973; Policy Statement, Staff-Resident Communication Committee, June 15, 1972.

36. Letter from then Warden H. J. Davis, Federal Correctional Institution, Tallahassee, Florida, March 31, 1967.

37. Letter from Warden Mason F. Holley, Federal Correctional Institution, Tallahassee, Florida, December 13, 1972.

38. Letter from Warden Paul T. Walker, Federal Correctional Institution, Terminal Island, California, December 12, 1972.

39. Letter from Warden Frank F. Kenton, Federal Correctional Institution, Lompoc, California, January 30, 1973; "Policy Statement," Inmate Advisory Committee, December 7, 1972.

40. Letter from Warden C. F. Campbell, Federal Correctional Institution, Fort Worth, Texas, December 27,

1972; Policy Statement, Resident Representation
Councils, April 3, 1972.

41. Letters from Warden William F. Zachem, Federal
Correctional Institution, LaTuna, Texas, December
6, 1972; Acting Warden J. Torreno, Federal Correctional Institution, Texarkana, Texas, December
11, 1972.

42. Letters from Supt. Robert W. Grunska, Montgomery,
Alabama, December 11, 1972; Supt. Alfred Ulibarri,
Safford, Arizona, December 13, 1972; Supt. Robert
L. Hendricks, Eglin Air Force Base, Florida, De-
cember 1972.

43. Letter from Director P. J. Ciccone, M.D., Medical
Center for Federal Prisoners, Springfield, Missouri, December 11, 1972.

Part IV

OTHER JURISDICTIONS

CIVIL

Although there are numerous facilities administered at other than the federal or state level, information was sought from only four such sources all known to the author, through references in corrections literature or by first-hand knowledge, to have past or present advisory council programs. The account of the Effort League at the Westchester County Penitentiary, Valhalla, New York, was given in Part I.

THE DISTRICT OF COLUMBIA

Department of Corrections

The Department of Corrections is comprised of three Services: Detention, Adult, and Youth. Information received in 1966 and 1967 was reviewed by the present administration and updated by the inclusion of data on the current status of advisory councils at the various institutions. [1]

Detention Services. The organization and operation of an inmate advisory council at the District of Columbia Jail is not feasible due to the rapid turnover of population. [2] The Women's Detention Center in Washington, was established in 1910 at Occoquan, Virginia, as the Reformatory for Women, moving to the present site in 1966. An Inmate Advisory Council is active there, convening once a week.

In 1966 the administration of the Reformatory for Women reported a favorable reaction to the results of the Inmate Advisory Council. Under the by-laws, one representative from each housing unit was elected to a six-month

term of office. Nominees must have been at the facility for
at least ninety days and have six months or more yet to
serve.   A councilwoman was expected to know all rules and
regulations, interpret them to others, and to encourage by
counsel and example a high standard of conduct.   She was
also expected to discourage and report any escape plans or
attempts and to lend her services to the staff in the event
of an escape.   Provision was made for removal from office
on any Councilwoman who became disinterested in her duties,
did not attend meetings regularly, continually discussed disapproved council recommendations, engaged in subversive
activities, or became involved in disciplinary incidents. 3

Adult Services.   The Lorton Correctional Complex,
Lorton, Virginia, consists of the Central Facility, formerly
designated as the Reformatory, which includes a Maximum
Security Facility, and the Minimum Security Facility, formerly the Workhouse.   Councils at the Complex have become inactive because of inmate dissatisfaction and lack of
participation.   The present administration states that revival
of the Councils rests with the inmates.

An Inmate Advisory Council at the Central Facility
was organized in November 1962, under a constitution and
by-laws.   Operating with the assistance of a Staff Committee, the council was the matrix for some successful inmate-
staff efforts.   Initially there was concern with inmate gripes
and somewhat superficial matters, but eventually the group
became engaged in activities regarded by the staff as more
constructive.   The constitution preamble emphasized the
blending of inmate-staff endeavors in promoting the resocialization goals of the institution.   A representative and an
alternate were elected by secret ballot to represent each
housing unit for a six-month period.   Those housing units
having more than one hundred residents elected an additional
representative and alternate.   Nomination qualifications included six months' residency at the institution, a minimum
of six months' time left to serve, no period in segregation
or forfeiture of goodtime credits during the six months preceding election, and the absence of any other penalty for the
immediate past sixty days.   A specific disqualification was
having been engaged in a collective action inimical to the
best interests of the institution.   At least thirty days prior
to an election, all office seekers were required to file written intention with the superintendent.   Those qualified were
given a certificate of eligibility.   The Council elected three
officers, a chairman, vice-chairman, and secretary.   The

Also, in 1966 it was reported that at the Maple Glen School, Laurel, students served as aides to the recreation supervisor, coaching and supervising the younger and newer boys. These junior coaches were regarded as having been very successful. Additionally, each of the facilities mentioned had a Clothing Committee made up of representatives from the cottages. Working from catalogues and samples furnished by wholesalers, the group assisted the administration in selecting student clothing. Each chaplain was assisted by student representatives in planning the religious programs. [7]

THE CITY OF NEW YORK

Department of Correction

The Department of Correction administers all detention and sentence institutions for adult and adolescent felony and misdemeanor offenders.

In 1957 there was a fairly sustained attempt by the Department of Correction to test the feasability of inmate advisory councils at the Correctional Institution on Rikers Island in both the Adolescent and Adult Divisions. Council members were elected on a fairly regular basis in each cell block. Meeting regularly with the warden and occasionally with the commissioner of correction, the councilmen presented suggestions by their constituents for improvements believed by them to be supportive of a good rehabilitation program. Although the administration considered the council program to be a potent factor in promoting the type of self-discipline most useful for success in both learning and community situations, the decision to abandon it had to be made principally because of the transient nature of the inmate population, overcrowded conditions, and lack of funds for required rehabilitation personnel. [8]

Guidelines were issued in late 1972 to assist all institutions in implementing a directive by the commissioner of correction regarding the formation, organization, and implementation of inmate liaison councils. [9] The principal points of the guidelines are:

1. The primary purpose of a Council is to develop new lines of staff-inmate communication as an attempt to promote the solution of problems arising as a result of

chairman was empowered to appoint ten standing committe whose chairmen, together with the three Council officers, formed an Executive Committee which had general supervi sion over the conduct of elections under the direction of th assistant superintendent for training and treatment. [4]

In 1966 it was reported that the administration of th Workhouse, now the Minimum Security Facility, was exper imenting with the use of an Inmate Advisory Council involv ing only a small segment of the population with the intention that should the activity prove satisfactory, all inmates would be given an opportunity to participate. [5]

Youth Services. Included in the Youth Services are two Youth Centers at Lorton, Virginia, the first opening in 1960, the second in 1972. An Inmate Advisory Council is active, meeting once a week. The Inmate Advisory Council, as reported in 1967, was composed of a representative from each of the eleven dormitories, elected by ballot to hold office for six months. The principal function of the group was to relay inmate wishes and ideas to the administration. At the weekly meetings with staff representatives, the Council considered proposals to be later discussed at an administrative staff meeting. Decisions on these proposals were usually made promptly. A maximum freedom in idea exchange was encouraged. The belief was expressed that this method of contact with inmates was a means of becoming advised of matters which have problem potential if not resolved. [6]

Bureau of Youth Services

The Bureau of Youth Services, Social Rehabilitation Administration, Department of Human Resources, administers ten facilities for the care and rehabilitation of delinquent youths. No information has been received regarding the current status of advisory councils at these facilities.

Information was received in 1966 that a Student Council at the Cedar Knoll School, Laurel, a co-educational facility, was sponsored by the administrator and the recreation supervisor. The Council advised on and made recommendations for recreational and leisure time activities such as dances, cottage parties, and special holiday programs. Council members acted as hosts or hostesses at these affairs and assumed responsibility for the conduct of other students.

institutional operations, by serving in an advisory, non-policy making capacity.

2.   Techniques for nomination, such as petitions requiring ten to twenty-five signatures, to be followed by announcements in the institutional newspaper, are suggested.

3.   Provision is to be made for closed ballot election in each housing area, to be followed by a run-off election involving the two to four major vote-getters, to serve as delegate or alternate, for a non-renewable term not to exceed three months.

4.   Frequency of meetings to insure the opportunity to resolve issues prior to their becoming crises.

5.   Staff members chosen to meet with the Council should be those recognized by inmates and staff as possessing both the interest and ability to communicate with inmates.

Additional purposes of the inmate liaison committee system are to provide the staff an opportunity to respond to legitimate grievances, in writing if practical, and to prove the good faith and commitment of the Department of Correction to remedy or to clarify the problems surrounding legitimate grievances; provide information to the administration for policy-making decisions; transmit to the institution population the attitudes, values, and commitments of the administration, and be an instrument to assist inmates in obtaining responses to grievances outside the jurisdiction of the Department of Correction.   Medical services and courts are cited as examples of the latter.

THE CITY OF PHILADELPHIA

The Department of Public Welfare has jurisdiction over the three prisons of the City of Philadelphia which are administered by the superintendent of prisons.   Each institution has an Inmate Betterment Committee and other groups, some being represented by attorneys assigned by the Community Legal Services.   These groups may request a meeting with the superintendent and his staff as the need arises. Two instances are cited as evidence of the value of recognizing and working with inmate organizations as opposed to attempts to suppress them.   A four-day food strike at the Holmesburg Prison in August 1972 was resolved as a result of negotiations with various inmate groups.   Also in 1972, two similar problems of shorter duration at the House of Correction were resolved through the inmate groups.

        The present superintendent of prisons relates that in
mid-1970 an Inmate Advisory Council was established at the
House of Correction on the recommendation of several staff
members.   Residents of each cell block selected a representative to meet under the supervision of correctional officers selected from volunteers believed qualified by tempera-
ment and attitude to discuss general conditions.   Four of the
Council members were selected to meet monthly with the
administration.   Initial meetings were regarded as being
very fruitful.   As recollected, seven of eight specific recommendations made by the Council at the first meeting were
immediately implemented. [10]

FEDERAL

DEPARTMENT OF HEALTH, EDUCATION AND WELFARE

        The United States Public Health Service opened two
hospitals in the 1930's for the care and treatment of both
term and voluntary narcotic addict patients.   Jurisdiction
of one of the facilities has already been transferred to the
Federal Bureau of Prisons.   The other is scheduled for a
like transfer in late 1973.

Clinical Research Center, Lexington

        The Clinical Research Center, Lexington, Kentucky,
was opened on May 25, 1935, as the United States Public
Health Service Hospital, for the treatment of persons addicted to the use of habit-forming drugs.   The population
included male and female prisoners, voluntary addicts, and
a limited member of non-addict neuropsychiatric patients. [11]
The first council of patients was organized in July 1956.
It consisted of twenty addict patients elected to represent
the various Units of the hospital.   It functioned until 1964,
disbanding because of inability of the members to present
and relay projects or programs, due largely to an exces-
sive attention to individual petty gripes. [12]

        A constitution drawn in July 1959, designated the
group as the Male Patients' Council and provided for ballot

election of two representatives from each housing unit to a
six months' term of office. No qualifications for office were
stipulated, but provision was made for expulsion "for cause"
by a two-thirds vote of the membership subject to concur-
rence of the medical officer in charge. The editor of the
patient newspaper was accorded all the privileges of an
elected member except the holding of Council office. A
chairman, vice chairman, recording secretary and sergeant-
at-arms were elected by the Council. Meetings with the
medical officer in charge were scheduled bi-monthly. Closed
meetings of the Council were held weekly. The president
was authorized to appoint standing and ad hoc committees on
the advice and recommendations of the Council. [13]

In 1958, a Puerto Rican group was organized by the
chief of general services to represent approximately 140
Spanish-speaking patients. Members acted as interpreters
of their language, culture, and customs for the staff and
other patients. Eight delegates from this group met bi-
weekly with the chief of general services. They provided
an orientation group for new admissions to promote racial-
cultural understanding, formed a Spanish music group, took
part in helping to lessen incidents of adverse behavior, and
organized an Alcoholics Anonymous chapter. [14]

The clinical director organized a Patients' Activities
Group in 1959. Its purpose was to encourage patients to
participate in the hospital programs, hold competitive meetings, and support special groups, such as Drama, Art,
Writers, Music and other talents, athletics and pastimes.
All of these were interwoven with mental health meetings
and closer relationships between and among patients and
personnel. This group existed until 1965. [15]

Following passage in 1966 of the Narcotic Addict Rehabilitation Act, the facility limited its patient load to narcotic addicts civilly committed to a six-months' in-patient
period and a thirty-six months' aftercare program. Autono-
mous living areas are provided, each comprising a small,
therapeutic community in which input from both residents
and staff provide the basis for all major decisions. Each
living area is encouraged to sponsor projects, including research. A Social Affairs Committee has been formed principally to plan extra-and intramural social events and to
select movies. A staff member and one resident from each
living area are the members of this committee. [16] This
facility was scheduled to be transferred to the jurisdiction of
the Federal Bureau of Prisons in late 1973.

Clinical Research Center, Fort Worth

From November 1938 until 1972 (when jurisdiction
was transferred to the Federal Bureau of Prisons and the
designation changed to Federal Correctional Institution), the
facility at Fort Worth, Texas, functioned as a United States
Public Health Service Hospital.   Until 1942 the patient population was composed of term and voluntary narcotic addicts.
From 1942 to 1949, the population consisted largely of
neuropsychiatric patients on active duty with the Navy, Marine Corps, and Coast Guard.   From 1949 until 1972 the
hospital cared for a wide variety of psychiatric patients,
about one-third of whom were addicted to narcotics. [17]

An Inmate Advisory Council was organized in 1951. [18]
Members, elected by popular vote, met with the clinical director and others of the professional staff.   An excerpt
from the 1951 annual report of the hospital indicated a positive impact on both program and patients:

Council presented to the Staff's attention many needed
reforms and changes which were adopted to the betterment of the patients in the hospital.   The council
served to disseminate information and staff attitudes
to the population through Ward Representatives.   It
played a therapeutic role in the lives of the individual
council members in that it gave them a greater sense
of responsibility and self-determination within the
hospital setting and helped them to resolve some of
their conflicts with authority.

In the same year the Honor Ward concept was established,
featuring single rooms and minimum security.   The selection of patients and the operation of the ward were functions
of the Classification Committee whose primary intent was to
develop a high degree of democratic self-government.

In November 1964, staff-led Self-Help Groups were
formed, in which patient-leaders encouraged the general patient group to a total involvement in the therapeutic program.   A patient-leader was allowed evening use of a group
therapy room which stimulated much enthusiasm among patients for the self-help concept.   It is known that between
March 1965 and March 1967 an entire ward was devoted to
the Self-Help Program.   It functioned as a minimum security
unit in which its thirty patients met twice weekly in ninety
minute afternoon sessions with a psychiatrist-psychologist-

social worker team. Each of the seven wards also had an eight-member Council, which sent one representative to a weekly Council meeting with the chief of addiction service, a security officer, and a nursing staff member. Minutes of these meetings were distributed to all wards. On its own initiative the Council assumed responsibility for influencing ward milieu favorably.

DEPARTMENT OF DEFENSE

The Departments of the Army, Navy, and Air Force, and the United States Marine Corps each operates correctional facilities for its members convicted and sentenced to confinement under courts-martial proceedings. There have never been inmate advisory councils at the Army facility known as the United States Disciplinary Barracks, Fort Leavenworth, Kansas, or the United States Army Retraining Brigade, Fort Riley, Kansas.[19] The United States Naval Disciplinary Command, Portsmouth, New Hampshire, does not have an inmate advisory council. The operation of the Mutual Welfare League from 1917 to 1921 at this facility, then designated as the United States Naval Prison, was recounted in Part I.

The Department of the Air Force 3320th Retraining Group was opened in 1952 at Amarillo Air Force Base, Texas, and relocated in 1967 to Lowry Air Force Base, Colorado. Several years ago a Retrainee Council was established on an informal basis. Two members each from five forty-man treatment groups, who are elected by retrainees or appointed by counselors and team staff, plus two additional members--selected at the discretion of the division chief from a Corrections Division program for men who have failed to be selected for Retraining Program participation or eliminated from it and returned to confinement to serve out their sentence--make up the twelve members.

Council meetings are held twice monthly at a specified time with the group commander and the security police superintendent present. Discussion topics range from petty complaints to the reorganization and revamping of Air Force penal and rehabilitation programs. The only topic not open for discussion is that of staff personalities. While members are cautioned not to expect action or immediate results on all topics considered, the frequency of changes occurring from their discussions is sufficient to cause them to realize they are taken seriously by the administration. Staff input has resulted in a more effective dissemination of information than by traditional written directives. [20]

No information has been received regarding the nine Correctional Facilities under the jurisdiction of the Security and Law Enforcement Section, Security Branch, G-1 Division, United States Marine Corps.

SOURCES

1.   Letters from Director Kenneth L. Hardy, Dept. of Corrections, Washington, D. C. , December 12, 1972; Special Asst. to the Director Eleanor Many, Dept. of Corrections, January 18, 1973.

2.   Letter from then Supt. Paul H. Preston, District of Columbia Jail, September 22, 1966.

3.   Letter from then Supt. Hallie C. Massey, the Reformatory for Women, Washington, D. C. , November 25, 1966; Inmate Council "By-Laws. "

4.   Letter from Asst. Supt. S. A. Knupp, the Reformatory Division, Lorton, Virginia, December 14, 1966; "Constitution and By-Laws, " Inmate Advisory Council, Reformatory Division, Lorton, November 1962.

5.   Letter from then Supt. M. C. Pfalsgraf, the Workhouse Division, Occoquan, Virginia, September 22, 1966.

6.   Letter from then Supt. Reuben S. Horlick, the Youth Center, Lorton, Virginia, February 8, 1967.

7.   Letter from then Deputy Director of Institutional Services Winifred G. Thompson, Dept. of Public Welfare, Washington, D. C. , September 29, 1966.

8.   Letter from then Commissioner George F. McGrath, Dept. of Correction, City of New York, October 10, 1966.

9.   Letter from Commissioner Benjamin J. Malcolm, Dept. of Correction, City of New York, March 23, 1973; "Guidelines for Inmate Councils, " October 30, 1972.

10. Letter from Supt. of Prisons Louis S. Aytch, City of Philadelphia, March 14, 1973.

11. Brochure, "Facts Concerning the U. S. Public Health

Service Hospital, " Lexington, Kentucky, 1966.

12. Letter from Robert W. Rasor, M.D., Medical Officer
     in Charge, Clinical Research Center, and Report by
     W. F. Owsley, Chief, General Services Section,
     USPHS, Lexington, Kentucky, March 17, 1967.

13. "Constitution, " Male Patients' Council, USPHS, Lexing-
     ton, Kentucky, July 1959.

14. Op. cit.

15. Op. cit.

16. Letter from Harold T. Conrad, M.D., Chief, Clinical
     Research Center, NIMH, Lexington, Kentucky, De-
     cember 5, 1972.

17. Brochure, "Our Hospital, " USPHS, Fort Worth, Texas.

18. Letter from James F. Maddux, M.D., Chief, Clinical
     Research Center, NIMH, Fort Worth, Texas, March
     21, 1967.

19. Letter from Colonel Harry J. Brockman, Chief, Cor-
     rections Division, Office of Provost Marshal Gener-
     al, Washington, D.C., December 1, 1972.

20. Letter from Colonel R. E. Blaun, Director of Security
     Police, Hq., USAF, Washington, D.C., December
     11, 1972.

Part V

THE EVOLVING PERSPECTIVE

In this decade in which America will embark upon
the third century of its history, the forces challenging the
social order are ever growing in number and in strength.
No institution of society is immune. None can escape un-
changed. Hopefully, each will meet the crisis it faces and
emerge renewed and strengthened.

The prison, too, faces a crisis. Through two cen-
turies of neglect, the prison has functioned apart from the
social mainstream, largely ignored, and fulfilling neither
the purpose for which it was established nor the dreams of
the handful of dedicated men and women who dared step off
the treadmill of tradition.

Prison management is caught square in the middle of
this situation. Increasingly the glare of publicity is pene-
trating the walls, exposing to public view what transpires
therein. The shame of the long neglect which has caused
the piecemeal fashioning of programming, the modus operandi of reacting to situations rather than planning for them,
and a host of other ills and shortcomings are ever in the
news. The lack of guidelines, the absence of evaluation or
of any means by which to evaluate the efficacy and efficiency
of correctional efforts has resulted in the sorry saga of
legislators continuing to pass laws, officials making policy,
and the expenditure of huge sums of tax dollars on ineffec-
tive methods.

Society and the prison--prison management--together
must define the role of the prison, say what it is and say
what it is not. And, most important, there must be at least
a first step made toward determining what the prison can be.
It has been said, and it will be echoed again and again, that
an objective of the prison--some assert it is the objective--
is to assist the individual prisoner to acquire modes of

coping in his life style which do not result in conflict with authority.   Direct participation by the individual in the process is essential, possibly mandatory, to insure the attainment of that objective.

As we review the scene from 1793 to 1973, it appears that the concept of offender participation in prison management as embodied in the advisory council has seldom been utilized in more than a superficial manner.   Many administrators regard the advisory council as simply a device for the communication of inmate complaints to the administration.   This narrow view has produced the term "gimme" groups.

The various rationales for the existence of advisory councils range from the pragmatism of providing an administrative peephole through which inmate plots may be discovered to the altruism of learning democracy by experiencing it.   Some practitioners accept the view that the inmate must be a part of the service process rather than simply an object of service, but have done little to translate the view into action.

The Manual of Correctional Standards, 1959 issue, of the American Correctional Association, states that inmate participation in planning and operation of institutional programs is slowly passing out of the controversial stage, and that many prison administrators recognize the approach and method as being sound in educational theory and practical as a means of prison administration.   Additionally, with the coming of more imaginative and socially-minded wardens and officials its use in institutions will come to be taken for granted.

The basis for that optimistic pronouncement and prophecy was an article published in 1931.   The statement is still valid, particularly with reference to the pace with which the concept of inmate participation is departing the controversial stage.

Views and pronouncements on the use and value of advisory councils appear to vary in accordance with the group, or the purpose of the group, doing the talking.   For instance, in May 1953, the Committee on Riots under the auspices of the American Correctional Association, reported on the unprecedented number of riots in American prisons during the period 1951-1953.   Effective communication

between management and inmates was mentioned in a report,
entitled "Prison Riots and Disturbances, " as one measure
that might prevent such outbursts of mass violence and
mutinous behavior.   A representative inmate council was
cited as one method of effecting this two-way communication.

In 1960, reportedly the Wardens Association of
America went on record as being opposed to the idea of inmate self-government (advisory councils).   The number of
persons present and voting is not known, but it is understood that prior to the meeting there had been a canvassing
of wardens on the issue.   Subsequently, the American Correctional Association was prompted to revise the 1953 report, "Prison Riots and Disturbances, " by the beginning of
a series of riots and major disturbances in correctional institutions in 1968.   The report of the revision committee
was made in an October 1970 publication entitled "Causes,
Preventive Measures, and Methods of Controlling Riots and
Disturbances in Correctional Institutions. "

According to the report, some administrators believe
that it is necessary to develop a formal structure for communications between inmates and administrative personnel.
The formation of ad hoc advisory groups was cited as ap-
pearing to be the most feasible way of dealing with particular problems or issues.   In the opinion of the revision
committee this practice would ensure inmate involvement and
at the same time prevent selected inmates from capitalizing
on their tenure on an advisory panel to exploit other inmates, since the ad hoc committees would be dissolved upon
resolution of the particular problem or issue.   The issue
of advisory councils occasioned a rather heated discussion
at the 1972 meeting of the American Association of Wardens
and Superintendents.   The consensus appears to be that the
ranks for and against were about even.

The history of advisory councils, since 1930 in particular, reveals that often the first step taken to create a
positive relationship between inmates and staff has been the
organization of an advisory council.   Additionally, advisory
councils have been organized following a crisis situation,
such as a riot, as an agency to bring order out of chaos.
In many respects, an advisory council formed under such
conditions may be likened to a peace tribunal to which each
side may send its most enlightened and capable representatives to determine upon what terms and by what means future
difficulties might be averted.

Then, on the other hand there are institutions where an advisory council has never been organized for any reason or under any circumstance. There is no evidence that the presence or the absence of an advisory council has had any marked influence on the destiny of an institution. The best evidence which can be adduced from the past and the present is that open communications between inmates and staff does seem to facilitate the adjustment of both groups.

Why do some correctional administrators look with disfavor upon inmate advisory councils while others turn to the concept for succor in periods of program malaise and in the aftermath of disaster? Further, why, during the course of our surveys, did many administrators qualify their admissions of no councils with statements reflecting a belief that councils offer many advantages to an institution program, that serious thought was being given to establishing a council, or that the organization and operation of a council had not been ruled out for the future. Certainly these reflect more than a suggestion of uncertainty about not having a council.

This ambivalence is believed to be the product of an erroneous equation of inmate advisory councils with self-government systems of the past in which inmates functioned as disciplinarians. This belief is buttressed by the results of a survey published in 1964 in the Journal of Criminology, Criminal Law and Police Science. The principal objection to advisory councils was that they permitted one inmate to have authority over another. Yet a properly drawn advisory council plan can easily and effectively rule out any possibility of this occurring.

The author is of the opinion that discipline is a part of the treatment process which must be retained in toto by prison personnel. The proper administration of discipline requires a degree of objectivity which is not to be found in the object itself. This does not imply an exclusion of inmate opinions and suggestions in determining the disciplinary process. However, it does imply that those who administer the process must be qualified to do so.

Many administrators are obviously concerned that some inmates will use membership on an advisory council to their personal advantage and at the expense of sound administration. It has been postulated that since many inmates have grievances they may tend to regard the advisory

council as a forum for the expression of those grievances.
All of this may well be true.   Also true is the fact that
some staff members may have views similar to those of the
inmates and in that light define their own role as one of
advocacy and align themselves with the inmates.   So, both
inmates and staff can use an advisory council to their personal advantage and at the expense of sound administration.

The foregoing should be regarded by the administrator
as a challenge to his correctional management skill rather
than as a reason not to have an advisory council if he believes that such a group will be of value.   The administration simply needs to recognize that this attitude may under-
lie the approach by some inmates and some staff members
to the advisory council concept.   A necessary part of the
development of both groups is to recognize the defined role
of an advisory council.   And only management can make
that definition.

Opponents of the advisory council point out that some
inmates will use their advisory council membership to create centers of personal power which can subvert the authority of the administration.   There is no doubt that politics
can be involved, since prisoners are people and people do
engage in politics of one fashion or another.   Properly designed and monitored procedures can do much to reduce the
creation of power centers--for instance, frequent elections
and rotation of positions in which power may be implied or
inherent, such as committee chairmanships.

If the decision is to have an advisory council, the
purpose and scope of the group's function must be fully
communicated to and understood by both staff and inmates.
This should be accomplished before a group is organized.
The method most frequently employed for this communication is the drawing up of a constitution and a set of by-laws.
Another approach is the issuance of a directive by the central authority setting forth the official policy regarding advisory councils--or staff-inmate communications, or inmate
organizations--and providing organizational and procedural
guidelines.   These approaches are adequate, but each lacks
any means or method of insuring that the intent of the decision maker is effected.

Despite the best structuring, the most careful planning, or the most meticulous implementation, there is no
absolutely certain method by which the intended purpose of

an advisory council, or any program for that matter, can be
assured. But we do know that people respond when their
personal interest is involved. A staff response of acceptance and support for an advisory council can be facilitated
if management makes it explicit that such acceptance and
support are factors in personnel performance expectations.

If an advisory council is organized, it is assumed
that the administrator is serious about it, that he is accepting the group as an element in the organizational structure, and perhaps even recognizing the inmates as members
of the staff, even though in a subordinate status. Granted
all of this, it is his intention then that the advisory council
function as an integral agency of the institution. He recognizes that in order for this intent to be translated into
reality, the involvement of staff at all levels is necessary.
A fatal defect of most of the early experiences with advisory
councils, and with many of those that came after 1930, was
the dependence of the organizations on a lone individual.
When that person departed the scene, the council ceased to
exist. To avoid this, the base of personnel involved with
council activities should be broadened. A warden and his
associate wardens should be actively interested in council
functions, of course, but can best demonstrate that interest
by insuring budgetary support, for instance, leaving operational contacts to other staff. Whatever staff works directly
with the council should be empowered to make decisions and
take actions, at least within limits in certain areas.

The question is often raised as to what are the
proper functions of an advisory council. The answer lies
in the purpose for which the organization is formed. Almost without exception, the expressed purpose of a council
is to effect or to improve inmate-staff relationships, and
consequently insure the proper functioning of the institution,
by providing a free-flow channel of communication. With
this as a basis, there is really no function of the institution
from which the input of council views should be excluded;
even in those involving personnel recruitment, selection,
and retention, management should be alert to the possibilities for staff development inherent in effective communication. Staff can learn much about itself by being attentive to
the nuances of that communication. The point is important
enough for a short digression.

Of all the techniques for changing behavior, the impact of one human being on another is probably the most

effective.   This imposes a tremendous responsibility on the
correctional worker, since the direction of that change may
rest in the hands of the worker.   It is this aspect of correctional work which lifts it from the ranks of ordinary pur-
suits and makes of it, if so perceived by the worker, one
of the most noble of all endeavors.   The correctional self-
potential of employees can be better realized when they are
in a communication with inmates that will provide the kind
of feed-back upon which progressive modifications of role
can be based.   The advisory council is one means by which
this meaningful exchange can be accomplished.

All functions of the advisory council should be con-
tinuously monitored and frequently evaluated.   Top management should be actively involved in this evaluation, according it the same serious consideration given to other program evaluations.   This brings us to what the author regards as the most powerful of all rationales for the inclusion of inmates in both the program and the programming
of corrections: the use of council membership as a treatment
method.   To do so offers an opportunity for effecting attitudinal changes through which more satisfactory modes of
coping with social-role demands can be realized.   A properly organized and functioning advisory council can be an excellent vehicle for the abundant energies and unusually high
abilities of many offenders that are not amenable to con-
ventional treatment forms.   Some men need an experience
of working for the welfare of others.   Others require ego-
satisfying assignments in which they can escape the feeling
of being engulfed in the crowd.

As the accounts in this volume reveal, council membership often changes recalcitrants to rather agreeable persons; often, too, the inward viewpoint of the self-centered
personality is redirected outward to a genuine interest in
others.   The use of membership in an advisory council as
a part of the development plan for a particular inmate certainly will call for a different method by which council members are selected.   One method would be to appoint members to the council.   There are reasons against this so obvious as to make discussion of them unnecessary.   However,
in that connection the best accepted and most dynamic advisory council the author has ever known of had 75 percent
of its members appointed by the staff sponsor.   The reason
for this was a series of vacancies created by transfers of
elected representatives to other housing units or to other institutions, and the brevity of the unexpired portion of their

terms made special elections not feasible.   Such appointments were provided for in the council constitution.

Probably the best method is to use the individual's
council membership as a part of his treatment development
plan, after he has attained membership through the regular
ballot process.   Those persons for whom it is believed that
advisory council membership would be beneficial can be encouraged to seek election.   In this regard, classes in the
principles of legislative duties, responsibilities, and techniques can be included in the educational program.

It has been the experience of the author, and the experience of many others as related in the accounts herein,
that placement in a formalized situation, such as an advisory
council, can have a salutary effect on dominating or aggressive individuals--those who demonstrate a big-shot complex.
In such a situation where discipline and ability, rather than
toughness or muscle are the factors important to personal
stature, a distinct toning down process can occur.   Conversely, those who are shy and withdrawn in the confinement situation, where a high value is placed on physical
powess and who have lost confidence in themselves because
of this, can attain some degree of stature and regain a
large measure of self-esteem in a formalized structure
where calmness and logic are superior to the strident voice
and the balled fist.

An advisory council, properly utilized, has a two-
way function.   It is an agency for communicating to inmates
the responsibilities which the administration expects of them
and to present a picture of administrative problems in the
areas with which inmates are concerned.   For instance, by
showing them the budget and soliciting their suggestions as
to how a better job might be done with available resources,
a structure is created which provides for and encourages
thoughtful, constructive feedback.   This approach involves
the same psychological principles basic to management efforts to provide employee job satisfaction--call it morale.

Whether or not the formalized structure of communication is an advisory council or some other method is really
not important.   What is important is that correctional administrators recognize and believe that communication with
their charges is vital to the proper functioning of the correctional process.   Just as the advisory council was an outgrowth of self-government, there is much evidence of the

evolvement of other forms of organizations in which the inmate is being recognized as performing an essential role in
the correctional system.

For example, in Wisconsin, the inclusion of inmates
on a committee to make recommendations on correctional
grant requests to the Council on Criminal Justice is definitely a new direction in inmate participation. An evaluation
of the experience will be of interest. The Residents' Advisory Council on Corrections at the Federal Correctional
Institution, Fort Worth, Texas, in which offenders are engaged in discussing correctional philosophy and current practice, is a good example of furthering the social education of
the participants.

Further, it is interesting to note the increasing number of jurisdictions in which the central authority has issued
official statements on the establishment of formal systems of
inmate-staff communications. When a vehicle for this has
been suggested, or mandated in some instances, it has usually been an advisory council or similar organization.
Guidelines for organization and implementation usually accompany the official statements. The implication of these
statements is the growing recognition of the value of communications. Such a recognition is undoubtedly a reflection
of an increasing number of professionally oriented persons
occupying top management positions, and a manifestation of
the results of efforts made during the last several years,
through LEAA funded programs, to provide for the professional development of correctional administrators.

A further implication of the foregoing is that throughout the nation, at all levels of government, there is a growing realization that simply because of his confined status,
the offender should not suffer the loss of all rights. With
increasing frequency the courts are mandating changes in
prison procedures. It is high time for corrections to ac-
knowledge an additional right, and to guarantee that right,
not under the compulsion of a court decree, but on the basis
of professional wisdom. Every person in a correctional
confinement facility should be assured of: the right to participate in matters relating to his personal welfare by contributing his point of view.

The author has previously stated that perhaps correctional administrators would be well advised to look again at
the modern counterpart of self-government, the advisory

council, and to consider it in its proper perspective as a
part of social education, and as a morale-raising device
for the entire institution through its facilitation of two-way
communication. This is certainly true but it is no resolution that an advisory council is the only or necessarily the
best method to accomplish effective communications. In
some situations, an advisory council may be the most efficient communication vehicle; in other situations, a different
approach may be best.

Decisions should be made by those who must justify
their choices and be held accountable for results. Although
it is fully realized that facts do not necessarily alter opinions, the historical and current accounts of self-government
and advisory councils contained in this volume can be of
assistance to the administrator interested in making an informed decision as to whether or not an advisory council is
the optimum of communication method alternatives available
to him. The conclusions on which he will base his decision
will be drawn from the best evidence--the facts of experi-
ence--rather than on the fictions, half-truths, misinterpreta-
tions, and prejudices that have heretofore beclouded the
issue.